Mediating the Family:

Gender, Culture and Representation

Estella Tincknell

Hodder Arnold

A MEMBER OF THE HODDER HEADLINE GROUP

First published in Great Britain in 2005 by
Hodder Education, a member of the Hodder Headline Group,
338 Euston Road, London NW1 3BH

www.hoddereducation.co.uk

Distributed in the United States of America by
Oxford University Press Inc.
198 Madison Avenue, New York, NY10016

The advice and information in this book are believed to be true and
accurate at the date of going to press, but neither the author nor the publisher
can accept any legal responsibility or liability for any errors or omissions.

British Library Cataloguing in Publication Data
A catalogue record for this book is available from the British Library

Library of Congress Cataloging-in-Publication Data
A catalog record for this book is available from the Library of Congress

ISBN-10: 0 340 74080 9
ISBN-13: 978 0 340 74080 4

1 2 3 4 5 6 7 8 9 10

Typeset in 10 on 13pt AGaramond by Servis Filmsetting Limited, Manchester
Printed and bound by Gutenberg Press, Malta.

What do you think about this book? Or any other Hodder Education title?
Please send your comments to the feedback section on
www.hoddereducation.co.uk.

Contents

Acknowledgements

This book had a very long gestation period, but has only really been 'in production' for a short time. I would therefore like to thank Jane Arthurs and my other new colleagues at the University of the West of England, who have been very supportive of my efforts to complete it over the last few months, especially by giving me the time and space away from teaching and administration that have helped me to focus on writing.

While at Nottingham Trent University I was grateful for the opportunity to develop some of the ideas explored here with Deborah Chambers, Joost van Loon and Richard Johnson, and especially Dave Woods, who always offered a lateral perspective on my opinions.

I would also like to acknowledge the hard work of Olwyn Ince, who formatted the manuscript and helped with some last-minute queries. Thanks, too, to Abigail Woodman, my editor at Hodder Arnold, whose encouragement and no-nonsense approach helped me to get on with it.

Finally, I would like to thank my dear friend, Parvati Raghuram, without whose moral support, intellectual stimulation and delicious meals I would have found it even harder to write.

The book is dedicated to my partner, Dave Jepson, who kept me going with endless cups of tea and, as night fell, the odd glass of wine.

The family, politics and identity

This is a book all about the family. It is not, however, a history of the nuclear family or even a sociology of 'familialism', although both history and social theory inform its theses. Nor is it purely focused on the specific media forms and genres that have been most central to family narratives, such as melodrama and soap opera, although these, too, are part of the story. Instead, it is interested in unpacking the ways in which ideas, values, beliefs and practices around kinship, sexuality, parenting, generational differences and identities have been produced and represented across a range of mainly textual forms, and in relation to a powerful cultural figure: the nuclear family ideal. The book's primary focus is on the articulations and discursive moves involved in this process, taking as its underlying theme the proposal that the politics of families and family relations have been significantly challenged and recast in a series of conjunctural moments throughout the last 50 years.

Therefore, this book has a starting point in the post-war period, examining what I have called the long cultural shadow of the nuclear family, which was absolutely central to post-war reconstruction in the west and to the 'modernization' of intimacy and kinship, and which has continued to loom over the power struggles that have been so central to the family's reinvention during the late twentieth century. The book then goes on to examine both the range and complexity of the various mediations of family life that dominate popular culture: from Hollywood films and television shows to the 'official' discourses of government, education and medicine. Not all of these forms are immediately and self-evidently about the family; they are all, nonetheless, part of the process by which it has been produced and by which we continue to make sense of it.

Rather than offering an account which reifies the family as a single institution or a wholly natural formation, this book explores its ongoing discursive and ideological production by examining the various pieces that have made up the jigsaw, especially at different historical, political and cultural moments. Each of these categories is dealt with in a separate chapter, which also foregrounds a specific configuration. Mothering is explored in relation to the popularity of the family saga and the Thatcherite female entrepreneur in the 1980s, while fathering is considered in the context of new claims to men's rights to family relationships – both the directly political and the more complexly cultural – during the 1990s. Childhood and adolescence are explored in relation to their long and contradictory histories within the development of modernity and the idea of a modern self, and also in terms of their sometimes

1

fractious relationship to a family ideal in which conflicting claims to rights and subjectivity have been a major source of tension. The book begins and ends with two chapters offering a 'long view'. Chapter 1 sets out the social context as well as the particular cultural articulations involved in the development of the nuclear family as an ideal from the late 1940s through to the 1960s, especially the importance of the 'companionate marriage' to post-war family values. Chapter 6 focuses more directly on particular media representations of family life since the counter-cultural and feminist critiques of the late 1960s, and specifically on the ways in which the family has been variously pathologized, scrutinized and problematized – in everything from Hollywood romantic comedies to reality television.

It is true to say, however, that slippages between a discussion of *families* and the singular ideological figure of 'the family' are not uncommon and can be difficult to avoid, even for those for whom recognizing that households have always been diversely organized is axiomatic. One of the reasons behind this must be the discursive pressure of the ideas around public and private spheres, in which 'the family' is always located within the latter. Another reason is the powerful mythology of family life, which frequently facilitates a reductively narrow model of 'normal' kinship relations. However, in all of this, the remarkable sticking power of a family ideal in an age in which non-familial relationships seem to be increasingly important is salutary and not to be dismissed lightly. That is why the emphasis throughout the book is deliberately not upon the family as an endangered institution, regardless of the hyperbole of some right-wing commentators. Rather, it is upon the idea of the family *in process*, a process in which identities and relationships are constantly reworked, contested and remade.

Family histories: public selves, private selves

The history of families has largely been bound up with a history of the public and the private spheres, which, while pre-dating the nineteenth century, were powerfully redefined and reconstituted during that period, especially in the work of polemicists such as John Ruskin (*Of Queens' Gardens*, 1864), and counter-polemicists such as John Stuart Mill (*On the Subjection of Women*, 1869). The public sphere has conventionally been understood as a masculine domain: the space where politics, history and economics are supposedly made and where men, in particular, are produced as subjects. The private, feminine sphere was where 'the family' was located – enclosed, domestic, ahistorical and timeless. Under nineteenth-century capitalism, the family, and especially the subordination of women within it, was thus seen as a necessary refuge from the dehumanization of a capitalist society that was perceived to stop at the front door (the 'haven in a heartless world'), and to some extent this model continues to inform contemporary idealizations of domesticity.

In all these configurations, the 'structure of feeling' that dominated the conceptualization of the family was that it was a space entirely separate from the outside world. Indeed, the defence of the family in much neo-conservative writing has been on precisely these grounds. Ferdinand Mount's *The Subversive Family* (1983), for example, argued that the family has had a crucial role as a bulwark against the excessive state control introduced by successive liberal and left-leaning governments. Such arguments, of course, would be more convincing if they had not been made by one of the main intellectual apologists for Thatcherism's highly interventionist family policies and far from liberal attitudes to sexuality in the UK during the 1980s.

While the restriction of sexuality to heterosexual marital relations continues to be taken as a given in some contexts, there can be little doubt that it has been subjected to contestation (and plain subversion) by the increasing visibility of households, relationships and domestic arrangements that do not conform to a hetero-normative ideal. During the late 1990s, especially, the idea that the family could still be represented as a single monolithic entity and as a space separate from the public world thus became much more difficult to sustain politically.

Thinking 'the family'

Of course, the state has always intervened in the family. Despite the repeated claims made for the family's uniquely ahistorical, timeless and therefore non-social nature, it has actually been the subject of a barrage of social, political and philosophical criticism and attempted transformations – not only by politicians. Marxist and socialist writers, in particular, have been exercised by the family's problematic role in capitalism, from Friedrich Engels' *The Origin of the Family* and *Private Property and the State* (1884, 1972), which identified the family as a crucial site for the reproduction of labour and of 'bourgeois ideology', through to Eli Zaretsky's *Capitalism, the Family and Personal Life* (1976). Yet Engels emphasized a productionist model in which work is the overarching category. Indeed, his account is so thoroughly materialist in its concerns that it can make little space for the intangibles of personal relations, which are the most difficult to transform. In addition, an attachment to 'scientific' socialism made it difficult to represent the apparently unscientific realm of the emotions.

During the 1960s and 1970s, however, the family was an important target for feminist criticism that in some ways took as its agenda the emotional aspects of domestic life. For early 'second-wave' feminists, such as Betty Friedan (1963), it had been precisely the way in which the personal sphere of family life – what we might now call its affective aspects – had been excluded from the political that needed to be addressed by a new feminist politics. Friedan's work was followed by important and more rigorously argued interventions by Juliet Mitchell (1971) on femininity and class, Ann Oakley (1974) on the politics of housework, and by a new salvo from Friedan herself in 1981. Perhaps the most important feminist work on the family, however, has been Michele Barrett and Mary McIntosh's *The Anti-social Family* (1982), which offers a sustained critique of the social relations involved from a socialist-feminist perspective.

Since that book was published there has been a proliferation of critical writing about gender, mainly concerned with sexuality and the production of subjectivity, the most influential of which must be Judith Butler's *Gender Trouble* (1990), which has helped to radically destabilize gender categories in its 'queering' of sexual subjects. Such work has rarely explicitly addressed family discourses, although it strongly influenced much research in the area, perhaps precisely because of the way in which the family has been bundled into hetero-normativity. Indeed, writing on the family has tended to remain clustered in the more 'social' areas of history, sociology and anthropology, especially in the work of Jeffrey Weeks, Carol Smart, Leonore Davidoff and Catherine Hall, and in film studies in the writings of E. Ann Kaplan, Lucy Fischer, Christine Geraghty and Sarah Harwood.

This book owes a debt to the work of all these writers and more. In addition, Jacques Donzelot's (1980) Foucauldian reading of the family as a site of a range of discursive intersections in *The Policing of Families* has in some ways influenced my own approach, specifically, the insistence on the importance of governance in the regulation of familialism and its recognition of the complexity of the relationship between the family and the social. However, contra Donzelot, I wanted to retain some attachment to the idea of agency in the production of meanings about family relationships and identifications, and a strong insistence on cultural specificity and material relations in their non-reductive sense. In this respect, the cultural studies tradition of studying contexts seems to me to be vital, in the context of what I would call the 'why this text *now*?' question. Equally important is the analysis of form as well as content – the way we tell stories about the family – in any consideration of cultural articulations. I have tried to pay attention to both these concerns in order to show how the process of mediation involves a web of silences and contradictions, as well as noise and affirmations.

Clearly, the power relations involved in the mediation of the family are a central concern here; but identifying and exploring those relations must also take into account resistance and refusals, as well as the ways in which power itself *produces* resistance, as Foucault (1981) has argued. While this book's focus on material relations is not very Foucauldian, I hope that I have been able to use the idea of discourse in a productive way. More than any other single theorist, however, I wanted to recover some of the historicizing ideas of Raymond Williams, a cultural thinker whose combination of intellectual rigour and critical breadth I cannot hope to match, but whose work remains an important touchstone for cultural analysis.

chapter one

Nuclear family values? Meanings and mediations from the 1940s to the 1960s

Introduction

In order to understand the changes that have taken place around mediations of the family, gender identities and relations of power and kinship over the last 50 years, we need to begin by locating such shifts within the specific cultural and historical context of post-war western society. In particular, the 1950s have been central to the way in which the family has been imagined and represented, both directly, in political discourse, and through more indirect but no less powerful cultural mediations. Certainly, the idea that this decade was a golden age of family values, the high point of bourgeois norms and certainties around sexuality, gender and the relationship between adults and children, persists in shaping contemporary assumptions and subjectivities.

Indeed, the repeated recirculation via cable channels of 1950s television series and films, such as *I Love Lucy* and the early Doris Day movies, together with the retro-nostalgia of advertising, has helped to construct a complex process of signification and cultural memory in which the family – or rather an idealized version of the white American nuclear family – is firmly locked into the 1950s. As Stephanie Coontz points out, 'our most powerful visions of traditional families derive from images that are still delivered to our homes in countless reruns of 1950s television sitcoms' (1992: 23).

It is important to recognize that while such representations offer a pleasurable opportunity to fantasize, they are just that: re-presentations, texts not mirrors, mediations not absolute truths about the past. *I Love Lucy* was part of a complex process of negotiations around the family, not a reflection of its stability; Doris Day's capitulation to marriage always came at a high price to her self-respect. The nostalgia for the 1950s family also ignores the political paranoia and fear of a real nuclear threat – the atomic bomb – that was always in the background, as well as evading the more evident power differentials of class, race and ethnicity in such texts. This chapter therefore sets out some of the fundamental structural changes that took place during the post-war period, and explores the extent to which they helped to shape the 'lived' culture of family life and its mediation in film, television and, equally importantly, official or quasi-official discourses. It also proposes that the particular family ideal that dominated culture during the 20 years roughly between the late 1940s and late 1960s was part of a dynamic involving struggles over meaning – and power.

Reconstructing the family

In the immediate period after the Second World War, from 1945 until the early 1950s, in the UK, the USA and much of Western Europe, the family was regarded as a central cornerstone in the necessary physical and ideological reconstruction of civil society. Because the war had largely secured popular support as a battle *for* democracy and *against* political totalitarianism – a 'people's war', if ever there was one (and there aren't many, as the invasion of Iraq in 2003 demonstrated) – the desire to build societies that were economically stable, socially inclusive, politically consensual and with a strongly defined sense of citizenship became central to the 'post-war settlement' (Henessey 1993). This is not to suggest that the consensus itself was not struggled over and debated. Neil Grant (1984) gives an incisive account of the way in which conscripted British soldiers were prepared for peacetime, through citizenship education during the last months of the Second World War, and points to the political contestations that developed over the process. There can be little doubt, however, that this, together with the mock parliaments that were set up, contributed powerfully to raising consciousness about the nature and purpose of democracy when it came to the general election of 1945. Indeed, contrary to the current emphasis on the 1950s as a decade which saw a return to traditional values, it is important to emphasize that the post-war moment was one in which modernity was an important organizing idea.

This commitment to national and international renewal focused intensively on the desire to restore the family life that war had disrupted; wartime anomie and chaos were supposed to be replaced with cohesion and familial stability. In the UK, for example, the development of what became known as the welfare state was central to this reconstructive move and to the way in which the family was cast as its central focus. As Jeffrey Weeks observes, 'the creation of a [British] Welfare State in the 1940s [was] based, however tenuously, on an ideology of social (and even sexual) reconciliation' (1989: 232). At the heart of this was the idea of reproduction in every sense: both social and sexual. The building of the modern state was powerfully bound up with a 'structure of feeling', to use Raymond Williams' (1977) phrase, that foregrounded family relationships. Yet the family was also subject to competing and sometimes contradictory claims to entitlement which did not always sit easily with these ideals. The post-war project would thus cast a long cultural shadow over the following decades, and especially over the ways in which the family was imagined.

Although the desire to rebuild the family was partly fuelled by concerns about the falling population rates that had preceded the war (frequently articulated in the disturbingly eugenicist terms of the need to 'breed for a healthy nation'), the reconstructive discourse also made space for an emergent set of priorities, in which the importance of forging a modern society, marked by shared responsibility and mutual dependence, took centre stage. In the

UK, the Report of the Royal Commission on Population of 1949 argued for the necessity of repopulating the country with 'good human stock' (Blackford 1995: 60). This was preceded by the 'Beveridge Report' (as it became known informally), published in 1942 as *Social Insurance and Allied Services*, which had established the principles of an integrated system of welfare provision that became the blueprint for the Labour government's new welfare state. Incorporating a commitment to 'welfare citizenship', the new system was particularly focused on improving mothering as the key to social transformation, and on mothers as the agents of such change (Riley 1983).

In all of this, the assumption that the state not only had the power but also had the *right* to intervene in the family was central to securing the hegemony of welfare reforms. The various versions of state welfare provision that developed at this historical juncture (even in the USA) were therefore wholly tied to a process in which the family's relationship to the state was actively redefined. It was to be subject to legitimate intervention by various government agencies in ways that were cast as consensual rather than coercive; as Leonore Davidoff et al. argue, such interventions would consistently 'reinforce particular boundaries of family obligation based on implicit constructions of the "normal" family' (1999: 48). This meant that while the principles of welfarism were generally consented to, the specific terms on which the state intervened in family life were often strongly contested in some popular articulations of family life.

In the film *The Happy Family* (1952), for example, the petit-bourgeois Lord family run a shop that is situated on the site planned for the Festival of Britain (a public jamboree that was intended to mark the end of post-war austerity and look forward to a confident future) and is therefore due to be demolished. This situation, as Christine Geraghty observes, 'sets the family in opposition to the state' (2000: 136). In fact, the film explores the Lords' battle with authority in the conservative populist terms of an uncaring bureaucracy versus honest family values, with the family becoming increasingly isolated in their attempts to resist change. Interestingly, the Lords win the battle, their shop is saved 'as a shrine' to the principle that an Englishman's home is his castle and the values of traditional family life are preserved. *The Happy Family*, although hardly a major film of the 1950s, oddly resonates as a staging of the conflicted relationship between the family and the state and of the particular terms – patriarchal and narrowly insular – in which the former continued to be defended in the UK against statist modernity.

In the USA, the post-war settlement was less explicitly linked to a particular reform programme, but reconstructivism undoubtedly informed the politico-cultural climate, making space for narratives that problematized – albeit in the conservative and populist terms of 'the little man versus big business' – the ruthlessness of monopoly capitalism and the personal costs it extracted, while also emphasizing the importance of family and community to national consciousness after the trauma of war. In *The Best Years of Our Lives* (1946), for example, the film's plot hinges on a loan that is awarded on the basis of personal character rather than financial equity, the guarantee for which is a serviceman's combat experience during the war – that is, his commitment to the nation and therefore, implicitly, to the renewal of family life.

In a slightly different take on these relations, *It's a Wonderful Life* (1947) has a hero,

George Bailey, who is finally saved from despair by the evidence that his selflessness as a family man and his community spirit have had an immeasurable impact on the lives of those around him. In both films, while the post-war desire for social transformation is translated into a celebration of small-town family life that seems to prefigure the more overtly ideological drive towards family values in the 1950s, the emphasis on the importance of the feminine space of domesticity, intimacy and social connectedness is notable. Yet this concern was at best double-edged when it came to women's rights, both within and outside the family structure.

Women, families, welfare: citizens or dependants?

While access to one form of political citizenship in the shape of the vote had been gained by adult women in most western societies by the late 1940s, women's status as autonomous citizens in the sense generally reserved for adult men was complicated by their continued economic subordination in marriage and by the effective institutionalization of this status in various welfare systems. In the USA, the assumption that a 'family wage' earned by a male breadwinner was the standard means by which most women were economically supported had already been established by Roosevelt's New Deal policy of public assistance in the 1930s. As well as naturalizing the economic dependence of married women, public assistance located the family at the heart of national welfare and identified the single mother as doubly unnatural. Indeed, as Linda Gordon points out, 'Long after the family wage was doomed . . . the charity of the public assistance system added to [lone mothers'] disadvantage – such as low wages and responsibility for children – by emphasizing domesticity as the only maternal virtue' (1994: 290–1). Indeed, the American mobilization of moral criteria when assessing women's entitlement to welfare (Mink 1991: 110) articulated these assumptions in highly instrumental ways.

The problematic status of the lone mother is exemplified by the film *Bachelor Mother* (1939), a comedy about single motherhood, which carefully ensures that the cinema audience knows long before Ginger Rogers' shocked co-workers that she has *found* the baby she is caring for – not that she has conceived it out of wedlock. As E. Ann Kaplan notes, by the mid-1950s American films were even more circumspect in their representation of motherhood, stifled by the paranoia surrounding McCarthyism and the fear of being thought 'un-American' to stick to largely 'safe' accounts of family life (1992: 173). Even in those films that attempted to posit the possibility of familial or marital conflict, such as the very odd *Young At Heart* (1954), in which a youthful and edgily urban Frank Sinatra finds himself clasped to the bosom of an all-American suburban family, an uneasy reconciliation was found to ensure a happy ending. Significantly, mothering is absent from the narrative, despite the film's sentimentalization of the family. Instead, a termagant aunt with a soft centre fills the role of domestic carer.

In the UK, as part of its intervention into the family structure, the Beveridge Report redefined women's entitlements within marriage, with the publicly expressed aim of revaluing housework and the role of the housewife. The report stressed the importance of seeing married women as partners in a marital team, with housewives defined as being in 'ungainful employment' (that is, doing unpaid work) rather than 'unoccupied' (Blackford 1995: 61). However, this also helped to embed more firmly married women's economic dependence on their husbands, while giving them no automatic right of access to the 'family wage' earned by the male. Housekeeping money thus largely depended on the goodwill and generosity of individual husbands. However, it might also, more complexly, mean the tradition in many working-class families whereby the weekly wage was automatically handed over to the wife, whose responsibility was to manage the household economy (see, for example, Richard Hoggart's account of the role of the working-class matriarch in *The Uses of Literacy*, 1957).

In other parts of Western Europe, similarly conservative models of the family were also incorporated into the new systems of citizenship and national restructuring. The West German version of the welfare state drew heavily on a corporatist-paternalist model in which, again, the married woman's dependence on a male breadwinner and 'head of household' was institutionalized, with women's caring and domestic labour effectively incorporated into the system as the primary source of welfare provision, as Lewis points out (1992a). The process of reconstruction and reconciliation during this period therefore involved a political marriage between two potentially contradictory discourses: an essentially modernist belief in technology and expert knowledge as the route to social improvement and a more conservative commitment to ideals of community and continuity, in which women's role within the family was highly prescribed.

The forging of an *ideological* relationship between the family structure and the state was a crucial dimension to these systems. As Elizabeth Wilson (1977) has argued, the role that women are supposed to play as mothers is reproductive both in its immediate biological and physical sense, and in its cultural sense. Mothers are expected to take responsibility for the transmission of particular cultural values and practices, for socializing children into particular roles and for mediating children's relations with the public world through their nurturing practices. With the post-war growth in the state's responsibility for and policing of family relationships, this role was placed under greater surveillance and was the subject of a host of different mediatory strategies and texts.

Managing the contradictions
Work

This approach – to the family and the relative economic status of women – was therefore full of tensions and contradictions. In the UK, despite a significant decline in female factory workers immediately after the war, the number of women still in regular employment by the early 1950s remained around six million, although many of these were unmarried (Philips and Tomlinson 1992). While in the USA systematic attempts were made to remind women workers that their presence had been 'for the duration only' (see the feminist documentary, *Rosie the Riveter*, 1980), the British Labour government made some attempt to encourage women to remain in work through exhortation. A Central Office of Information film,

Women Must Work, appeared in 1947, and the decision to close the children's nurseries, which had been opened during the war to enable women to enter the workforce, was not the consequence of a coherent strategy to send women back into the home, but rather one of short-termism and political expediency (Weeks 1989: 233).

At the same time, however, attempts to encourage women to work outside the home were undercut by the unexamined assumption that married women, in particular, remained a 'reserve army' of labour who would (and should) be committed to the family primarily. Most employed women were concentrated in low-paid jobs in factories, shops and offices and the scarcity of reliable forms of childcare meant that juggling work and domestic life was always problematic. Even middle-class women found that without the mainly female servants who had left for better paid and better regulated work during the war years, simply keeping up appearances at home often involved hard manual labour, as the novels of Elizabeth Taylor, published throughout the 1950s, exquisitely attest – the genteel struggles of managing with nothing more than a daily 'help' are portrayed with a detailed economy (*The Blush*, 1958).

Kinship

Throughout this period, the idea of the family was itself in the process of redefinition. It increasingly came to be understood to mean the *nuclear* family of father, mother and two children, rather than the traditional extended family that had remained a norm until the First World War in many western countries. This modern model emerged partly through the greater availability and acceptability of effective contraception to married couples – although the UK birth rate actually went up between 1943 and 1948 (Weeks 1989: 245) – together with the new emphasis on social planning, including family planning (exemplified by the establishment of the Family Planning Association in 1939). The long-term trend was towards limiting the number of children in a family to two or three, despite the pleas of the head of the Anglican Church, the archbishop of Canterbury, who apparently argued in a speech to the Mothers' Union in 1952 that 'a family only truly begins with three children' (Weeks 1989: 233).

The changing definition of the family was also a product of the increased affluence and social mobility that marked the post-war years. In the USA, where the ideal of the classless society was already a powerful component of the American Dream, the desire to achieve middle-class status was an important element in the post-war drive to social renewal, and the nuclear family was a powerful symbol of this. Even in the UK, where there was a more embedded history of class inequality and conflict, the political rhetoric around 'the affluent society' in the 1950s and 1960s helped to shape new expectations. These structural changes were also linked to the emergent forms of individualization associated with late modernity, in which social and kinship networks are increasingly understood as autonomous and relatively isolated from other social structures (Beck 1992). The family came to mean a relatively small-scale, intensely private unit, connected by immediate emotional and economic ties rather than a loose-knit, broadly linked community of 'kith and kin'. Culturally, however, the most significant factor was a new emphasis on the emotional and relational aspects of domesticity – family life – and the social good.

Housing

Throughout the post-war years, family housing was thus increasingly associated with suburban developments of individual, privately contained homes, each with its garden, drive, garage and separate bedrooms for two children, rather than the city apartment or cramped terraced house. Such housing represented a cultural as well as an economic investment in a domesticated version of modernity (and the modern family) for many (Silverstone 1997: 4). To move to the suburbs was to express confidence in the future and one's place there. However, this process was largely confined to white populations, especially in the USA where the move to the suburbs also marked the beginnings of 'white flight' from the older industrial cities whose infrastructure was beginning to crumble. (In the UK, of course, the new black and Asian populations tended to be clustered in the inner cities.)

The growth of suburban housing estates and new towns of modern, purpose-built dwellings outside the old urban spaces represented more than a change of domicile during the 1950s: it marked an emergent change in class position, as large numbers of urban working-class families found themselves newly affluent and socially aspirational. 'The move outwards [was] also a move upwards', as Willmott and Young observed (1960: 3). For the first time, they could look forward to a steady income, a well-equipped kitchen and bathroom, a planned family and middle-class status. This shift also marked significant changes in patterns of work and social life, including reductions in weekly working hours, the increase in white-collar jobs, and the 'suburban separation of "work" and "life"' noted by Raymond Williams (1961: 211), in which 'life' meant leisure time spent at home with the family.

Indeed, the idea that families would automatically benefit from (largely male-dominated) technological and scientific expertise was central to the way in which the future was imagined in these post-war estates, often with little reference to the desires or experiences of married women, who actually found themselves living the suburban dream. As Judy Attfield has shown (1995), attempts by British post-war planners to impose a modernist aesthetic on the newly suburbanized working-class families who moved out to one new town, Harlow, was strongly resisted by women who wanted to retain a very different set of ideas about taste and domesticity. By the early 1960s, the suburbs would be cast as one of the sources of Betty Friedan's 'problem that has no name' (1963): the discontent that affluent white middle-class American women were beginning to feel at being marginalized (literally) from the sources of decision-making and power, through their 'imprisonment' in the suburbs. The combination of increased social mobility, the fragmentation of older family and kinship networks and family planning in various guises all contributed, therefore, to the emergence of the normative model of familialism and domestic life that came to dominate the post-war years – and to increased critiques and resistance.

The family, femininity and domestic life

Unsurprisingly, the main burden of the domestic ideal fell upon women's shoulders. Throughout the two decades following the end of the war, the family was increasingly represented as the primary ideological centre of women's lives. Although by 1957 one-third of married women were employed in the UK (Lewis 1978: 64), the ideological emphasis of femininity and feminine cultural forms remained focused on domesticity as the only legitimate site of female identity. In the USA, the emphasis of the Truman and Eisenhower administrations on economic progress and America's growing affluence, together with anxieties about un-American values, meant that the ideology of familialism and its centrality to accounts of national identity were difficult to disentangle. The American way of life continued to be powerfully linked to the ideal of the white, Anglo-Saxon and patriarchal family in its picket-fenced small-town home, mythologized in the 1930s and 1940s by Norman Rockwell's sentimental paintings.

It is, however, important to recognize that, while this powerful discourse of familialism was not without critical resistance, its hegemony articulated a genuinely popular (if contradictory) response to the war itself, and to the kind of economic and social freedoms that war work had offered women. While these freedoms were frequently cast as a threat, both to the successful reincorporation of ex-servicemen into mainstream civilian society and to the future of the family itself, the special role of mothers as the moral guardians of the family was offered as an appealing alternative. Married women who 'chose' to go out to work not only risked being accused by others of taking jobs from the men to whom they supposedly rightfully belonged, but they were also likely to become part of the value system that set up polarized versions of 'selfish' versus 'self-denying' femininity. This powerful set of oppositions, around a nurturing and dutiful model of femininity and a thoughtless and narcissistic model that sought outside employment largely for frivolous reasons ('pin money'), informed much of the discursive shift around women, work and the family that took place during the late 1940s and early 1950s.

By the mid-1950s, the enormous growth in affluence in western countries and the consequent emergence of a vibrant and thriving consumer culture meant that the housewife became identified as a pivotal cultural figure, responsible not only for the physical labour of caring for the family but also for the less tangible emotional and cultural labour of consumer decision-making. In 1953, the political imperative for married women was not to work – it was to buy.

Modernizing femininity

Women's magazines best articulated this remarkable transformation through their own shift in emphasis during the early 1950s. The focus on service in the public sphere, political engagement and cheerful sacrifice that had been a mainstay of such journals in the immediate post-war period gave way to a new preoccupation with private space and domesticity. Janice Radway traces this move in her account of changing discourses around women's aspirations and concerns in the most popular women's magazine of the period in the UK, *Woman* (1984: 188–211). Until the late 1940s, *Woman*, like other popular journals, remained dominated by the war-time ideology of national duty, 'make do and mend' and public responsibility, in which the nation as well as the individual woman was a central figure. As Radway observes, at this point, *Woman* fully endorsed state-funded nurseries as a necessary part of the modernization of women's lives, away from the drudgery of the pre-war years. By the early 1950s, however, the magazine had radically changed its position: it was now emphasizing the role of the full-time mother and housewife as the modern way to care for the family. It did this explicitly through its newly expanded focus on childcare and 'expert' knowledge, and also in its colourfully seductive features about cordon-bleu cookery and home decoration – activities which frequently necessitated hours of intensive labour unavailable to those in paid employment. In this way, *Woman* and other popular magazines both articulated the changing currents of opinion around femininity and helped to manage them.

Such magazines therefore represented a significant discursive site around which a modernized ideology of femininity was developed and tested – the production of what Radway calls 'conservative modernity'. The modern woman of the 1920s and 1930s had largely been a class-specific figure – the bourgeois housewife with a cook and other servants – and her modernity also entailed a necessary degree of detachment from domesticity, even if this was bought at the expense of other, working-class, women (to be modern thus involved moving out of the devalued domestic sphere). In E. M. Delafield's *Diary of a Provincial Lady* (1930), for example, the eponymous author earns her own living as a journalist, despairs of yet often ignores her tetchily disengaged husband and is politically independent, while retaining an interest in the feminine concerns of fashion and beauty. The version of modernized womanhood that became hegemonic in the 1950s, however, while less class-specific, was marked by a powerfully insistent focus on domestic life and the home as the primary concern for women. Far from rejecting domesticity, the truly modern woman of the 1950s was encouraged to embrace it and remake it in her own image.

This discourse drew on a number of elements. It mobilized the idea of a modern consciousness, strongly influenced by popular Freudianism, in which individualism and notions of self-fulfilment were central: the modern housewife used her domestic labour creatively in order to generate pleasure and interest. It drew on the currency of the post-war commitment to rationalism and technology as a problem-solving mechanism: the modern housewife demonstrated her technological competence through her use of the new kitchen appliances, such as washing machines and refrigerators (Walley 1960). Cookery books habitually offered examples of 'menus for a week' that included detailed suggestions for an efficiently managed schedule for every meal. The discourse also represented domestic labour in the flattering register of management and professional knowledge: the modern housewife was not a drudge, she was a 'home economist' or 'domestic scientist', someone whose expertise in cooking or cleaning could match (and perhaps even exceed) her husband's skills at the office or workshop – although *The Jackson Cookery Book* (1953) sternly advised the 'Cook-Hostess' to 'leave the drinks to some male member of the household'.

In this way, housework was re-presented as a form of skilled labour and the housewife as the expert manager of a specialized domain. Importantly, these concerns also spoke to the pleasures and the autonomy that women found in the home and in their work there, as well as a sense of the dignity of domestic labour and its intrinsic value – as an expression of care, love and nurturing. For many women, getting married was the gateway to independence, in which managing household tasks and organizing one's day at home was an expression of personal freedom.

Coupledom, 'the age of marriages' and the reproductive imperative
The companionate marriage

Linked to the changing form of the family structure during the post-war years, an important shift in the meanings attached to marriage was also taking place at the level of cultural production. Whereas marriage in traditional or pre-modern societies had been largely an alliance between families or clans, with the individual partners playing a less important role, modern marriage was predicated on a narrower, but much more intense, conceptualization in which the primary allegiance was between the couple and was based upon personal commitment to each other. The Beveridge Report's formal commitment to marriage as a partnership of equals was one very concrete symptom of this. The other was the growing dominance of the discourse of romantic love as a prelude to matrimony. For women especially, the idea of romance as a cultural entitlement became part of the more general expectations produced around marriage throughout the 1950s and into the 1960s.

It is important to stress here that this model of intimacy was not invented in the 1940s; nor was it an overnight transformation. The emphasis on romantic love within marriage can be traced back at least to 1920s sexology (e.g. Havelock Ellis) and to works such as Marie Stopes' *Married Love* (1918), which tended to glorify marital sex as an intensely spiritual shared experience, which depended on mutual respect as well as desire. In the post-war period, however, it was becoming newly democratized, although this does not mean that everyone felt an equal entitlement (Giles 1995).

The popularization of psychoanalysis in the 1940s and 1950s also helped to boost the sexualization of the marriage ideal, and this was correlated by the rather differently conceived but equally significant sex 'reports' of Alfred Kinsey in the late 1940s and early 1950s (published in 1948 and 1953), and Masters and Johnson in the mid-1960s. Women's magazines also contributed to the management of the boundaries of marital relations at this time: they asserted women's right to expect romantic love and, in a coded way, sexual pleasure, while simultaneously insisting on marriage as the only 'healthy' context for women's sexual expression. The 'companionate marriage' thus made space for the recognition of mutual desire on the part of women as well as men, even if it did not always accord that desire the same status. By 1948 the Marriage Guidance Council was arguing for the desirability of 'satisfying orgasms' for both husbands and wives as an essential component of a happy marriage (Weeks 1989: 237). However, as Wilson suggests, the sexual ideal was complementary rather than egalitarian, emphasizing 'sexual potency in men and sexual responsiveness in women' (1977: 66).

For men, 'sexual potency' was further legitimated by the wider availability of (hetero) sex as a recreational (as opposed to procreational) activity, in the form of glossy, well-designed and respectable 'girlie' magazines such as *Playboy* (which first appeared in 1953 – a year that seems to be the *annus mirabilis* of this chapter in many ways). While the 1950s were marked by the growing sexualization of women in the public domain, helped by the crossover textuality of films and pin-up magazines, exemplified by the career of Marilyn Monroe (Dyer 1986), the emergent sexual liberatory discourse of the later 1950s also spoke to women. The idea of sex as recreation was crucial to the new dynamic around coupledom and marriage, as Richard Dyer has pointed out.

Indeed, popular culture more generally was heavily dominated by a preoccupation with recreational romance. Popular music during the 1950s and well into the 1960s featured balladeers such as Bing Crosby, Rosemary Clooney, Nat King Cole and Frank Sinatra, whose material celebrated and wryly problematized marriage as the inevitable legacy of heterosexual desire. Sinatra's work in this period, for example, tended to oscillate between a celebration of heterosexual coupledom, overtly linked to moneyed sophistication ('Come Fly with Me'), an emphasis on old-fashioned morality ('Love and Marriage') and half-serious warnings addressed to men about the dangers of matrimony ('The Tender Trap'). This, as well as the popularity of paperback romantic novels and the cultural reach of Hollywood romantic comedies and musicals, clearly contributed to the hegemony of romance and the companionate ideal from the 1930s and 1940s onwards. In films as relatively divergent as *Top Hat* (1935), *It Happened One Night* (1936) and *I Was a Male War Bride* (1949), the companionate relationship of the romantic couple is further emphasized in (but also potentially troubled by) wisecracks and wordplay.

One example of how seriously all this was taken by middle-class couples can be found in Richard Johnson's revealing and thoughtful analysis of his own experience as a young husband during the early 1960s, in which he reflects on the importance of sex to marriage in what he calls 'the Age of Marriages':

> Sexuality was central, for both man and woman, as part of an ideal of 'companionate' marriage. Perhaps it was central primarily for the husband and the many male commentators on marriage, but women's sexuality (however subordinated) was also recognised in ways it had not been before . . . This meant that such couple relationships, especially if pursued rather 'seriously' . . . could be very intense and all-encompassing.
>
> (Johnson 1997: 248)

This intensity was especially important within the context of wider social shifts towards greater privacy and the closing down of the family into the nuclear model. Couples were to depend upon each other for emotional support and shared interests as well as for economic stability, and this was recognized as a new challenge for men as well as for women.

Yet, as Geraghty points out, while many film comedies of the mid-1950s helped to clear a space for this new kind of relationship, they frequently ended by reasserting male dominance in new and subtle ways. In the British film, *Genevieve* (1953), for example, whose narrative about two couples taking part in the London to Brighton vintage car rally seems to embody the ideology of the companionate marriage, it is still the female characters (played by Kay Kendall and Dinah Sheridan) who are required to subordinate their own interests to the charms of rallying in order to produce the heterosexual couple as a companionate alliance – and to ensure that Kendall's character is 'rewarded' with the promise of marriage. As Geraghty says, 'the final resolution of the narrative, which refigures the couples on the basis of heterosexual companionship rather than gender alliances, is achieved . . . by the women making the move into a more sympathetic position with their men' (2000: 164). The marriage of companionship, if it was to involve shared interests, was still to be dominated by male hobbies or occupations.

Modernity v. tradition

The 'modern' marriage in which men and women were supposed to be 'different but equal', and in which partners invested considerable emotional work, was therefore crucial to the new economy of desire. It was also frequently favourably compared to an imagined older, reductive model – often linked to the working class – in which couples stayed together for economic and social rather than emotional reasons. In *The Catered Affair* (1956), for example, a film that is all about marriage and the family, the narrative revolves around the emotional conflicts and anxieties submerged in a New York blue-collar family's relationships with each other. These concerns are brought to the surface by the mother's (Bette Davis) plans for an elaborate and expensive wedding for the only daughter of the household. The film contrasts the relaxed attitude towards sex and the easy companionship of the young couple who are to be married (Debbie Reynolds and Rod Taylor), with the bride's parents' uneasy and evidently desexualized relationship. In a key scene, the daughter realizes that her mother's coded warnings about the pressures of marriage – 'I'm just saying it isn't all a bed of roses' – are an indication of her parents' estrangement from each other and the absence of love from the relationship.

The film's commitment to the ideal of the companionate marriage and its assumption that this represents something new is articulated in the way in which it works to contrast the young couple's shared interests and activities (they do the washing-up together, go out to the cinema and are uninterested in a complicated wedding) with the older couple's rigidly separated roles within marriage and their uncommunicative dealings. Indeed, the film ends with a recuperative gesture that is not wholly convincing, but which confirms the importance of the companionate model to contemporary ideologies of marriage: the parents rediscover their commitment to each other and begin to rekindle their relationship.

However, the appearance of so many texts about marriage clearly suggests, not that marital contentment was a given at this point, but rather that it was a source of anxiety and struggle. As Peter Evans and Celestine Deleyto point out, debates about sex and marriage were central to popular films during this period: '[t]he cycle of "sex comedies" of the 1950s and early 1960s appears at a time of unprecedented open discussions of sexual matters in the

USA and one in which marriage is increasingly perceived as a repressive institution' (1998b: 6). The idea that marriage was particularly repressive for *men*, especially as a limited sexual outlet, together with the pitfalls that could befall the couple who made the wrong choice, was the subject of a wide range of texts, both popular and 'serious', during the 1950s and early 1960s. For men in the early 1960s, especially, and before the liberalization of the divorce laws, marriage represented a lifetime commitment to supporting another person economically, regardless of whether there was much affection left on either side – and even if there never had been. The assumption that a married woman remained the economic responsibility of her husband thus coloured the way in which even the companionate marriage was represented.

One example of this is Stan Barstow's novel, *A Kind of Loving* (1962), which successfully expresses the tensions felt by a young man 'trapped' into marriage by pregnancy yet retaining a belief in the possibility of true love. Such texts articulate very clearly both the desires and the anxieties involved in the establishment of the couple, as well as showing the growing importance of sexual, emotional and intellectual compatability to contemporary ideologies of marriage. Barstow's work is also interesting because of its relationship to the counter-discourses around marriage that circulated during this period, especially those expressing male resistance.

Male resistance and anxieties

It would be a mistake to assume that there was no resistance to the hegemony of this ideal, especially within specifically masculine cultural spaces and forms. Lynne Segal (1988, 1990) carefully delineates how a large part of masculine popular culture and, more subtly, many elite cultural forms (which were heavily male-dominated) in the 1950s and early 1960s were saturated with a particularly vicious misogyny, in which marriage was figured as a female trap to be avoided by sensible men. Women were habitually represented as intellectually inferior, their 'value' to a man in marriage largely dependent on a transient desirability and on the social prohibitions that made non-marital sex so difficult. The new men's magazines, such as *Playboy*, also helped to articulate this double discourse (as well as the double standard), of women as desirable objects and marriage as a trap, in their emphasis on masculine freedom from domestic constraints.

As Segal points out, much of the celebrated work of the 'Angry Young Men' of the decade, such as John Osborne and Kingsley Amis, expressed a profound hostility towards women. In Amis's comic novel, *Lucky Jim*, for example, the eponymous sort-of-hero, Jim Dixon, is constantly finding himself unwillingly caught up in a vaguely amorous relationship with the neurotic and selfish Margaret Peel, a woman whose sexual attractiveness is limited – she is described as 'small, thin and bespectacled, with bright make-up' (1992: 18) – and whose attempts to secure Jim's affections are close to blackmail. Margaret is unfavourably compared to the beautiful Christine Callaghan, who is both younger and, importantly, sexually passive rather than threateningly desiring. For Amis, Jim's final sexual conquest of Christine is linked to his triumph in the public world, a reassertion of dominance. As Segal ironically muses:

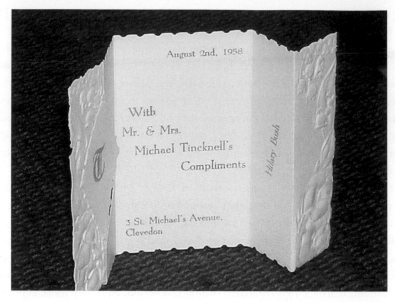

August 2nd, 1958

With
Mr. & Mrs.
Michael Tincknell's
Compliments

Hilary Bush

3 St. Michael's Avenue,
Clevedon

Figure 1.1 My parents' wedding cake gift cards make it clear that even in the era of the companionate marriage, Hilary Bush must become the appendage of her husband as Mrs Michael Tincknell.

> A stifling domesticity has killed the spirit and ripped out the guts of men, and who is there to blame but women? Who indeed, if, like Osborne and most of the other 'Angries', you are a rebel without a cause and believe that class struggle is obsolete and Marx a fraud?'
>
> (Segal 1990: 15)

The ideology of the companionate marriage thus effectively worked to conceal the continuing power imbalance inherent in the institution. As Segal observes, there was a powerful residual sense that 'separate spheres' for men and women were still inevitable, even within the home, and the gendered division of labour was only intermittently challenged (1988: 73). In the public sphere and in the official discourses of legal and governmental instruments women remained even more overtly subordinated. 'Mrs John Smith' and 'Mrs Jack Jones' were not only expected to disappear beneath their husbands' names, especially in formal and official contexts, but they were also customarily required to gain their spouses' written assent for bank accounts, credit or major purchases, despite the privileged cultural status of the housewife consumer.

Working women, career girls and female fulfilment

It is in this context that we can see how work outside the home for women was (mis)represented in terms of a 'choice' between careers: one, the 'natural' career of the family and motherhood; the other, paid work of almost any kind, which, if undertaken full-time for a lifetime, meant that the woman must compete with men in the workplace and might suffer all sorts of psychological consequences. The influence of Freudian theory made anxieties about women's 'healthy fulfilment' (with its coded sexual references), whether as mothers, lovers or (sexually repressed) librarians, a central thread of any debate about the issue. To attempt both to be a mother and to have a career was potentially dangerously transgressive.

Yet this psychosexual discourse also disguised the extent to which meaningful career development was almost entirely tied to class. The expansion of the 'caring' professions facilitated by the modern state during this period, as well as the emergence of new careers utilizing feminine cultural competences linked to artistic or design skills (see, for example, the films *The Constant Husband*, 1955, or *Designing Woman*, 1957), mainly meant making space for middle-class women in the workplace. Prohibitions on the 'working wife' were made slightly more problematic by the figure of Queen Elizabeth, who, as Geraghty points out, 'epitomized the "new woman" who was such a feature of the 1950s . . . [as] that most troublesome of creatures, a woman who went out to work (2000: 156). If these particular tensions were mainly managed by recourse to the ideology of duty and tradition in much description of the queen's work, it did not completely erase the fact that she operated in the public sphere and was the most important person present wherever she went. And, as Philips and Tomlinson point out (1992: 38), in the USA especially, 'careers books' for girls, such as the Sue Barton series, contributed to a sense that there was a new attitude towards working women.

Notwithstanding these circumstances, routine office work was the most likely 'career' open to most young women. It was seen as appropriately feminine (it serviced the 'real' labour being done by men) and might be relatively glamorous, not because the work itself was intrinsically interesting but because it facilitated entry to a 'man's world' of commerce and competition, and therefore increased the chances of meeting a suitable husband. For example, in Barbara Pym's novel, *Jane and Prudence* (1953), Prudence Bates has an ill-defined job as an 'assistant', based in what Pym amusingly describes as a 'vaguely cultural organisation' somewhere in Bloomsbury, helping the eminent but clearly wholly self-satisfied Dr Grampian, with whom she believes herself to be in love and about whom she daydreams, ('the thought of Arthur having to go without his elevenses was quite unbearable', 1953: 42). Prudence's self-delusion, as well as her sense of cultural superiority as a career girl over her married and comfortably muddle-headed friend, Jane, is the source of much of the book's comedy. While Prudence has a good degree of cultural investment in an idealized image of herself as a working woman, the novel's ironic voice makes it clear that what she really wants is to be loved and to be married.

The extent to which the figure of the 'career woman' or (sexually unfulfilled) 'girl' was a source of tension can be illustrated by a brief consideration of an unlikely text: the Nat King Cole song, 'Dance, Ballerina, Dance', which was an enormous popular hit in the USA and the UK in 1963. An up-tempo ballad, with an eminently hummable chorus, 'Dance, Ballerina, Dance', turns out to be a modern morality tale in which the subject of the song, the threateningly ambitious prima ballerina, is warned of the consequences of her professional commitment. She has jeopardized her chance of marriage and children, and is, presumably, condemned to a lonely old age: 'once you said love must wait its turn, you wanted fame instead / now love is gone . . . I guess that's your concern, dance on and on . . . so, on with your career' – and on with the song.

The identification of the career ballerina as a problematic figure is particularly interesting. Ballet had undergone a significant cultural revival in the post-war period, and it was characteristically cast as an exemplary feminine cultural form, with its emphasis on grace and balance and its subordination of real physical strength to an appearance of lightness and fragility. Here, the ballerina's physical autonomy and bodily control seem to suggest a wider social independence and resistance to patriarchal power; as though, by devoting her body to dance rather than sex and maternity, the ballerina is challenging one of the most powerfully asserted precepts of the post-war period: the insistence that motherhood was not only a social imperative but also fundamental to a healthy femininity.

Anxieties about women's place in the public sphere, the economic freedom which paid work offered and deeper fears about the threat to the family posed by the working mother had serious consequences. Indeed, although the marriage bar to women's employment in the civil service and teaching professions was officially abolished in the 1940s, unofficial restrictions on married women's access to and promotion within many careers remained in place well into the 1970s.

Consequently, this often meant that single women were automatically seen as 'career girls' who had rejected the 'natural' path of family and motherhood, regardless of the specific circumstances involved or the opportunities and status of their job. Spending your life as a low-paid typist, while you struggled to look after aging parents and your siblings married, thus qualified you for this designation, even though the nature of the 'career' itself was unlikely to lead to the board of directors.

Domesticated leisure, gendered labour and the home

Ready, steady, cook!

By the early 1950s, the growing affluence and leisure time of middle-class and lower-middle-class families in the USA and the UK, together with the emergent culture of domestic life as a space for the fulfilment of modern individualized selves, led to a growing interest in hobbies, especially those which were supposed to articulate specifically *gendered* skills. The idea of 'home cooking' (perhaps even more than the actual practice) became especially central to post-war ideologies of domesticity, resonating particularly powerfully in a cultural context in which memories of dried egg were still vivid. It also tended to be represented in two idiosyncratically 'Anglo-Saxon' ways: baking, which was devoted to supplying the family with freshly made cakes and biscuits, and home entertaining, which was linked to other shifts in domestic leisure and family life.

The idea of the housewife in the kitchen, constantly planning, preparing and eventually producing an endless array of meals, was central to the way in which familial femininity was represented in women's magazines, films and television. Advertisements, too, deployed a dual discourse of the home economist, who required precision tools and a streamlined kitchen to work efficiently, and the fulfilled woman, whose discovery of her deep femininity lay in fairy cakes and a well-turned-out Victoria sponge for her family. Complex and labour-intensive recipes and menus in women's magazines (for choux pastry, soufflés or pavlova), were an important part of the emergent discourse of home entertaining, in which the housewife reinvented herself as a glamorous hostess, whipping up delicious dinners for her husband's work colleagues and deftly wheeling a heated trolley around her lounge. The style of cooking demonstrated by one of British television's first real stars during the late 1950s, Fanny Cradock, was almost entirely about spectacle and performance, focusing on such visual delights as flambéing, sugar sculpture and radish carving (which must have been rather less spectacular on a 9" television screen).

This emphasis on entertaining as fun also helped to reconfigure housework as a project of a properly feminine self, as I have said. However, the emphasis on home cookery also frequently carried with it an implicit (sometimes very explicit) competitive element, in which showing off domestic skills also invited an envious gaze from other women. Karal Anne Marling (1994) even points to the public competitive 'bake-offs', staged by flour producers in the USA such as Pilsbury, into which women were recruited. Indeed, industrially produced convenience foods, such as cake mixes and TV dinners, while marketed as aids to the busy housewife whose domestic chores occasionally prevented her from producing a completely home-cooked meal, frequently reproduced – even as they claimed to solve – the cultural pressures on women to provide such meals for their families.

It was not only cookery that was supposed to express a true feminine self. Cleaning might also bring out the real woman lurking beneath an unprepossessing exterior. One of the most ideologically coercive scenes in the musical, *Calamity Jane* (1953), for example, is that in which Calamity (Doris Day) and her friend Adelaide set up house together and proceed to transform a filthy shack into a cosy cottage, complete with gingham curtains and flowers arranged in a vase. In a musical montage to the song 'A Woman's Touch' (what else?), the sequence both neatly erases the real labour through rapid editing, while also emphasizing the 'magical' housewifely skills of the heroine. It is this scene that tells the viewer that, despite her protestations to the contrary, 'Calam' is really a proper little woman at heart.

Furthermore, housework itself had a tenuous and problematic value in relation to the paid labour done in the public sphere. Not only was it unpaid and explicitly feminized, but it was also too heavily bound up with the expression of love, care and nurture to be readily disentangled from these, and its invisible character devalued it further. Being a housewife was frequently conflated entirely with consumption or with doing nothing very much, a dyad of work/not work, despite the competing claims about 'home management'. As Janet Thumin argues, 'women were assigned the domestic sphere as their workplace, yet frequently addressed within it "as if" they were at leisure' (2002: 215).

Man about the house

Perhaps for many men in the period, the opportunity to undertake creative, relatively undemanding and therefore pleasurable kinds of manual labour, such as gardening, carpentry or fancy woodwork, represented the recovery of an 'authentic' masculinity, dispersed or displaced by the white-collar jobs of the middle-class male. More than this, however, the properly companionate marriage required husband and wife to have a shared commitment to domestic leisure pursuits. In contrast to the spatial or monetary restrictions faced by the 'ordinary' married couple of the 1930s, the post-war family was supposed to play together as well as eat together. Indeed, as Segal observes, married men were supposed to be at home when they were not at work, enjoying domestic coupledom (1988: 70).

This new togetherness was most fully articulated in a very specific take on the emergent consumer culture of the post-war period: the growth of do-it-yourself. In the UK, the stimulation of a desire for domestic comfort, combined with the relatively impoverished range of consumer goods available in British shops in the early 1950s and the economic constraints imposed on couples dependent on a limited income, meant that while more sophisticated consumer tastes were being produced through advertising, films and television shows, the economic means to purchase furniture or appliances remained limited. Families therefore found themselves encouraged to develop an impressive range of building, carpentry, decorating and upholstery skills in response to these constraints.

Even in the USA do-it-yourself, although differently expressed, became a major feature of domestic life during the mid-1950s, as Karal Ann Marling notes. For men, '[do]-it-yourselfism . . . was the last refuge for the exercise of control and competence in a world run by . . . bosses and bureaucrats' (1994: 56). It was also enthusiastically endorsed by the Eisenhower administration as a morally improving way of spending family leisure time, as fathers and sons shared a workshop, making shelves or fitted cupboards for the home. The rise of do-it-yourself also led to the growth of new kinds of industry, producing power tools, fretwork kits and instruction manuals for aspirant home improvers. The popularity of these activities was further mediated by the growth of magazines such as *The Practical Householder* and *Do-It-Yourself*, and advice and hobby guides (such as the *Hobbies* annual in the UK), as well as by public exhibitions and fairs such as the Do-It-Yourself Show in New York and the annual Ideal Home Exhibition at Earls Court in London.

(The Daily Mail Ideal Home Exhibition began in 1908 and coincided with the growing establishment of the suburb as the primary residential space of the middle classes in the UK. With the development of the newsreel and television it became a regular feature and was fixed as an annual event. Its exposure in the media helped to consolidate the meanings it offered related to domesticity, marriage and consumption (Andrews and Talbot 2000: 10–22).)

Perhaps inevitably, doing-it-yourself also entailed a set of cultural negotiations around the division of labour in the home, around class identities and aspirations and around the power relations involved in domestic life and the patriarchal family. As Jen Browne (2000: 144) points out, it was women who tended to be directly addressed in terms of social aspiration and the acquisition of cultural capital in magazine articles about home decoration and advertisements for the paint, melamine and chipboard that were to transform their houses into homes with dream kitchens or fitted furniture. The aesthetic labour of taste and decision-making was thus assumed to be part of the work of femininity. Men, on the other hand, were supposed to do the actual manual labour involved, as well as paying for the raw materials. This combination of appropriately gendered skills meant that the production of 'the home' – the triumphant outcome of husband and wife working together – expressed in a (sometimes literally) concrete form the ideological values invested in the companionate marriage.

Shared pleasures

Domestic leisure was also considerably transformed during the 1950s and 1960s by the relatively rapid increase in the availability of new kinds of entertainment technologies, especially radios, record players and television sets. By 1955 there were 37,590,000 television sets in the USA (Parks 2002). In the UK, in contrast to the provision of practical domestic technology in the home, which, despite the ideology of modernization, was surprisingly slow to become normalized (in 1949 one-third of all British households still heated all water on a stove, Davidoff et al. 1999: 217), radio and television enjoyed a rapid and widespread take-up amongst all social classes (perhaps this isn't so surprising, though, given that men tended to control domestic spending on such appliances and would presumably have prioritized their own interests when given a choice).

Certainly, the success of television, in particular, as the site of shared leisure in the form of family viewing was an important cultural development. It was linked to the dramatic changes in the availability and use of various kinds of space that suburbanization instigated, including the reduction in family cinema-going and in female audiences occasioned in the USA by the middle-class move to the suburbs. Alongside this, there were transformations in time management, with the weekend newly set aside for leisure and family life and domestic time increasingly mediated by radio and television, both in the form of the official clocks and routine schedule that marked the day's passing, and also in the rhythm of programme preferences and pleasures. Families 'made a date' with a particular show on a nightly or weekly basis (Morley 1992).

Broadcasting was also an important site for the mediation of public forms of national consciousness (the 'unified nation') to the family, as in the live television transmission of the coronation of Queen Elizabeth II in 1953, which, it was claimed, was watched by at least half the British population (Street 2003: 100), and in the screening of President Eisenhower's inauguration in the USA in the same year. The ideological relationship between an individual, their family and a wider national community, with a set of shared interests and concerns, was powerfully forged during this period, especially in the context of the cold war. The family's inscription into a community that was defined in national or regional terms was a significant feature of the securing of consent to the modern state's function and status: by mediating the channel between a public world of politics and a private sphere of the family, broadcasting also helped to *construct* these relations in quite specific terms (Frith 1983).

Figure 1.2 The 1950s family gathered around the 'television hearth': an idealized image of domestic leisure. © Hulton-Deutsch Collection/CORBIS

Indeed, the idea of the family watching television together effectively constituted an 'imagined community', to use Benedict Anderson's phrase. It is certainly familiar from the history of popular representations of the domestic context, in which idealized images of the nuclear family gathered around the hearth-like glow of the television set are familiar. The family audience has even contributed powerfully to the organization of television's specific style and address: particular genres, especially sitcoms and soap operas, have not only figured as peculiarly appropriate for family viewing, but they have also tended to be dominated by family narratives, as is discussed later in this book.

Furthermore, television's peculiar status as the primary medium through which the public becomes private has informed television's long history of censorship and regulation, which, although locally varied, tends to be grounded in the shared belief that there are particular taboos around the representation of sex within a domestic sphere in which the whole family (that is, the nuclear family) watches together (see, for example, The Annan Report 1977). Importantly, this complicity between the state and broadcasters in the regulation of the family was further marked in television's educational role, with mothers specifically addressed by radio and television in particular terms as the moral guardians of the household and as 'monitors of the domestic sphere' (Moores 1988: 35).

From here to maternity: mothering, regulation and the family

Mother Nature?

If the 'naturalness' of the relationship between marriage and reproduction that became so central to post-war accounts of the family seems to be one that has always prevailed, it is instructive to compare this discursive focus with the range of representations of marriage found in popular texts from earlier periods. Throughout the nineteenth century, a period commonly assumed to be the high point of ideologies of domesticity and marital fertility, it is interesting to see that most literary texts, while they offer crucial ideological work on gender relations, sexual desire and the social role of marriage, make remarkably little space for mothering as an essential component of femininity. Even Dickens, the most sentimentally 'domestic' of the major English novelists of the period, makes no automatic link between marital contentment and reproduction and certainly does not represent a dependence on nursemaids and other servants as evidence of maternal deprivation.

Motherhood, in such work, is necessary and probably unavoidable, but it is not a career in itself, nor is it represented as essential to female psychological health. If anything, mothers are offered as physically fragile and emotionally dependent on their children while the more robust, independent and self-assured women are unmarried and contentedly childless: Betsy Trotwood in *David Copperfield*, Mrs Gaskell's community of single women in *Cranford* and Charlotte Bronte's *Shirley*. By the early twentieth century, however, eugenicist and social Darwinist models of mothering that linked the private act of reproductive labour with a public responsibility to breed for race and nation had begun to dominate discourses around marriage (Bland 1995).

The increased regulation of mothers and mothering by the state was effectively facilitated by welfare and medical systems throughout the UK and the USA during the late 1940s and early 1950s, although it was done in different ways and through different instruments at a local level. In the UK, the new National Health Service made special provision for pregnant women and new mothers, but this also meant that pregnancy and mothering were increasingly subjected to state intervention via local healthcare professionals. Giving birth became a matter of intervention by (usually) male doctors, hospital care and professional surveillance. Working-class women especially 'were subjected to close supervision from health visitors and other authorities on childbirth and child-rearing, whose advice often conflicted with traditional wisdom' (Davidoff et al. 1999: 209).

In the USA, the 'medicalization' of mothering was largely effected by the expansion of technological innovation into health, combined with authoritarian models of professional power and the growing centrality of psychoanalytical and psychological frameworks of emotional and physical development. Women generally were subjected to an intensified 'pathologization' during this period, with housewives in particular diagnosed as suffering mental health problems specifically linked to femininity (Carol Warren, quoted by McCracken 2002). Paradoxically, this increase in medical and state intervention in childbirth was underpinned by an ideological emphasis on the naturalness of mothering to femininity, in which the maternal instinct was supposed to guide and shape the experience, and to which the work of John Bowlby was central.

Maternal deprivation and 'bad mothers'

Bowlby's work on the importance of mothering to the proper development of children originated in 1948 as a World Health Organization report investigating the crisis in family relations produced by the physical displacement of the war. However, his report became a crucial part of a larger cultural shift in attitudes towards the family, parenting and the status of childhood during the post-war years. Published by Penguin as *Childcare and the Growth of Love* in 1953, Bowlby's book became (with the work of Winnicott and Roberts in Britain and Dr Benjamin Spock in the USA) an instrumental text in the emergence of a new ideology of family life and child-rearing that emphasized the centrality of attentive and nurturant mothering to childcare. Strongly influenced by Freudian psychoanalytical theory, Bowlby argued that the emotional and psychological bond between mother and child was both instinctive and the crucial factor in the development of healthy children. These arguments were to be effectively institutionalized in medical, welfare and popular discourses from the 1950s to the 1970s (and remain powerful), particularly as regards the concept of 'maternal deprivation'.

Like other researchers before and since, Bowlby minimized the role of fathers in parenting as he privileged and helped to mythologize the figure of the nurturing, absorbed mother whose every absence threatened the psychological health of her child. The absolute necessity of constant maternal attention to the infant was further legitimated by the proposition that mothers, too, benefited emotionally and psychologically from this arrangement. Bowlby argued that,

> [j]ust as a baby needs to feel that he [*sic*] belongs to his mother, a mother needs to feel that she belongs to her child, and it is only when she has the satisfaction of this feeling that it is easy for her to devote herself to him. The provision of constant attention night and day, seven days a week and 365 days in the year, is possible only for a woman who derives profound satisfaction from seeing her child grow from babyhood . . . and knows that it is her care which has made this possible . . .
>
> (Bowlby 1953: 78)

This was not, however, a straightforwardly conservative ethic of childcare, despite the insistence on the mother's absolute devotion to her infant, as Elizabeth Wilson points out (1980: 188). In fact, the new 'experts' of the 1940s and 1950s were remarkable for suggesting that childcare should be child-centred and permissive. Nonetheless, while this new style of permissive, child-centred mothering represented an acknowledgement of children's importance to the new kind of society being built, it also meant that working mothers were placed in an impossible double-bind: responsible both for the health of their children and for their economic well-being. The demonization of bad mothers alongside the canonization of the good became an important feature of post-war models of family life, particularly those deployed in moral panics about youthful deviancy. Although such models were neither simple nor one-dimensional, they generally contributed to the powerful over-determination of mothering in the ideology of the family. Bad mothers were usually taken to be those who went out to work, leaving their offspring to become latchkey children, who would roam the streets getting into trouble rather than being cared for at home. Maternal deprivation was thus implicitly linked to the psychoanalytic idea of lack – a fundamental and traumatizing absence. Such children, it was claimed, were in danger of becoming tearaways or delinquents, whose lack of moral reponsibility would lead to crime.

Crucially, while the theory of maternal deprivation was institutionalized into the common-sense of post-war health and education systems, like other regulatory discourses it was usually applied to the policing and supervision of working-class women and their children by largely middle-class health professionals, precisely because the unequal power relations between these two groups was already embedded in the system. As Deborah Chambers (2001: 54) observes, the British middle- and upper-class practice of boarding children at school was rarely defined as maternal deprivation or subjected to the same direct scrutiny and intervention as the habits of working-class families. Moreover, while maternal feelings were supposed to be entirely natural, mothering skills were increasingly incorporated into the formal education of mainly working-class girls, who received classes in childcare and 'mothercraft' (*The Mothercraft Manual* apparently ran to 12 editions between 1923 and 1956, according to Davidoff et al. 1999: 208).

These class-based assumptions about the 'right' kind of mothering skills and the role of state intervention in family relations appeared in British films dealing with social problem, especially in the mid- and late 1950s. In *No Time For Tears* (1957), for example, Geraghty points to the way in which the narrative distinguishes between the right kind of love and the wrong kind, and focuses on one character, the 'slatternly' working-class Mrs Harris, who is too busy worrying about herself to offer her children the care they need: 'the film resolves the problem of their mother's inadequate care through an ending in which their father voluntarily gives his children back to the hospital . . . the care of the middle-class professional is deemed to be best for the working-class child' (2000: 151).

In addition, bad mothering was not only defined in terms of lack; it was also sometimes understood as a form of excess. Women who offered their children, and especially their sons, 'excessive mothering', who smothered them, over-protected them or failed to ensure that they grew away from maternal dependence, were equally demonized. Indeed, as Segal argues, maternal deprivation and bad mothering began to be used to explain almost every conceivable social problem – from divorce to delinquency (1988: 77).

The polarized oscillation of anxieties about mothering, together with the insistence on female self-abnegation, suggests that the uniquely powerful role that mothers occupied within the nuclear family was the source of deep anxiety. Yet such theories tended to accentuate this concentration of power in the mother's hands. Indeed, a new wave of social fears about mothering appeared in the USA during the 1940s in a range of texts that were clearly, in part, a response to the changes in gender relations produced by the war. One,

Philip Wylie's virulently titled *Nest of Vipers* (1942), argued that American culture had been warped by something he called 'Momism', compared mothers to Hitler, castigated them for sending their sons to war while they stayed at home, and expressed a barely concealed hatred for menopausal women who had the audacity to survive into old age. Another, *Modern Woman: The Lost Sex* (1947), drew heavily on Freudianism to identify 'mom' as the cause of delinquency and male psychological disturbance (Fischer 1996).

Screen mothers: manipulative matriarchs

That such theories entered and powerfully shaped common-sense assumptions about mothering during this period is evident from the way in which the figure of the bad mother began to appear in film and television texts. One film which powerfully articulates some of these anxieties – the family melodrama, *Imitation of Life* (1959) – is described by Lucy Fischer as 'an encyclopedic treatise on the working mother'. As Fischer goes on to summarize: 'The film's narrative counterposes two maternal heroines: Lora Meredith (an actress) and Annie Johnson (her maid). Both women are blamed for their parental inadequacies; Lora for being absent and placing career above motherhood; Annie . . . for being omnipresent and suffocating her child' (1996: 14). As if this playing out of the impossibility of contemporary maternal roles were not enough, *Imitation of Life* is also a powerful story about racial identity and transgression. Indeed, its foregrounding of black characters, albeit ones who are largely defined by and narratively structured through 'race', is relatively exceptional for a mainstream film of the period (although its appearance was in the context of the emergence of other 'social problem' films, such as *Rebel Without a Cause* which, while featuring black and Latino Americans, made them part of the problem), and its resolution depends upon the transgressive figure of the mulatto girl who passes for white being restored to her 'natural' place, just as it endorses the punishment of the mother.

In Alfred Hitchcock's horror classic, *Psycho* (1960), although the ending – in which 'mother's' voice is heard over an image of the psychotically murderous son, Norman Bates (Anthony Perkins) – is relatively ambiguous about questions of moral responsibility, it is clear that the film depends on post-war theories about mothering (and about maternal power) derived from psychoanalysis to 'work' as a text. Norman is still psychologically attached to his dead mother and deals with the danger that other desirable women present to this attachment by murdering them. In the final scenes, in which Norman's psychosis is 'explained' by a reassuringly patriarchal psychiatrist, the mother's excessive love for her son is expressly blamed for his criminality. Indeed, Perkins' portrayal of Norman Bates articulates precisely those 'feminine' qualities that excessive mothering was supposed to induce: he is shy, courteous and sexually passive – he is also feline, treacherous and mentally unstable. In addition to the dangers of excessive mothering in *Psycho*, the absence of an appropriate paternal model seems to confirm Norman's gender ambiguity and his moral inadequacy: without a strong father he is doomed. In what is perhaps an even more paranoid fantasy of manipulative maternity, and one that links these fears to the politics of the cold war, *The Manchurian Candidate* (1962), the bad mother not only smothers her son emotionally and psychologically, but is also revealed to be a Communist spy.

If the bad mother sacrifices her son to a foreign (Communist) state, then the good mother tended to sacrifice herself for the good of her children, although this might well be within the terms of wider social contradictions around appropriate femininity. During the late 1930s and the 1940s, films such as *Stella Dallas* (1937) and *Mildred Pierce* (1944) had articulated the difficulties for women of negotiating maternal love within a society that was morally conflicted. For Viviani, these films show how a mother recovers her dignity while helping her child re-enter society thanks to her sacrifices (Viviani 1980: 14).

In post-war melodramas, however, and especially in Douglas Sirk's women's films, women's desire – for 'unsuitable' men or for personal freedom – is both situated within the family and problematized as in some ways unachievable without other sacrifices. In *All That Heaven Allows* (1955), for example, following the death of her husband, Cary (Jane Wyman) resists family pressures to settle for a respectable man of her own age and to stay in with her newly purchased television set (here represented as the symbol of domestic boredom), choosing instead a daring romance with a younger man (Rock Hudson). Arguably, Sirk's specific use of colour and an excessive *mise-en-scène* helps to ironize the film's centralizing of the family and conventionalized relationships, by expressing the emotional and ideological contradictions involved, thus potentially inviting a reading that sees Cary's desire for love as liberatory. However, as Kaplan remarks, the use of irony in such a text indicates the inadequacy of the expectations it subtly critiques, and prefigures a later, more overt assault on the family (1992: 177).

Baby boom

Despite the social fears about the power of mothers, the relationship between marriage and reproduction remained central to the post-war reconfiguration of gender roles and representations, as did the insistence on domesticated maternity as the only appropriate role for married women. This can be identified in the marked shift in the style and narrative focus of romantic or sex comedies from the 1930s to the 1950s. In the six *Thin Man* films made between 1934 and 1947, which featured a sophisticated Manhattan couple, Nick and Nora Charles (played by Myrna Loy and William Powell), for example, the marital relationship is located in the profoundly anti-familial context of nightclubs, bars and restaurants, while domestic love is lavished on a dog (Asta) rather than children. And in many of the 'screwball' comedies of the pre-war and immediate post-war years, which played out the complexities of gender relations as farce, such as *Bringing up Baby* (1938) and *My Favorite Wife* (1944), motherhood is only problematically represented as the 'true' career of the female protagonist. In contrast, popular romantic comedies later in the post-war period tended to insist on the indivisibility of matrimony and reproduction. For example, in the sex comedies made in the 1950s and early 1960s, which paired Doris Day with Cary Grant and Rock Hudson, the plot repeatedly circles around the fear, possibility and *necessity* of reproduction to marriage.

In both *Pillow Talk* (1959) and *Lover Come Back* (1961), Day is cast as a glamorously ambitious 'career girl' – an interior designer and an advertising executive respectively – who fails to recognize and therefore resists her 'natural' desire to marry and reproduce, a desire

Figure 1.3 Doris Day's career girl is overpowered by the physical strength (and ideological force) of Rock Hudson's masculinity. (Photo: Ronald Grant Archive)

that is only finally confirmed by the 'happy ending', which in both films features the birth of the child that will confirm Day's true career as a mother. Marriage and maternity are therefore effectively fused and Day's resistance is represented as a symptom of her refusal of a biological calling. Indeed, this factor is particularly violently emphasized in the final scenes of *Lover Come Back*, in which Carol Templeton (Day), having been impregnated by the playboy, Jerry Webster (Hudson), as a consequence of a drunken night in a motel, is finally forced to agree to marry him as she is wheeled into a hospital room to give birth to his child. As Frank Krutnik argues, '[t]he final image of Carol, prone and powerless on the hospital trolley, constitutes an overpowering vision of the "taming" of the independent career woman' (2000: 226). It is also oddly evocative of the shotgun marriage that was such a common feature of an age in which premarital sex remained taboo – although the film invites a reading of its conclusion as a happy ending.

Day's own star persona during this period contributed significantly to the possibility of reading her career women as unknowingly maternal and in need of patriarchal control. From the domestication of Calamity Jane in 1953 through to *The Glass Bottom Boat* in 1966, Day represented a version of femininity that appeared to safely reconcile the contradictions presented to women in the post-war years. While she generally played spirited, economically and emotionally independent women, in a way that was attractive to female audiences and which successfully articulated female resistance to excessive forms of masculinity, her films almost unfailingly managed to return her to the structure of the patriarchal family by the end of the narrative, and insisted on her willing submission in the process. Yet while these films represent domesticity as both unavoidable and problematic for men and desirable and necessary for women – with the arrival of children an appropriate consequence of matrimony

– they rarely propose that fathering might be a matter of voluntary and active emotional investment.

Life with father

If the 1950s saw the emergence of a new ideology of maternal responsibility in which mothers rarely found themselves permitted to be playful, it is noticeable that the idea of the playmate father began to assume more importance. Adrienne Burgess argues that the change from father as authority figure to father as playmate began in the 1920s and 1930s, claiming that, 'throughout the first half of the twentieth century the image of the father as his children's pal and confidante was relentlessly promoted' (1998: 18). However, fathers in the early post-war period tended still to be represented primarily as providers, and often also as distant, mystified figures whose work could only intermittently be reconciled with the feminine sphere of domesticity. In both *Father of the Bride* (1950) and *Father's Little Dividend* (1951), for example, the Spencer Tracy character is represented as mildly baffled by the flummery surrounding the 'feminine business' of weddings and births, confining himself to paying the expenses and reflecting facetiously, if indulgently, on the situation he finds himself in. Certainly, in many children's books of the period fathers are either permanently absent or unsympathetic authoritarians; in Richmal Crompton's *William* stories (1919–70 – a span which is, admittedly, stretching the period!), for instance, Mr Brown is regularly cast as the kind of father who demands silence at the breakfast table and is likely to impose curfews for misbehaviour.

The move from provider to playmate seems, then, to have been much more tentative than Burgess suggests. By the mid-1950s, dads were beginning to be cast *both* as playmates and as authority figures; although their role as playmates was confined to specific times, spaces and places – the evening, weekend, on holiday, at the football match or for a few hours – in contrast to the mother's continual responsibility. In addition, the father's role as moral arbiter of family rules was emphasized by material absence. 'Wait until your father gets home' was the anxious threat of tired and harrassed mothers who were attempting to fulfil their maternal destiny without turning into bad mothers.

However, fathering was undoubtedly undergoing some modification. The new ideal of the playmate dad was distanced from an imagined older version – the Victorian patriarch with his absolute authority. Indeed, John and Elizabeth Newson concluded that men were spending more time with their families by choice: 'At a time when he has more money in his pocket, and more leisure on which to spend it, than ever before, the head of the household chooses to sit at his own fireside, a baby on his knee and a feeding bottle in his hand' (1963:145). Men were being urged to help out at home and especially to interact with their children, although the extent to which this actually happened was often exaggerated (Roberts 1995). Segal points out that working-class fathers, especially, took little part in the active nurturing of their children, regarding this as exclusively 'women's work' (1990: 8–9).

Yet what is noticeable about post-war representations of fathering is their ambiguity about the relationship between men and domesticity. Nurturing is offered as a profoundly and innately feminine skill, yet anxieties about 'excessive' mothering focus on the importance of appropriate role models for boys. Fathers were a necessary presence in the home, but their roles were specific and circumscribed. Such anxieties were frequently coded around questions of sexuality and the possibility that boys who were 'over-mothered' would either become feminized (and homosexual) or delinquently masculine and therefore unable to take up their proper place in patriarchal power structures.

Figure 1.4 The source of Jim Stark's distress is the domestic conflict he witnesses between his over-bearing mother and 'hen-pecked' father. (Photo: Ronald Grant Archive)

A striking example of this anxiety can be found in the melodrama, *Rebel Without a Cause* (1955), in which the source of the teenage anti-hero's distress is identified as the domestic conflict he witnesses at home. In a key scene, Jim Stark (James Dean) arrives home to find his henpecked father in an apron, abjectly cleaning up after his wife: the moral is obvious – if rather too obviously Freudian. As a 'castrated' male, the father is unable to take up his proper role, thus producing the crisis of identity in his son that leads to later disastrous events. The post-war period was thus marked by an incoherence around fatherhood, which articulated the presence of a number of competing discourses: first, in Raymond Williams' (1977) paradigm, a dominant ideology of fathering as emotionally distant but economically reliable, and an emergent ideology of father as an emotional support to his wife and friend to his offspring; second, a set of conflicting concerns about masculine identity, gender roles and sexual power.

The times they are a-changing

Nonetheless, there were important and noticeable shifts in the way in which both fathers and families were being represented by the mid-1960s, and in the relationships between familial structures, class identities and cultural assumptions about what should be perceived as a norm. The first family melodrama to feature a black family, and to situate that family within a recognizable nexus of class and gender tensions, rather than asking the members simply to represent 'blackness' as a totalizing category, was probably *A Raisin in the Sun* (1959), adapted from Lorraine Hansberry's play. By representing the various generations of an African-American family, and by dramatizing the conflicts between competing political positions and subjectivities, *Raisin* worked to set out the issues that were central to black consciousness during the period. In this respect, and with its origins in theatre, it differed from other melodramas whose political themes tended to be less overtly stated or were submerged beneath the apparently wholly personal tensions of family life. Yet *Raisin*'s success was also linked to larger shifts in the representation of family life and in the idea of the family itself.

By the late 1960s, and with the powerful impact of youth culture and, in more overtly politicized ways, second-wave feminism and the counter-culture, the family was itself the subject of intense criticism and hostility. Betty Friedan's critique of 'the feminine mystique', while overtly (and wholly non-self-reflexively) preoccupied with the idea that educated, white and middle-class women were wasting their talents by being confined to suburban conformity, had nonetheless been an important intervention in the assumptions that underpinned the family ideal. Later feminist writers, such as Germaine Greer (1971), Shulamith Firestone (1971) and Kate Millet (1970), developed a more sustained (if not always very sophisticated) analysis of the relationship between the culture of femininity, patriarchal power, women's subordination within marriage and the reproductive labour involved in family relations.

Symptomatic of the convergence of various anti-familial discourses drawn from left politics, counter-cultural values and 1960s iconoclasm in the early 1970s was the British television 'documentary' play, *Family Life* (1971), directed by Ken Loach and based on R. D. Laing's controversial 'anti-psychiatry'. Although *Family Life* was focused on the traumatic relationship between a mother and daughter and claimed a radical position on the family, its underlying trajectory was deeply anti-feminist and, indeed, marked by a visceral dislike of middle-class femininity that articulated itself in the figure of the dominant, stifling mother, who is held responsible for the collapse of the family. In its gender politics, *Family Life* was not so very different from *Psycho*, although rather less enthralling.

Conclusion

It would therefore be more accurate to identify the 1950s and 1960s as a moment of struggle over ideologies of fathering as well as mothering, rather than a simple reinforcement of traditional models. Indeed, the post-war period saw significant cultural shifts around all kinds of popular representations of gender in film, literature, music and other forms, undoubtedly partially produced by the post-war breakdown in gender regulation and its attempted reconstruction. The post-war 'moment' saw the hegemonic ideal of the nuclear family forged and popularized, but this did not mean that real families always subscribed to it – or even that it would be a permanent social formation.

chapter two

The impossibility of maternity: the family saga and entrepreneurial femininity in the 1980s

Introduction

The complex relationship between textual representations, lived gender roles and discursive tropes becomes especially interesting when we consider a narrative genre which achieved particular success in the 1980s: the family saga. The ways in which the saga was developed, reshaped and newly invigorated as a vehicle for changing ideas about the family, femininity and the social realm during this decade may be read as symptomatic of what I will call the 'conjunctural moment' of the 'New Right' governments of Margaret Thatcher and Ronald Reagan and, especially, of the emergence of entrepreneurial femininity. Dominated as it was by the ideology of economic neo-liberalism, the New Right was also characterized by a politics of 'authoritarian populism' (Hall and Jacques 1983) when it came to social and cultural issues.

In the UK, the ideology of Thatcherism explicitly linked the changes in family structures and relationships that had begun in the 1960s and 1970s to Britain's economic and political decline during the same period. Emergent shifts in attitudes towards sexuality, gender roles and traditional forms of authority were cast as symptoms of moral decline. In the USA, the incremental successes of the civil rights, feminist and gay liberation movements were frequently identified as a threat to individual freedom, and certainly to a specific version of an American way of life in which patriarchal power, white dominance and conservative values were central. In both instances, a complex set of moves around gender identities, power relations of class and race, and anxieties about the increasing rapidity of social change helped to secure hegemony for the New Right – but this was not a simple or uncontested process. In cultural terms, the impact of feminism on representations of gender and familial relations was significant, and was especially marked when it came to media forms and texts that, like the family saga, made the family their defining discursive focus.

The New Right, Thatcherism and family values

In both the UK and the USA (and, to a lesser extent, other Anglophone cultures), the discourse of traditional family values became increasingly hegemonic as a central political trope throughout the 1980s and early 1990s, with the moral superiority of conventional heterosexual relationships loudly and insistently proclaimed, in direct policy initiatives, such as the establishment of the Thatcher Government's Family Policy Unit in 1982, as well as in the populist punditry of the tabloid media. Indeed, in a whole range of political speeches which reasserted conservative moral values, Margaret Thatcher herself explicitly 'promoted the family as the source of freedom, liberty and dignity; of national pride; of moral values; and, most importantly, of consumption' (Franklin, Lury and Stacey 1991: 38). This rhetoric of the family was underlined by attempts at social engineering that sought to remarginalize gay and lesbian identity.

'Section 28', for example, which was passed as an amendment to the Local Government Act in 1988, made it illegal for local state authorities to 'promote' homosexuality through educational initiatives or support for gay rights groups. Yet far from helping to protect a traditional family structure, with hindsight, these initiatives seem to have articulated a Canute-like inability to stem the tide of social change. Political responses such as Section 28 were undoubtedly reactionary, and may be identified as part of a conservative backlash against feminism and other civil rights movements. However, as Jackie Stacey points out, the very introduction of Section 28 represented a tacit recognition that gay and lesbian sexuality was increasingly part of contemporary culture and identity. Legislation designed to stifle these emergent subjectivities thus actually helped to produce the meanings it sought to suppress by calling into being resistant identities that informed oppositional groups such as the national Anti-Section 28 movement (Franklin et al. 1991: 301).

Furthermore, in the context of changing gender roles, the figure of Margaret Thatcher was frequently identified by commentators as an example of feminism's triumph rather than its defeat. Indeed, her personal emphasis on individualism and the will to power effectively helped to create space for a new version of femininity, even if it was not 'feminist' in strictly leftist or radical terms. It is therefore better to see these events as part of a series of – difficult and often vicious – struggles over power, sexuality, identificatory positions, gender roles and social formations, not all of which confirmed the reassertion of conservative values. As we will see, such contradictions were bound up with the ways in which the family itself was problematically recast during this period.

The New Right's insistence on the market as the primary medium of social exchange also involved reconfiguring the family as a defensive structure, both against the necessary privations of the market place and against the intrusions of the state. Ironically, the centrality of the emphasis on familialism to New Right ideology took little account of the destructive effect many Thatcherite and Reaganite policies actually had on real families. 'The family' was invoked as a form of imaginary identification, a powerful symbol of stability and security in the face of the confusion and instability brought about by economic change. However, while this insistence on a defensively anti-statist model of the family explicitly invoked a Victorian or nineteenth-century ideal, it by no means constituted a simplistic return to an ideology of 'separate spheres'.

First, the specific identity of the housewife had become increasingly fractured by the late 1970s, despite Thatcher's own appeal to housewifely principles in her political language. The dominant idea of the 1950s and early 1960s, that managing the home was the definitive feminine career, was being increasingly replaced with the principle that juggling work and home was an inevitable – and necessary – component of femininity. As male industrial unemployment increased and new modes of labour developed in the late 1970s, women

Figure 2.1 Margaret Thatcher's apparent ability to run both a home and the country using 'housewifely' common sense was underlined by media representations of her shopping for groceries.

found themselves increasingly in demand as a flexible and cheap workforce within the emergent service sector and post-Fordist technology industries. Alongside this, feminism's limited take-up as a form of liberal individualism had begun to inform the kinds of new enterprises that were emerging: these not only addressed the increase in female wage-earners in terms of consumption, but they also drew on feminine skills and interests at the level of production. The Body Shop, for example, established in 1976 by Anita Roddick, became the paradigmatic example of a business that combined the traditional feminine concern with beauty culture with a 'feminist' entrepreneurialism, in which ethical values and employee care was emphasized. In addition, Roddick's own marital status and the contribution made by her husband to the Body Shop's success suggested that the principle of the family business could be successfully developed and transformed without overturning the system.

At the same time, the actual work of the family – the emotional and reproductive labour of childcare and housework, nurturing and home management – continued to be deemed largely the responsibility of women. The extension of state provision in the form of pre-school education was rejected by the governments of the Anglo-American New Right as fundamentally unnatural, linked to the idea of a demonized left-wing 'nanny state'. Instead, true freedom (as in 'freedom to' rather than 'freedom from') for women as well as men, it was argued, could come only through exercising personal – and, of course, privatized – choices about families into which governments should not intrude. If this meant that women had to take on the 'double shift' of full-time employment and childcare, it was up to them to manage these responsibilities through the mechanisms of the market place.

Both in Thatcherism's claim that 'society' did not exist beyond 'individual men and women and their families' (1987)[1] and in Reaganism's insistence on the family as a bulwark of a powerfully imagined 'moral majority', familialism was recovered – but also recast, reworked and reinvented. Crucially, the family was intensified as a consuming unit during this period, partly through the new patterns of work noted above, partly through the growth of domestic goods and commodities that were offered as consumer options (Franklin, Lury and Stacey 1991: 228). Yet the hegemony of family values was itself challenged by continuing and radical changes in household structures, sexual identity and marital models – and by the ideology of 'consumer choice' itself. Sexuality and marital status, it became increasingly accepted, were lifestyle choices rather than moral imperatives. Despite the political rhetoric, then, the 1980s saw an increase in single-parent households, a decline in marriages and a significant growth in divorce.

Indeed, even as responsibility for the family was firmly returned to the private sphere by one strand of Thatcherite political rhetoric, the 1980s were dominated by the powerful public persona of the woman herself, which strongly paralleled that of the fictional superwomen who began to appear in the popular sagas of the time. A crucial dimension to this was the idea that Mrs Thatcher evidently successfully managed both the demands of the masculine arena of public debate in the House of Commons and those of the feminine domain of housekeeping. Thatcher herself even claimed that she had brought to politics the common-sense skills of an 'ordinary housewife',[2] and this version of her career was kept in the foreground through media represention of her shopping – representations that effectively evaded questions of gendered responsibilities within the family. Thatcher's own apparent ability to command the political stage while also running a home thus became the dominant paradigm of a particular kind of successful femininity, condensing a whole range of problematic issues, desires and struggles within a single powerful idea of the superwoman.

The 1980s family saga also articulated the contradictory discourses of familialism, femininity and power found in Thatcherism and in Thatcher's public persona; its emphasis on competitive individualism struggling to make narrative space for the family and the

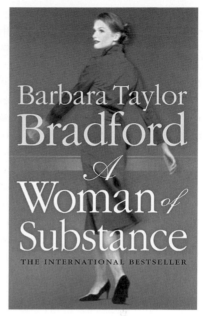

Figure 2.2 Barbara Taylor Bradford's public image was closely bound up with the project of entrepreneurial femininity that her novels advocated. © Alex Gotfryd/CORBIS

demands of mothering, despite a rhetorical focus on both these issues. Indeed, as a site for the staging of debates, desires and conflicts about the family during a decade of accelerated economic and social change, the saga offered the same contradictory nostalgia for an age when kinship structures were apparently more stable that was expressed by the conservative right. The resurgence of the genre during the 1980s may therefore be seen as part of the complex process of 'thinking the family' under Thatcherism.

The discursive link between property, social identity and femininity that had always been an important strand in the classic saga was further intensified through the focus on consumption and consumer culture that marked the 'superwoman' sagas of the 1980s. The paradigmatic version of these stories was, I will argue, Barbara Taylor Bradford's *A Woman of Substance* (1979), a book which clearly attempted to intervene in the dominant discourses of femininity and entrepreneurialism in order to change them. This novel therefore becomes the focus for the latter part of the chapter.

The family saga as popular genre
Generic conventions, timelessness and 'history'

The family saga first appeared in a recognizable form in the mid-nineteenth century, as part of the development of romance as a feminized and commodified popular literary genre (for more on romance generally, see Modleski 1982; Radford 1986; and Radway 1987). 'Domestic' or 'sentimental' romances, focusing on family life, struggles over inheritance and the complexities of kinship relations, and largely addressed to a female readership, became increasingly popular in both Europe and America from the 1840s onwards, with stories such as Ellen Wood's *East Lynne* (1861) and, in a more overtly literary vein, Anthony Trollope's *Palliser* series (1864–80) achieving widespread success (Tompkins 1989). In the twentieth century, the development of popular publishing, together with the establishment of public library services in the USA, the UK and other parts of Europe, helped to ensure the continued presence of the family saga as a popular women's genre. Multi-volumed series, such as the *Jalna* stories by Mazo de la Roche, originally published in the 1930s, and Fanny Cradock's *Castle Rising* novels in the 1970s, suggest that the saga retained a powerful pull for readers.

Indeed, the genre's distinctive identity as a cultural space for the exploration of the relationship of women to the family and to familialism, and its tradition of largely female authorship has been central to its continuing popularity with a female readership. While the best known family saga is probably John Galsworthy's *The Forsyte Saga*, published between 1906 and 1921, it is important to see this as an exception rather than a direct precursor of a popular genre. The Forsyte stories are not only identifiably part of a more overtly 'literary' tradition, but they also fail to place what might be called feminine consciousness firmly at the centre of the narrative. It is precisely the narrative centrality of this feminine consciousness, and its overt address to the woman reader, that makes the genre particularly interesting in the context of its new popularity and visibility during the 1980s, with the emergence of the single-volume blockbuster, typical of the work of Catherine Cookson, Danielle Steel and Barbara Taylor Bradford. By the end of that decade the paradigmatic contemporary version, *A Woman of Substance*, had sold millions and had been made into a highly successful television miniseries. The revival of the genre as a vehicle for the staging of new versions of femininity and familialism during the 1980s, particularly that of the entrepreneurial, self-willed 'superwoman', was thus intimately connected to the emergence of other changes within the political and cultural spheres.

The popular saga had always depended on a cyclical repetition of narrative incident, suggesting continuity through its focus on births, marriages and deaths, as well as emphasizing the female territory of family relations. As Christine Bridgewood observes, 'the saga differ[ed] from other popular fiction genres in its lack of drive towards narrative closure and in its tendency to begin at the point where Romance stops' (1986: 167). The genre thus dealt not with the achievement of marriage, but with its maintenance and renewal; and with the ongoing process of cultural negotiation around gender relations within marriage. Because this narrative structure is overtly cyclical it also tends to affirm the common sense that the events described (whether real or simply realist) are part of a natural and continuous process to which women are central. *A Woman of Substance*, for example, offers only a temporary closure, since two sequels (*Hold the Dream* and *To Be the Best*) 'continue' the story of later generations. Similarly, Catherine Cookson's Tilly Trotter stories are a trilogy in which each text is both discrete and part of a larger narrative. The family saga thus offers a paradigm in which femininity is a category outside the linearity of conventional history.

However, historical authenticity or documentary verisimilitude is also very important to the genre's claim to realism. The saga is often implicitly ascribed a status that verges on the true or the almost-true, and is set apart from the escapism supposedly offered by other popular women's genres, by publishers and readers alike.[3] Indeed, sagas can be a powerful site for the airing of profound grievances about women's oppression and exploitation; accounts of rape, infidelity, humiliation and sorrow are routine, while individualized male power is frequently problematized. The details of everyday life and what might be described as 'local colour' in the form of phonetically rendered regional accents and detailed descriptions of specific locations are crucial to these claims to truth. Yet, as Roger Bromley points out, such details may work to obscure the contradictions of the past:

> Marx's 'noisy sphere' can be related not only to the mechanisms of story and plot, but also to the status details and locations (historical and territorial) which are often meticulously researched and the result of months of 'leg-work'. The detail is like noise, in so far as it silences the contradictory by filling in the interstices of the text.
>
> (Bromley 1978: 46)

Family sagas therefore deploy a discourse of history which is fundamentally binary. On the one hand, it is a matter of the contining cycle of birth, reproduction and death, in which the feminine arena of the family and familialism are the 'real stuff' of history; on the other, the past becomes a pageant of political and social events in which 'history' takes place wholly outside the domestic realm. While this offers women a seductive narrative, a 'natural history', which seems to valorize the family's and women's centrality to social relations, it also reaffirms the naturalness of women's exclusion from the public sphere. By offering an account of the past in which the public and private realms are so firmly split – as social pageant or private story – the continuities between the two are obscured. The idea that oppression may be systematic as well as personally experienced fits uneasily into the cyclical, so that any sense of continued struggle or of the potential links between different struggles becomes difficult to discern. As Bridgewood argues,

> history in the saga works as a double-edged discourse: it is at once the shared nudge of awareness of historical process . . . and the soothing balm of an ideology of stoical acceptance which naturalises the social and sexual status quo and is ultimately dependent upon essentialist categories of femininity . . .
>
> (Bridgewood 1986: 178)

In other words, history may appear as both a process of change and a process of continuity; but the means by which those two discourses are held in tension by the text is often incoherent and contradictory. Such contradictions would be intensified in the sagas that appeared during the 1980s, which attempted to foreground women's roles within the public realm, while also articulating an emergent 'heritage' model of the past. Here, an uneasy relationship appeared between the emphasis on competitive and individualistic modernity and a yearning for a stable, organic past social order.

These tensions are also identifiable in the way that family sagas were marketed. Not only was the saga's explicit engagement with history made part of its address, the *familial status* of the author was emphasized, rather than her professional or scholarly authority. Clearly, this manner of presenting the saga author, with its repeated emphasis on the familial, works to narrow the gap between the writer and the reader, making the possibility of shared experiences *as women* the primary focus. It even 'appears to be directing the reader back into the potentialities of her own experience, into her family history as a potential saga, to writing as a "natural product of living" (Bridgewood 1986: 171). Women's authorship, then, is also returned to the ahistorical realm of the timeless, so that the specific skills of plotting, narrative structure and literary address are cast as a natural extension of feminine consciousness.

New versions for the 1980s

In *The Alienated Reader* (1991), Bridget Fowler argues that during the 1980s the saga changed markedly. The revival of the genre is traced by Resa L. Dudovitz (1990: 114) to the publication of Colleen McCullough's *The Thorn Birds* in 1977, a novel whose epic sweep and narrative focus on women's emancipation prefigured the emergence of the 1980s version of the family story in which individual female ambition and eventual success was expressly tied into larger social transformations. The most significant of these changes focused on the complex figure of the saga heroine, around whose emotional toughness and ability to survive the novels had always been centred. This toughness had never been figured as a masculine trait. On the contrary, it was clearly signalled as feminine: as an underlying resistance to the vagaries, dangers, temptations and tests of the public world or as an essential (and therefore unchangeable) emotional strength.[4] By the 1980s, however, the public realms of work and what might loosely be called history had become much more narratively pivotal, encompassing a new model of femininity in which the traditional desire for a perfect and completing heterosexual union as the apex of female ambition was now linked to a project of entrepreneurial success. The saga heroine therefore had to operate both in terms of 'feminine' rivalries for love and 'masculine' rivalries for power: she must succeed in both spheres.

This shift constitutes an important intervention in discourses of femininity, power and the family. *A Woman of Substance*, for example, is underpinned by the myth that 'success' in the world is a matter of individual willpower, and that 'femininity', far from being a problem, can be mobilized as a tool of advancement. Emma Harte, its heroine, has a poverty-stricken childhood, gives birth to an illegitimate daughter at seventeen and is left an orphan at the same age with nothing but her resilience, ambition and determination to depend on. By the end of the book she is described as 'one of the richest women in the world, ruler [*sic*] of a business empire stretching from Yorkshire to the glittering cities of America and the rugged vastness of Australia' (1979: 53). A powerful fantasy indeed.

Family fortunes: television versions of the saga

Interestingly, many of the main tropes of the 'superwoman' sagas of the 1980s were partly prefigured and later reworked by some of the most popular and significant television dramas of the period, which were also versions of the family saga. The most successful of these television sagas, *Dallas* (1977–87), *Dynasty* (1980–90), and a British drama which attempted to do something similar, *Howard's Way* (1985–90), represented the family as the primary site of an entrepreneurial capitalism that worked by uniting a buccaneering individualism with the stable structure of the family unit. Initially, however, such dramas tended to represent the family in terms of conventional gender roles. Indeed, they offered plenty of strong male characters, who frequently dominated the drama, in particular contrast to the British tradition of social realist soap opera, as Geraghty points out (1991: 121).

In *Dallas* in particular, the contrast between home and work, the private realm of morality and the public realm of risk-taking, was discursively organized through the structural distinction the programme made between the Ewing family ranch, Southfork, where the guardian of family morality, matriarch Miss Ellie was invariably found, and the downtown skyscraper housing J.R.'s wood-panelled office, in which (usually dubious) business schemes were hatched and executed. This binary divide not only worked to underline the conflicted ethical values within the Ewing clan, but it also firmly emphasized the gendered character of the division. At the same time, *Dallas* consistently returned to the family – and to Southfork – as the site of narrative resolution. Indeed, this privileging of the family was most visible in the way in which all the Ewings lived together at Southfork, in a set of relationships that exceeded the normally valorized nuclear unit. This unconventional emphasis on the extended family not only made *Dallas* a more complex text in terms of the available reading positions (see, for example, Liebes and Katz 1991), but it also helped to foreground the centrality of the female characters to its narrative coherence.

This does not mean that marital and family relations were represented as harmonious, and in *Dallas* especially the family could be identified as a site of continuing conflict between wives and husbands. As Jane Feuer observes, 'it might be argued that prime-time family dynasty serials in particular offer a criticism of the institution of bourgeois marriage, since marital happiness is never shown as a final state' (1984: 14). While the younger Ewing brother, Bobby, and his wife, Pamela, were initially cast as dewy-eyed newly-weds, and the elderly patriarch, Jock, was devoted to Miss Ellie, the machiavellian J.R. and his spouse, Sue Ellen, were repeatedly represented as caught in a complex and destructive emotional relationship that effectively subverted the ideal of marital harmony. Marriage was thus rarely a permanent or certain institution in the American serials: divorce, widowhood, even bigamy, was nearly always a shadow on the horizon. Indeed, *Dynasty* featured two competing wives, Krystle and Alexis, with an almost equal claim on the patriarch of the Carrington clan, Blake. Nonetheless, marriage, however emotionally unsatisfactory, was both taken for granted as the natural and socially endorsed framework for heterosexual relationships and repeatedly valorized through the ideological framework inhabited by the serials – it was part of their common sense. This became especially clear when the female characters' attempts to claim control over their sexuality was invariably represented as a threat to the family structure, as Geraghty observes (1991: 71).

Neither *Dallas* nor *Dynasty* was an ideologically closed text, however. Indeed, in later series of both programmes excessive forms of patriarchal power were increasingly subjected to critical interrogation, with J.R.'s conniving explicitly identified as a form of oppressive behaviour towards his wife. Furthermore, the emphasis on familial rather than conjugal relations worked to displace the usual focus on the couple (whether heterosexual or homosocial) as the key dramatic site in popular television, concentrating instead on a sometimes bewildering variety of relationships. In *Dynasty*, for example, Blake Carrington's son, Steven, was represented as a gay man who was also married and a parent; the show explicitly setting out to stage a dialogue about homosexuality in which a liberal assertion of individual rights to 'difference' was brought into relief (Finch 1990).

Perhaps what is most important about this aspect of the American serials is the degree of incoherence which was produced as a result of their attempts to incorporate liberal and liberal feminist values within the framework of a deeply patriarchal family structure. Interestingly, both *Dallas* and *Dynasty* were to draw on some of the conventions which were developed by the popular sagas like *A Woman of Substance* in order to do this. Both shows changed in order to make space in their representation of popular capitalism for the female characters to enter through the establishment of highly 'feminine' businesses, such as fashion stores. This meant that by the late 1980s the notion of a family with a *unified* business project and corporate identity was partially abandoned, either in order to make the main female characters closer to the tough businesswomen of the sagas, or to incorporate new characters who fitted this role. This became an important feature of both *Dallas* and *Dynasty*, and of the *Dallas*-related serial, *Knots Landing*. In all three texts, the binary division between the public/masculine world of work and the private/feminine world of home was disrupted and then partially reconstructed as characters such as Pam, Sue Ellen and Alexis were increasingly asked to operate in the public sphere as newly-fledged 'businesswomen', while retaining an allegiance (however troubled) to the patriarchal clan. However, the resolution to the narrative and discursive problems this presented turned out to be the continued return of business conflicts to the family – the women found themselves competing against husbands or fathers – so that they became recuperated as signifiers of an older, safer battle of the sexes rather than signs of radical change. Moving outside the family for business purposes was also firmly linked to the production of conflict *within* it, so that the women's career ambitions always had to be reconciled to maintenance of the family structure (Geraghty 1991: 68).

The 1980s BBC drama, *Howard's Way*, attempted a British take on the glossy family-based serials discussed above, but was (as tends to be the case with British television) more firmly located within the specific social conditions produced during the decade (discussed earlier in this chapter), such as unemployment and the simultaneous growth of a hard-edged consumerism. Structured around the various conflicts and achievements of the Howard family – affluent, middle-class, keen sailors on the south coast of England – the programme articulated a Thatcherite optimism about enterprise and rugged individualism tempered by middle-class conscience liberalism. Essential to the programme's success was the emergence of the figure of housewife, Jan Howard, as an entrepreneur. Like the *Dallas* women (and like Emma Harte in *A Woman of Substance*), Jan was able to transpose feminine skills apparently rapidly, painlessly and successfully to the sphere of business. In contrast to *Dallas*, however, *Howard's Way* was markedly ambivalent about the character of Jan, about her materialism, her place within the family as a 'dependant' and, especially, her ambitions for her husband. The process by which she became an entrepreneur in her own right through the establishment of a fashion business, thus worked to legitimate her as a sympathetic figure in terms of 1980s ideologies of femininity, as multi-skilled and, if not economically independent (which might present too great a threat to the family), a contributor to the family income.

In each of these texts, the family was also clearly marked by its identity as a site of spectacular, voracious and demanding consumption. From the luxurious interiors of their 'ranches' and mansions to the restaurants and offices where they wheeled and dealed, the *Dallas* and *Dynasty* characters were engaged in a constant round of conspicuous consumption. Plots were hatched over dinner in expensive clubs, dramatic climaxes occured at parties or the oil barons' ball, and each of the glamorous female stars wore a variety of elaborate – and carefully showcased – costumes in each episode. Arguably, this is due to the way in which the conventions of such texts bear important similarities to the melodrama or 'women's film' of the 1940s, with their focus on emotional excess and their glamorous production style. However, this emphasis on the 'spectacle of consumption' was such an intrinsic part of the visual and narrative pleasures offered by these texts, so much a part of the texture of the lives being represented, it seems important to remark on its centrality to 1980s saga. Just as the reader of *A Woman of Substance* could vicariously share Emma Harte's luxurious home and wardrobe (as I explore later), the viewer of *Dallas* or *Dynasty* was effectively invited into a world in which abundance and plenty were taken for granted.

The 'conjunctural moment' of *Dallas*, *Dynasty* and *Howard's Way* in the late 1970s and 1980s was, then, profoundly marked by the construction of a very specific relationship between discourses of the family, enterprise and consumption. Yet these intertwinings served both to confirm *and* to disrupt the pleasures to be gained thereby. In *Dallas* and *Dynasty* this was largely because the main characters were repeatedly portrayed as unhappy or emotionally unstable; being rich was represented as an unlikely path to happiness; and owning desirable objects was not always seen as helpful in lessening the pain of betrayal – although it may have helped the recovery. Indeed, excessive materialism, an inappropriate preoccupation with money, things or oneself was invariably represented as morally dubious, punished in *Dallas* and made the site of conscious and camp excess in *Dynasty*. The texts could not *contain* the contradictions of consumer culture and Protestant morality that tended to be their primary features; they could only hold them in uncertain tension.

A Woman of Substance: the paradigmatic text?

Contexts and contradictions

A Woman of Substance was published at a significant moment in British political history, for 1979 was the year in which the real Margaret Thatcher became quite as much a woman of substance as the fictional Emma Harte. The success of both women may be understood now as part of a complex response to feminism and its critique of patriarchy on the part of the political right; an attempt to rework femininity within the terms of competitive individualism, without destroying patriarchal structures. This is not to suggest that fact and fiction should be confused, however, but rather to point out that values, beliefs and discourses inform a wide range of formations and shape identities in complex ways. *A Woman of Substance* was a component of the ideological shift to neo-liberal economics and social conservatism that was most clearly marked by the elections of Thatcher and Reagan; it worked imaginatively through the narratives of nationhood, sex, class, consumption and, most importantly here, familialism, which the British Conservative Party and the US Republicans also articulated in more overtly political terms. The contradictions in the ideological framework of *A Woman of Substance* mean that the text itself is incoherent and confused. Nonetheless, its powerful account of one woman's achievements also successfully engaged with the aspirations of contemporary readers. This success is what makes the novel a paradigmatic text for the superwoman sagas of the 1980s: however improbable or lacking in coherence the book may be, the figure of Emma Harte, in particular, exceeds these limitations.

Interestingly, the increased focus on individualism and personality politics that marked the Thatcher/Reagan years was complemented by a similar shift towards author-branding in the world of publishing. The growth of the family saga as a market leader in popular fiction during the 1980s was thus facilitated by major changes within the publishing industry itself, in which authors were themselves branded or used in the battle for sales. Writers such as Cookson and Taylor Bradford became central to the intense competition of the world of the popular bestseller, not only in terms of sales but also at the level of personal recognition and image. Cookson's modest 'Geordie' persona and Taylor Bradford's Yorkshire-girl-makes-it-in-America image thus became as important as the novels themselves. What was being 'sold' was not simply a novel or even a saga series; it was an idea of success in which the novelist's own rags-to-riches story was closely bound up with the fictions she offered her public. This process took the tendency to naturalize female saga authorship discussed earlier and developed it into a discursive move around entrepreneurial achievement. Taylor Bradford's novels of enterprising businesswomen, in particular, were linked to her own story of success within the corporate world of the global market place. Her books were central to the process by which the genre increasingly stitched an idea of feminine entrepreneurship into its concern with the family.

Alongside this, the saga's focus on the preoccupations of a consumerist femininity became increasingly elaborated. Lengthy – and highly detailed – descriptions of clothes, decorations or food not only occupied extensive textual space, but they also generally exceeded the narrative requirements of the plot. These concerns were given a space and value that demonstrated the saga's relationship to other feminine textual forms, such as women's magazines. The centrality of consumption and consumer culture to the heroine's project – both entrepreneurial and personal – worked to draw the reader in and secure her (our) pleasure.

Consumption, pleasure, desire

For women, especially, the intensification of consumer culture during the 1980s also involved its recasting as a form of empowerment – a consumer feminism in which the (temporary and contingent) sovereignty of the purchaser was widely conflated with social change. The articulation of women's central relationship to consumer culture thus became more visible, and more problematic. As Janice Winship observes:

> For women in particular . . . it is the commodities you buy and what you do with them which signal to others, as well as to yourself, who you are, what kind of woman. And for these reasons consumption is an odd mix, associated both with leisure, pleasure and fantasy *and* . . . with work, anxiety and individual expression for women. Any pleasure to be derived from consumption is thus a *fragile* one organised around the potential conflict of that mix . . .
>
> (Winship 1991: 27)

The conflicted pleasures of a fiction about shopping might therefore be understood to be part of the ideological work which makes sense of consumer culture and women's place in it: a way of articulating a model of femininity within late capitalism. As Margaret Marshment points out, the best known female entrepreneurs, such as Laura Ashley, Coco Chanel, Helena Rubinstein (or, indeed, Anita Roddick) are generally presented as capitalizing on distinctively feminine skills and pleasures, in beauty culture or interior decoration, and as having a 'purchase on the public world through this link' (1988: 35). The changes in the family saga of the 1980s, therefore, included the incorporation of a consumerist discourse as part of the narrative strategy. They also included a tendency to locate stories within businesses or enterprises perceived as particularly feminine, such as fashion, the jewellery trade, hotels, and – especially – the department store.

The department store has a long history as a symbolic figure in popular fiction, especially in relation to narratives exploring changes in discourses of femininity, such as Emile Zola's *Au Bonheur des Dames* (1882). In its heyday, in late nineteenth-century bourgeois culture, the department store also represented a utopian ideal – akin to the position of the country house for the *ancien régime* – as a symbol of plenty and of the efficiency of the free market. David Chaney points out that,

> the department store was a significant element in the emergence of a consumer culture [because] . . . as all transactions are essentially equivalent the willingness to engage endlessly in accumulation must be motivated by a

combination of the attractiveness of the place of sale and a general conviction that an independent identity can be exhibited through the range of commodities purchased . . .

(Chaney 1983: 27)

This 'independent identity' was thus firmly tied into consumption practices, and the freedom to exercise the specific kinds of choice that such practices seemed to offer to women within the context of nineteenth-century modernity. As Mica Nava argues, 'Women played a crucial part in the[se] taxonomies of signification – in the acquisition of goods which conveyed symbolic meanings about their owners – since it was women who went to the department stores and did the shopping'(1996: 48). Department stores were thus claimed as a 'feminine' or 'respectable' space in which middle-class women, in particular, could exercise their economic capital as consumers and their cultural capital as arbiters of good taste. Indeed, store owners such as Gordon Selfridge were quick to identify a link between middle-class women's right to access the public sphere as consumers and their claims to political enfranchisement; seeing 'no conflict of interest between women's growing independence and the economic success of the stores' (Nava 1996: 55).

Moreover, the department store is also important to the development of discourses of the family in relation to capitalism and entrepreneurialism, precisely because of the confluence of these concerns in the nineteenth century. The department store's comprehensiveness, its promise to clothe, feed, furnish and entertain the whole family was important to its feminized status. And, as Rachel Bowlby (1985) points out, the primary 'moment' of the department store in the nineteenth century was also the moment of the Great Exhibition and other spectacles of looking. In other words, the pleasure of the department store was – and is – a pleasure of a consumerist gaze in which, as in the women's film and the television family serial, aesthetic delight is wedded to the desire for commodity ownership.

It is therefore significant that, while for the most part the real women whose business was the department store at this key moment in the late nineteenth century were either the wealthy middle-class customer or the poorly paid and often thoroughly exploited shop assistant, the *idea* of the store as a space in which the female entrepreneur might succeed by deploying exactly the same kind of cultural capital – taste – as her customer, becomes a seductive mythology in 1980s family sagas. Indeed, throughout the 1980s, popular sagas were thoroughly engaged with the business of consumption, deploying the richly detailed register of goods and premises that such a theme permits, while simultaneously offering a plausible space in which the heroine's feminine skills could legitimately be deployed for profit (see, for example, Cynthia Freeman's *No Time for Tears*, 1981; Vera Cowie's *Fortunes*, 1985; Judith Gould's *The Love-Makers*, 1986; and Danielle Steel's *Pearls* 1991). By looking back to the nineteenth century for their subject matter, and especially in their attention to the 'period detail' that suggested historic truth, such sagas also helped to invent a tradition of female entrepreneurialism that supported the ideological emphasis of the 1980s.

The department store therefore appeared as an increasingly powerful vehicle for these cultural articulations in such sagas, its cultural resonance tied to three concerns that would become central to the 1980s. The first was the accelerated and intensified development of consumer culture and its complex relationship to spectacles of desire and plenty, as I have noted. The second was the way in which the department store represented (contradictorily) both the present and the past, both contemporary consumer culture and a nostalgia for an ideal of service and luxury that by the 1980s had begun to disappear. The third and most important was the way in which such stores were already tied into the discourse of the family, partly through the mythology of family ownership expressed in nomenclature (Harrods, Lewis's, Jenners) – which the sagas readily rehearsed – and partly through their apparent comprehensiveness when it came to the range of goods on offer and an appeal across generations to the whole family. The availability of the department store to popular fictions that spoke to and elaborated the feminine discourse of consumption together with an emergent discourse of the entrepreneurial woman is, then, hardly surprising.

In *A Woman of Substance*, for example, Emma Harte's own career is wholly tied up with the development of a retail business centred on a chain of department stores, Harte's. As with the women of *Dallas* and *Dynasty*, Emma's is an emancipation of consumption rather than enfranchisement. Her ability to act in the world is fused with access to desirable commodities rather than access to democratic structures. Indeed, differentials of power are invariably linked to differentials of taste and self-determination as well as class. Emma's 'good taste' sets her apart from her working-class origins from the first, aligning her with a network of relatives, friends and fellow entrepreneurs who will constitute a new middle-class, fully entitled to the power it claims. At the beginning of the book, for example, the reader is treated to a virtual inventory of the contents of Emma's drawing room at Pennistone Royal, a large seventeenth-century house in Yorkshire: '[t]he palest of yellows washed over the walls and gave the whole room a sunny, airy feeling and everywhere sparkling silver and crystal gleamed richly against the mellow patinas of the handsome Georgian tables, consoles, and cabinets and the large elegant desk' (Bradford 1979: 75). We are then assured that 'Emma's unerring eye for colour and form and her skill at placing and arranging furniture were in evidence everywhere' (Bradford 1979: 76). These passages are important because of the way in which they seek to establish the legitimacy of the book's distinction between characters and their different fates wholly in terms of access to a good taste that is itself naturalized. As Pierre Bourdieu argues,

> The ideology of natural taste owes its plausibility and its efficacy to the fact
> that, like all the ideological strategies generated in the everyday class struggle,
> it *naturalises* real differences, converting differences in the mode of acquisition
> of culture into differences of nature; it only recognises as legitimate the relation
> to culture (or language) which least bears the visible marks of its genesis . . .
> (Bourdieu 1984: 68)

However, such descriptions also directly address the reader, who is invited to consent to and take pleasure in both the material detail of things as things (much as the viewer of *Dallas* or *Dynasty* is also called upon), and to recognize the cultural value of particular commodities. The act of reading thus functions as part of the creation of the consumer-subject, in which material pleasures not only help to define a fictional character, but also speak to the reader as a participant in consumer culture.

More than this, however, the book insists that it is Emma's specifically feminine competences, her ability to exercise taste and judgement in food and dressmaking and to turn those skills into profit, combined with an extraordinary will to succeed, that secures her position. This emphasis on domestic skills transformed into business acumen is a central theme throughout the novel. The food halls in Harte's Knightsbridge store, for example, are, 'an extension of [Emma's] instinctive good taste, her inspired planning and diligent purchasing; in the whole hierarchy of Harte Enterprises no one could lay claim to their creation but she herself' (Bradford 1979: 62). This insistence on feminine competences as the route to entrepreneurial success in *A Woman of Substance* and other similar sagas is, I think, oddly akin to Margaret Thatcher's analogy between housewifely bookkeeping and managing a national economy noted above. It attempts to clear a space within patriarchal capitalism for women to exercise skills that are unthreateningly feminine (and thoroughly bourgeois), while also asserting their economic as well as their emotional value. In this respect, *A Woman of Substance* was part of a wider incorporative move around feminism that marked the politics of the 1980s.

This may have operated in complex ways nonetheless. Notably, the book's repeated and elaborate descriptions of food, houses and clothing all work to situate the novel very firmly within the 1980s 'moment' of the celebration of wealth as the rightful reward for entrepreneurial success. However, the chintz covers and Chippendale cabinets that furnish Pennistone Royal are explicitly identified as part of an unbroken tradition of English craftsmanship, which is about authenticity and truth. This organic notion of nationhood, in which England features as a timeless Arcadia untouched by the grime, disarray and fragmentation of industrialization, is in stark contrast to the clean modernity and consumerism of Emma's project, the department store, yet her taste is described as belonging to that other narrative of England, the narrative of national continuity. In this respect, the book powerfully locks into the specific ways in which Thatcherism attempted to stitch together a hybrid account of Englishness in which entrepreneurial 'modernity' was allied to a notion of 'heritage' and 'tradition'. The figure of the family is crucial to this. It offers a model of continuity tied to individualized identity that seems to connect these elements naturally. It is the emphasis on the family in the family saga, then, that helps to forge a link between the present and the past, between Victorian values (which naturally prioritize the family) and Thatcherite values (which attempt to reassert the value of the family).

Emma Harte's *entitlement* to her wealth is, therefore, central to *A Woman of Substance*'s intervention in dominant discourses of femininity. She begins her climb to the top, we are told, with ' the most grinding and merciless work schedule ever conceived and willingly undertaken by a seventeen year old girl' (Bradford 1979: 512), a schedule that involves working at the local mill every day, dressmaking in the evenings and baking at weekends. Such a puritanical emphasis on hard work and sacrifice, together with an amply fulfilled promise of deferred gratification, not only fails to address the probability that a life spent in hard work will rarely offer such rewards; but it also means that the *cultural* labour of building a business, and especially the network of masculine, homosocial bonds and power structures that characteristically exclude women, are only partially acknowledged. Emma's story is told as a narrative of individual struggle, with her fictional success working to affirm not only that capitalism is natural and inevitable, but that it is also open and flexible – to women as well as men.

Indeed, there is something additional – and contradictory – at work here and that is the articulation of a very particular ideological figure: the figure of the exceptional woman. Emma Harte is identified as 'different' and 'special' from the very beginning of the story; as her brother, Winston, observes at one point in the text, '*Abnormal* ambition. *Abnormal* drive . . . That's the difference between Emma and most people' (Bradford 1979: 701). This means that while *A Woman of Substance* attempts to suggest that success in business is open to women as well as men, it simultaneously insists that only the most driven and ambitious individuals are likely to achieve their desires. The comparison with Margaret Thatcher refuses to go away.

In addition, most of the difficulties which Emma confronts as a businesswoman are explicitly linked to her own emotional history, so that her business triumphs are clearly offered as motivated by desire not for money but for revenge. As Dudovitz (1990: 166) points out, the desire for revenge, having been wronged by a lover, tends to be cast in popular fiction as the only legitimate motivation for women's ambition. In *A Woman of Substance,* however, this personal revenge is explicitly linked to ambition in the public sphere, so that it is not enough for Emma to punish the Fairley brothers emotionally, she must buy out the factory and mill that they own and take up her place in a new economic order. Just as Margaret Thatcher represented herself as an anti-establishment figure, challenging entrenched power and the corruption of vested interests, so Emma Harte is offered as a condensation of an entrepreneurial modernity which is enhanced by her sex. As Fowler points out, ' From this point of vision, the social relations of capital and labour virtually disappear from the text – symbolically dissolved in the cult of entrepreneurial personality' (1991: 105).

Maternity matters?

Clearly described on its dustjacket as a *family* saga, *A Woman of Substance* nonetheless struggles to deal with the requirements of cyclical familialism adequately. Certainly, the family is a recurrent ideological motif throughout the narrative, in the form of the Polish Jewish Kallinskis, for example, who feature as an early model of familial closeness. Family relations are, moreover, absolutely central to the rhetoric of the novel, the way in which it directs us to 'read' Emma Harte. Yet there is very little sense that maternity, nurturing or the prosaic aspects of domesticity are fully present or meaningful. While it is true that the novel shows Emma's early businesses as benefiting from financial support or inheritance from two of her male partners, the text makes little space for the details of domesticity. On the one hand, as Marshment points out, 'Emma Harte . . . lives an unorthodox family life, but does not reject its principles: she is a (serially) monogamous, devoted mother' (1988: 40). On the other, the very fact that the family is generally absent from the story suggests an underlying problem.

Interestingly, the book expressly represents Emma's sexuality in highly conventional terms; having been married to two evidently unsatisfactory and inadequate men during the period of her initial empire-building, Joe Lowther and Arthur Ainsley, Emma dutifully subordinates her own business interests when she meets the powerful and assertive Australian, Paul McGill. Both Lowther and Ainsley are clearly marked as 'shadow-males' in Tania Modleski's terms (1982); either unable or unwilling to take on a proper masculine responsibility, and sexually aggressive or inadequate in ways which are presented as excessive. Yet, as Dudovitz observes, both characters conform to the standard heroic stereotype found in conventional romantic fiction (1990: 170). As partners for the superwoman figure of Emma Harte, they are, however, clearly inadequate. In their place, McGill appears as an ultra-male, a man who is even more powerful than Emma herself. This is important precisely because of the way in which the novel attempts to deal with its (and the wider culture's) anxieties about Emma Harte as a 'castrating' woman whose success represents a threat to male autonomy and power. The woman of substance, it seems, is still nothing without a man of substance to guide her.

This is not to suggest, however, that the impressive career forged by Emma Harte and other superwoman heroines within family sagas is represented as unproblematic to conventional gender and familial relations. *A Woman of Substance*, like other sagas of its historical moment, such as Freda Bright's *Decisions* (1985), stages the threat that the achieving, entrepreneurial woman poses both to most men other than her male equivalent (the Paul McGill figure, whose fortune, will-power and personal magnetism are even greater than her own) – through the disastrous series of personal relationships she has with various husbands and would-be lovers – and to the family itself. As Dudovitz argues, 'Superwoman, having entered the business world and found the man of her heart, must still straighten out the mess this has all created in her family circle' (1990: 171). Just as the newly flexible working woman juggled job, childcare and the emotional labour of family life as a condition of entry into consumer culture under Thatcherism, so the saga heroine's equally demanding obligations to her business and her family were reiterated.

Yet the complexities, pleasures, rivalries and contradictions of family life occupy relatively little narrative space. *A Woman of Substance*, therefore, has great difficulty in reconciling the story it wants to tell, of achieving and desiring womanhood, with the demands of an ideology of femininity which insists on maternity as the defining experience for women. The dominant tropes of motherhood – sacrifice, nurture and self-abnegation – are profoundly difficult to reconcile with the vigour and self-centredness of entrepreneurialism. This produces a range of contradictory and oddly fatalistic strands within the novel in which the repeated assertion of Emma's maternally sacrificial nature is contrasted with her driving ambition. 'She had given up her youth, her family, her family life, much of her personal happiness, all of her free time, and countless other small, frivolous yet necessary pleasures enjoyed by most women' (Bradford 1979: 63).

The text therefore struggles to make space for maternity and, perhaps more surprisingly, for the family as a safe space for its heroine. Mothering, it seems, is the 'problematic' (Althusser and Balibar 1979), struggling to emerge in the family saga. This is not simply because Emma Harte so thoroughly dominates the book, although that is a factor. It is more that Emma's relationship with her children and her role as a mother are actually shown to be irreconcilable. This is especially notable in the episodes concerning the birth of Emma's illegitimate daughter, Edwina. Much is made at the level of rhetoric about Emma's strong maternal feelings (and it is important to note how central the desire for children remains to the construction of the popular heroine), but Emma is clearly shown as having to give up her child to be looked after by a distant relative if she is to become economically independent. Interestingly, rather than being presented as an act of selfishness, Emma's preparedness to leave her child is offered as a heroic and necessary action. Yet it is here that *A Woman of Substance's* radical departure from conventional discourses of mothering turns back into a defence of bourgeois individualism. As an 'exceptional' woman, or rather, an entrepreneurial one, Emma cannot be judged on the same terms as others. Instead, the incipient selfishness of an act of child abandonment is transferred onto the figure of the child. Edwina becomes a demonized figure, offered as dangerously sexual, knowing and malicious. Indeed, the child's traits are pathologized through their connection with the bad blood of the Fairley family, which has, among other things, a sprinkling of madwomen in its attics.

The failings of Emma's other three children are similarly ascribed to genetic inadequacy – the bequest of the 'shadow-males', Lowther and Ainsley, whose failed masculinity taints their children. The alienation of the four eldest children produces the climax of the book, in which Emma accidentally discovers their financial conspiracy against her just in time to avert it. Yet the reasons for the children's betrayal are never fully explained, nor is the source of their animosity, especially since the text repeatedly insists on Emma's sacrifices as a mother. Only Daisy, the daughter fathered by Paul McGill, grows up to be affectionate and loyal to her mother. This account of genetic responsibility, in which Emma appears as an 'empty vessel' for the deposit of alien seed from her first two husbands, also figures her as strangely passive in the whole process of motherhood. It is as though the active, desiring woman cannot also be an active mother. The problematic nature of motherhood is thus raised, but Emma is absolved of responsibility.

As I noted earlier, the attempt to reconcile the pleasure of consumption with the puritanical requirements of a work ethic is sometimes unsustainable, and I think that is why the problem of maternity keeps returning. Anxiety about the implications of Emma's power for hetero-orthodoxy permeate the story, and one of the functions of the prologue and epilogue sections, where her family relationships are explained, is their reinsertion of Emma into a familial and domestic discourse. The family plot is important as a device to return Emma to the family at the end of the novel and, indeed, it establishes her very firmly as a matriarchal and powerful figure. Emma's business interests and her position as the central locus of the family are thus clearly signalled as belonging together, although this has hardly been evident throughout the main body of the text. Furthermore, the text cannot, ultimately, construct itself as a narrative of maternal love in any material sense; it can only claim that its heroine is mother as well as businesswoman at the level of rhetorical assertion.

Conclusion

Emma Harte's role as a fictional figure condensing a number of complex problems around the family, femininity, power and capital during the 1980s is a significant one if we read her historically. For she offers a promise which is highly seductive, suggesting that skills and talents which are represented as specifically feminine competences – the exercise of taste, the manipulation of men – may be successfully transferred to the public sphere of business. While this is hardly progressive in a feminist sense, and may certainly be understood as anti-feminist in important ways, it also signals that the challenge to social relations produced by feminist critiques had begun to lead to a shift in the common sense about femininity and power. However, the emphasis on exceptionality works in a double-edged fashion. It is made clear that the success of the achieving woman is dependent on her class difference (and separation) from others: in the world of Emma Harte there is only room for one woman to sit at the boardroom table.

Most importantly, the way in which *A Woman of Substance* repeatedly emphasizes a kind of rhetoric of family values, which undoubtedly echoes and rehearses the ideology of the family that was central to New Right politics in the 1980s, is remarkable. Not only is the assertion of the family's importance to social structures a central component of the novel's underlying values, but also the impossibility of making space for human relationships within capitalism is inadvertently emphasized. Just as Thatcherism and Reaganism presided over a wave of major shifts in family structures, sexual identities and personal relations, while simultaneously insisting on the validity of one traditional kind of domestic arrangement, so *A Woman of Substance* presents itself as a family saga, while only really being interested in the competitive, striving and ultimately selfish individual at its heart.

Notes

1 This assertion originally appeared in an interview with Mrs Thatcher for the British women's magazine, *Woman's Own* in October 1987. In full, she was quoted as saying, 'There is no such thing as society. There are individual men and women, and there are families'. This particular observation would later be taken by Thatcher's opponents as the quintessence of Thatcherism's brutally antisocial character, and continues to be used as evidence against her to this day (most recently around the 25th anniversary, in 2004, of her becoming prime minister). To be fair, it is unlikely that Mrs Thatcher could have anticipated that her words would come back to haunt her in quite this way, and it is true to say that she clearly made this argument in response to the equally meaningless tendency, on the part of many liberal-left apologists, to claim that society was entirely responsible for individual behaviour.

2 Or rather, Thatcher's invocation of 'what every housewife knows' in her appeal to common-sense models of the political.

3 For example, in a small-scale informal research project I conducted during the late 1980s, I interviewed seven female readers of popular family sagas. In response to my questions about the value of the books, many of them directly and deliberately asserted their belief that the historical dimension to the stories made them more worthwhile than popular romance (i.e. they had a higher cultural value) and more credible as cultural documents.

4 Such testing of the heroine, in which her ability to endure emotional and physical assault is repeatedly staged, has some similarities to the conventions of the traditional male romance, such as the James Bond novels.

chapter three

Paternity suits: reclaiming fatherhood

Introduction

Fathers have traditionally been represented in all kinds of texts primarily as breadwinners and disciplinarians, as we have seen, but these representations underwent a fundamental shift during the 1980s and 1990s, as struggles over the family intensified and parenting became increasingly subject to scrutiny from both official (political, governmental, psychological) and unofficial (popular) agencies. Indeed, fathers were increasingly visible and celebrated in contemporary popular film and television texts, while being lamented as materially absent from family life in the real world, and some interesting contradictions arose around these tensions. While popular film and television versions of fathering began to transform the playmate father discussed in Chapter 1 into a newly nurturing figure, governmental discourses re-emphasized the importance of financial responsibility and moral authority.

Such contradictions were symptomatic of the relatively incoherent ways in which the reclamation and relocation of fathering was taking place: on the one hand, a backlash against feminism produced what became known as 'laddism', or a form of resistance to taking up adult responsibilities; on the other, fathering was recast as a newly acceptable form of emotional empowerment for men. Both these formations had as their root, however, a shared and profound disquiet and resentment among men (especially white men) that the privileges they had historically enjoyed as the dominant gender, and to which they felt a strong sense of entitlement, were being unreasonably challenged or undermined. It is this sense of masculine entitlement that continues to structure the way in which the family and the power relations that operate within it are represented and mediated in contemporary culture.

The cultural shift away from a narrow economically supportive model of fatherhood formed part of broader changes in meanings about gender identities in the late twentieth century. Masculinity, in particular, was increasingly perceived and represented as being in a state of 'crisis' from the early 1980s onwards (Segal 1990), a crisis that was often identified as having been precipitated by the feminist critique of patriarchal power and women's changing social roles. Continuing struggles over women's participation in the public sphere of paid work and men's roles in the home tended to crystallize most conflictually around parenting, fertility and reproductive rights, and around the 'proper' relationship which women and men should have with their children. These struggles were also polarized through the pathologization of 'bad' mothers and the valorization of 'good' fathers in all kinds of cultural and political texts. While the development of new models of the family during the 1980s, to include step-parenting, same-sex relationships and cohabitation, seemed to shape and consolidate changes in gender roles, as I explore in Chapter 6, women's increased economic and social power was often represented as being at the expense of both men and children. Politicians and social commentators argued that the family had become a beleaguered and increasingly residualized institution.

At the same time, the greater centrality of men's emotions (and the emotional man) to popular media of all kinds during the 1980s and 1990s was striking. 'Feminized' men, expressing emotional engagement and paternal tenderness in film and television, were most often found in the feminine genres of melodrama and soap opera, yet female characters were often displaced or marginalized by this new emphasis, as though the representation of 'feminine' concerns or anxieties did away with the necessity of representing real women. This appropriation was symptomatic of responses to the 'crisis' in masculinity which sought to reaffirm men's place at the centre of discourse, even where the discourse had changed. As we will see, many of the new lad/new dad narratives, including films, television shows and confessional baby books, effectively worked to locate *men*, not women, at the centre of the family romance.

The 1980s and the 'new man'

By the 1980s the transition from childhood to adulthood had become less clear-cut than it had been in the early or mid-twentieth century, as marriage became more casualized, youth – or its 'structure of feeling' (Williams 1977) – was prolonged from 10 to 20 years, and young people no longer marked their entry into the adult world through the wedding or the workbench. At the same time, the 'emotional sphere' of relationships – including parenting – had undergone a degree of democratization, with the ideology (if not the practice) of parenting as a shared role becoming increasingly pervasive. The partial recognition by some parts of official culture (such as the law, government, education and the media) of the oppressively patriarchal elements to adult masculinity, together with the gradual disappearance of many traditional forms of male employment, especially those in heavy and manufacturing industries, helped to produce two key cultural figures of the period: the 'new man' of the 1980s and his antithesis, the 'new lad' of the 1990s.

Both these figures were highly mediated, by which I mean that their appearance, style and meaning were primarily produced and organized through media representations, which condensed and aestheticized a range of complex tropes about these 'new masculinities' very effectively. The 1980s new man was represented as a direct contrast to an imagined 'old man' against whom he was defined: a figure whose supposed increased emotional sensitivity represented a degree of feminization and an acknowledgement of the validity of nurturing. (Although it should be noted that this argument had been made before in relation to the 'new men' of the 1950s, who were compared favourably with an even older version of masculinity, as discussed in Chapter 1.) The iconic representation of the new man was perhaps the 1988 Athena poster that showed the head and bare torso of a young, rippling-muscled man, holding a tiny baby to his chest. The new man was supposed to have voluntarily relinquished some of the powers and privileges of masculinity in exchange for a greater emotional investment in his relationships and a more feminized approach to the balance between work and domesticity.

Yet, as Rowena Chapman points out, the new man was a suspiciously assimilable creature, whose centrality to the advertising and style cultures of the 1980s suggests that he was more important as an *image* of reformed masculinity than as a representative of deeper social change. Indeed, the emphasis on style and appearance meant that,

> [t]he original new man welded together the possibilities of the nurturer and the narcissist into a flawed whole; but in reality the new man was always an uneasy mixture. And the tensions began to emerge with the increasing importance of advertising in propagating the ideal of the new man. With its emphasis on artifice, on style over content, it caused a fragmentation in the image that the new man presented to the world . . .
>
> (Chapman 1988: 230)

Nonetheless, two important elements emerged from the reconfiguration of masculinity that the new man represented. One was the greater availability of the male body as a site of desire and erotic potential; the other was the emphasis on emotional sensitivity and nurturing as a central dimension to masculinity. It was this latter quality that made it possible for the representation of fatherhood to become increasingly important to the discursive remodelling of masculinity that took place during the 1980s.

In *Feminism Without Women* (1991), Tania Modleski argues that during the 1980s female characters had increasingly disappeared from mainstream popular texts, as men moved in to occupy 'feminine' terrain and as narratives in which the 'absent mother' was a crucial empty space to be filled by others, particularly men, appeared in their stead. As Sarah Harwood also observes in her discussion of the absent mother in a range of 1980s films,

> the mother was so firmly collapsed into the family that creating additional space for the father meant dislodging the mother. Rather than negotiating power relations within the familial space, many of these films opted simply to remove the mother from it. Rooting her out of it, however, threw the family into crisis, a crisis which most narratives found impossible to allay.
>
> (Harwood 1997: 104)

This is a crucial point. The appearance of films such as *Three Men and a Baby* (1987) signified a cultural moment in which the dramatic representation of fathering as nurturing was only possible through the exclusion of mothering from the discourse: mothers are dead, lost or criminally negligent in order for fathers to take up a nurturing role. They are rarely simply doing something else. This also meant that the wider social implications of nurturing fatherhood (including issues of pay differentials between the sexes and socialization and education) were never fully addressed; instead, men continued to be offered as naturally incompetent when it came to the practical skills of nurturing, but successfully competent in the appropriately 'masculine' realm of play. In *Three Men and a Baby* the main characters are, in effect, shown to be *playing* at nurturing and this is expressed through the film's comic register. I will return to this problem later in the chapter.

Where mothers *were* present in a number of popular Hollywood films in the 1980s, their fundamental passivity often became a crucial feature of their characters: they were either rewarded for recognizing the necessity of patriarchal authority and control or punished for refusing this. In *Look Who's Talking* (1989), for example, Molly (played by Kirstie Alley), the mother of the narrator baby, Mikey (he's the one who is doing the talking – in the voice of Bruce Willis), is in search of a 'perfect' husband and father, yet the film displaces this preliminary concern and, indeed, Molly's agency by representing Mikey as the ultimate arbiter of this. He effectively 'chooses' James (John Travolta), the cab driver who takes them to hospital, and the former's suitability as a social – if not a biological – father is confirmed when Mikey's first word is 'daddy'. Indeed, Molly's attempts to act independently are continuously thwarted and represented as misguided or driven by an inappropriate desire for control. Molly must not only learn how to mother from the expert knowledge of the two main male characters, but she must also learn to willingly abandon her claims to agency.

It is important to point out, however, that Hollywood films throughout the 1980s did not simply and unproblematically replace the figure of the mother with that of the father; nor did they systematically offer representations of nurturing paternity. Instead, the crisis of the family was powerfully linked to the crisis in masculinity in a range of often generically diverse but thematically linked films. In texts as apparently different as *Fatal Attraction* (1987), *Back to the Future* (1985), *Rain Man* (1988) and *Kramer vs Kramer* (1979), it is the failure of patriarchal authority and of the father to support his family and sustain familial relationships that precipitates a struggle over parenting and becomes the motive for the narrative (although in the latter this responsibility is ultimately shifted back to the mother). Such struggles were therefore represented both directly, in films like *Kramer vs Kramer* or the role-reversal comedy, *Mr. Mom* (1983), and indirectly, in films which were not, strictly speaking, family melodramas, but which nonetheless located a threat to the family at the centre of the narrative.

Fatal Attraction (1987) is an important text to explore here precisely because it is usually its representation of the 'psycho-femme' in the form of the character of Alex Forrest (Glenn Close) – whose mental and emotional instability threatens to destroy a family – which is analysed. Yet a further look at the film reveals that it is the problematic status of the main male character, Dan Gallagher (Michael Douglas), as a father and husband that is central to the narrative. In the film, Dan meets Alex through his business as a publisher and is tempted to have a brief adulterous weekend with her while his wife is away in the country. However, she becomes increasingly erotically obsessed with him and refuses to end the relationship, eventually stalking Dan, threatening his child and finally breaking into his house to kill his wife, Beth (Anne Archer), so that she can take the latter's place. While the figure of Alex is undoubtedly disturbingly anti-feminist and her final destruction by the 'good mother', Beth Gallagher, seems to symbolize the triumph of domestic femininity over a threateningly independent (and therefore pathologized) version of womanhood, it is important to note that it is the weakness of the father which produces the crisis. Dan's weekend of sex with Alex signifies his transgression from the role of protective father, as Harwood points out

(1997: 120). Indeed, Dan's inability to deal with the increasingly monstrous Alex is played out in the final scenes where he attempts to drown her. It is Beth, the avenging wife, who reclaims her husband and family by finally killing Alex, thus restoring equilibrium, but also leaving behind the uneasy suggestion that Dan is ultimately too weak to deal both with his desires and his responsibility as a father to protect the family.

Significantly, then, while the new man was able to express an *emotional* engagement in the project of fatherhood in ways that had not been seen before, his ability to sustain responsibility became a site of considerable cultural anxiety. Indeed, it would even be difficult to sustain an argument which claimed that the character of Dan Gallagher is credible as a new man in a meaningful sense, given his dependence upon his wife's domestic support and his sexual proclivities. *Fatal Attraction* suggests instead that holding the family together is still a woman's job. It may therefore be better to see the considerable impact that the film had as a symptom of a current of anxiety about men's relationship to power within the family, and the increasing claims to masculine beleaguerment and confusion that will be explored in more detail below.

The new fathering and masculinity
Political claims . . .

Political anxiety about the social role of fathering also became a powerful feature of the official debates about the future of the family that took place throughout the 1980s and 1990s in the USA and the UK. Indeed, while the perception that there was a crisis in the family was not new, what was relatively novel was the increasing ideological focus on the father as a central figure in the family narrative. Panics about family values throughout the 1980s and 1990s were marked by their demonization of the figure of the single mother (and especially the teenage mother), who appeared recurrently throughout both decades as a troublesome source of anxiety (see Chapter 5). By the 1990s, however, fears that the social demands of fathering were being abandoned (by young, white, working-class men, in particular) helped to foster a new focus on fatherhood in a wide range of political, psychological and social discourses.

The British government's establishment of The Child Protection Agency in 1991 as a way of enforcing the economic role of 'absent' fathers is one example of this, although social concern about fathering was marked by its incoherence and ambivalence. The explicit purpose of the Child Protection Act (1991) was to 'shift the burden' of supporting children of divorced parents, from the state, back to fathers. The Child Support Agency was set up in its wake to trace 'recalcitrant' fathers, who would be forced to pay a calculated amount towards the support of their children. The Act also empowered the Agency to place financial penalties on claimants (mothers) who withheld information pertaining to absent fathers, thus reinforcing their continued economic dependence on a male partner from whom they were separated (and possibly estranged). Furthermore, the circulation of renewed debates about the legitimacy of current divorce law, through the emergence of interest groups seeking to defend male entitlement, such as Families Need Fathers (established in 1974, but which became more visible during the 1990s, especially via the media) in the UK and The Promisekeepers in the USA, meant that fathering became an increasingly intense site of antagonism between men and women, focused on the problematic and conflicted issue of parental rights and their relationship to nurturing or breadwinning. Fathering became subject to anxious public scrutiny, precisely because ideas about the constitution of masculinity and its relationship to adulthood, power and male agency were themselves perceived to be in a state of crisis.

Yet the process of reclaiming and redefining fatherhood was also linked to the continuation of patriarchal power in a new form and with a new style. Fred Pfeil points out that political rhetoric during the 1980s and 1990s increasingly represented traditionally feminine skills and qualities as valuable, while problematizing traditionally masculine ones as undesirable; yet this shift failed to address the continuing gap between men and women's economic power and continued to take for granted as natural a whole range of social relations and expectations that perpetuated patriarchy, leaving many men uncertain about their proper role. Indeed, while this produced attempts at left/liberal and pro-feminist 'new mannism', it also led to a range of anti-feminist responses, such as the reactionary and essentialist 'Iron John' ideologies of some men's movements, which loaded the blame for social change onto women (see Robert Bly, 1990, *Iron John: A Book About Men*, for a powerful articulation of these). Pfeil's self-reflexive account of his own involvement with the American men's movement describes – alarmingly – how a liberal feminist language of self-determination, empowerment and liberation was happily appropriated by men as a way of casting themselves as the 'new victims' in order to recover patriarchal power:

> in recasting themselves as yet another minoritized, marginalized and oppressed tribe, the white men in the movement have not only been expressing a real if partial truth about their place on the cusp between straight and alternative culture, but claiming their 'difference' in the same terms and on the same ground rules by which other groups within left-feminist alternative culture have constituted and 'empowered' themselves.
>
> (Pfeil 1995: 227)

This re-empowerment on the part of the American men's movement frequently involved the invocation of the figure of the father as a benign authority. Patriarchy was both deconstructed and reconstructed – simultaneously problematized when it exceeded appropriate expression (in domestic violence, for example) and recuperated through the feminization discussed above. Fathers, it was sometimes argued, were being deliberately excluded from participation in family life by over-powerful or obsessive mothers, who had taken feminism 'too far'.

And refusals . . .

In the UK the culture of 'new laddism' which began to appear in the early 1990s, and which was most visibly articulated in the highly successful men's magazine, *Loaded* (and in similar magazines such as *Maxim* and *FHM*), presented a more coded reactionary and anti-political response to feminism than that of the American men's movement (*Loaded*'s original 'ironic' strap-line was 'for men who know better'). The new lad was physically and economically mature, but emotionally and culturally attached to adolescence; in his crudest form he espoused hedonism, misogyny and a flight from adult responsibility, a two-fingered refusal of the ideal of the new man, as well as a backlash against the gains of feminism. Peter Jackson, Nick Stevenson and Kate Brooks point out that such 'laddism' was originally characterized as little more than a return to a more 'natural' form of masculinity, after the unreasonable expectations forced on men by feminism's hegemony during the previous decade (2001: 116–19). It is worth emphasizing, however, that this 'authentic' masculinity is itself highly constructed. The celebration in *Loaded* of 'birds, booze and football' as the epitome of contemporary masculinity was as retro-fixated on an imaginary golden age (some point in the supposedly pre-feminist 1970s) as it was culturally impoverished.[1]

Indeed, while the lads' magazines vigorously (and anxiously) emphasized the centrality of heterosexual desire to contemporary masculinity, they also simultaneously dissociated it from an emotional commitment to – or even simple friendship with – women, while valorizing apparently more 'authentic' (homosocial but certainly not homosexual) attachments to other men. This was largely articulated through a discourse of ironic knowingness and 'cool', in which women figured as threateningly desirable objects – or simply as threats. Rarely has the profoundly conservative nature of irony been so dismally demonstrated or the inventiveness of magazine journalism so nihilistically employed (for a more detailed discussion of this, see Tincknell, Chambers, Van Loon and Hudson 2003).[2]

Interestingly, and despite the magazines' resistance to paternal responsibility on the part of their readers, fathers reappeared as senior authority figures in *FHM* in the ironic device of the 'Expert Dads', a panel of older men (including a retired priest and a gardening expert!) who could, allegedly, be consulted on a range of issues, instead of the more usual sex advice column. Perhaps unsurprisingly, the page was nonetheless consistently dominated by sexual problems, but the symbolic presence of 'dads' in the role of advice-givers is interesting here. Clearly, for the lads' magazines to explicitly imagine their readers as fathers would have presented too many unresolvable contradictions (around parental responsibility and commitment), but that does not mean the relationship between 'lads' and 'dads' was not present elsewhere. Indeed, important aspects of the lads' magazines' voice or register would appear allied to the feminine subject matter of the family.

'Laddishness' was also an increasingly visible element in British television sitcoms and game and quiz shows throughout the 1990s. Programmes such as *Fantasy Football*, *Men Behaving Badly* and *Have I Got News For You* occupied a discursive space in which the 'gang culture' of lads explicitly and defiantly set itself against an ascribed form of female power that had to be effectively reduced, silenced or made over into objectification if it was to cease to be a threat, while simultaneously pleading men's innate inability to change. As Imelda Whelehan observes of *Men Behaving Badly*, the plea for men's fragility 'is also a plea for women to indulge masculine "weaknesses" not necessarily because they are inevitable or right, but purely because they are so absurd' (2000: 26). To quote *Loaded*, men really should know better, then, but can't be expected to change as long as they continue to have a sense of natural entitlement to privilege.

Or negotiations

Yet the excesses of the lads' magazines' anti-feminism concealed the extent to which middle-class and media-friendly versions of remodelled masculinity had already taken on board feminine discourses of emotional intelligence and nurturing. Indeed, during the 1990s this began to be expressed in a new genre of masculine confessional semi-autobiography that was to become extremely popular and which seemed to condense elements of both the new man and the new lad. For example, Nick Hornby's fictionalized memoirs (*Fever Pitch*, 1992 and *High Fidelity*, 1995) shared a register and an agenda both with some elements of the *Loaded* model of adolescent obsession (with football and music) and a form and style of address more usually associated with the tradition of female journalism.[3]

Such writing was personal, self-reflexive and highly knowing about masculinity, while its focus was on the interior space of emotions as well as the trials of domesticity. Moreover, Hornby's novel, *About a Boy* (1998), an account of a relationship between a thirtysomething man and a boy of 12, effectively located the author at the very centre of a new nurturing masculinity. The book displaced biological paternity to focus on the increasingly important *social* role of fathering, and its account of the developing emotional relationship between man and boy is offered as a defining experience for contemporary heterosexual masculinity. The deployment of a highly personalized yet masculine 'voice' in such work thus enabled Hornby and others in the genre (such as Tony Parsons with *Man and Boy* in 1991) to appropriate an area hitherto largely dominated by women. Hornby's work is an effective apologia for contemporary masculinity and it is significant that his confessional, factional stories are precisely about both the emotional contradictions of modernized bourgeois masculinity and the symbolic role of the male leisure rituals of record collecting and football. Hornby's literary success tells us much about the changes which have taken place in discourses of masculinity, and especially about the central position occupied by recreational rather than work skills, and the increasing availability of an emotional language to describe them.

Public articulations/official knowledge
Political performances

As traditional forms of masculinity were increasingly represented as redundant, and as changing reproductive technologies made biological paternity more uncertain during the 1980s and 1990s, the social agency involved in 'proper' fathering became one way in which patriarchy could be legitimately produced and reproduced. Thus, the increasing visibility of 'active fathering' as a moral project was one of the key cultural and political shifts of the period, and one which was manifested in political public discourse as well as in popular texts.

This is particularly pertinent if we look at the ways in which the two leading figures in British and American politics of the 1990s were presented and represented in terms of their familial relations, and, indeed, as new men: the British prime minister, Tony Blair, and the American president, Bill Clinton. Both men deployed similar but locally nuanced versions of

Figure 3.1 The Blair family posed together outside the door of No. 10 Downing Street the day after the British general election in 1997: a very visible symbol of Tony Blair's 'new dad' masculinity.

a 'new politics' (The Third Way, Clintonism), which focused on the realm of the individualized, the personal and the therapeutic in their political address. Indeed, Clinton's very specific personalization of politics articulated his own response to individual problems – 'I feel your pain' – *as* individual problems. Blair's less overtly sentimental but no less personal address involved the mobilization of himself as a moral rather than a political figure, 'the people's friend', in which, as prime minister, he was above party politics. In both cases, Clinton and Blair responded to the critical problematization of masculinity by taking on those aspects of a feminine discourse that seemed most viable in the public sphere. Blair's astute response to the death of Diana, the Princess of Wales, in August 1997, for example (in his 'People's Princess' speech), demonstrated his own ability to empathize with the public expression of grief in a highly feminine way.

Significantly, but somehow unsurprisingly, the feminization of politics during the 1990s in the figures of Clinton and Blair also meant the continued marginalization of real women in the political arena, despite the hovering presence of the 'exceptional woman', Margaret Thatcher.[4] Most importantly, both Blair and Clinton effectively used their own status as *fathers* in ways that had not been seen before, by mobilizing the discourse of responsible fathering into their political rhetoric and through the visual signifiers of their children. Chelsea Clinton became a key figure in securing Clinton's continued legitimacy, despite the scandal of the Monica Lewinsky liaison in 1998. The Blair children also featured very symbolically in media representations of their father's entry into Number 10 on 1 May 1997, since every British newspaper carried a picture of the Blair family posing together outside the front door of their new home on 2 May. Later, the children came to be a marker, not of a return to family values in politics, but of a new kind of normative masculinity in which fathering was central – and the arrival of baby Leo in the spring of 2000 seemed to confirm Tony Blair's paternal authority. Patriarchal power was thus re-presented, literally, in the form of the father who was both publicly responsible and privately caring.

In these political narratives, the figure of the father as *both* responsible breadwinner and carefree playmate was central. In contrast to earlier prime ministers, Tony Blair had to be seen both at play with his children and responsibly working for them. Media representations of the prime minister repeatedly showed him at home with the family, as well as at work in Downing Street, holding his newborn baby, Leo, in August 2000 and playing football with his teenage sons. In other words, it was the *staging* of fathering in the public domain which was important: and both Clinton and Blair were, in their different ways, 'playing dad'.

Interventions and ideology

In addition to the symbolic staging of fatherhood in the political arena, however, the attempt to recover fathering for a new patriarchy was made more overtly through openly ideological work. *Fatherhood Reclaimed* (1997) by Adrienne Burgess, for example, was a sustained attempt to develop a model of modern, bourgeois fathering for New Labour that was in many ways anti-feminist. While acknowledging the feminist critique of masculinity, the book was evasive about the power differentials involved, of race or class as well as gender, and clearly addressed an implied readership composed of highly educated, professional, middle-class white women. Its solutions to the problem of men's absence from parenting thus required women – not men – to change:

> The challenges to women would be considerable. Since employing men substantially in education and welfare is crucial to broadening the definition of fathering, women would find themselves facing job losses in those areas they currently dominate. They would also have to give up their dominance over their children and acknowledge fathers as equal partners in parenting, while finding the *obligation* to be breadwinners imposed on them as it currently is on men.
>
> (Burgess 1997: 217)

Burgess's book is important largely because it is one of the few examples available of a sustained attempt at a consciously popular political intervention in the ideological reconstruction of fathering. It sought to construct the figure of the 'new father' in contrast to an 'old' version, just as the new man depended upon an imaginary outmoded version of masculinity. However, as Deborah Lupton and Lesley Barclay point out, claims about new kinds of fathering are almost as old as fatherhood itself (and as old as the arguments about new men, perhaps), and the idea that men are *now* starting to become involved in family life in ways that they have hitherto failed to do is a recurrent feature of fatherhood's reinvention over the decades (1997: 15; see also above and Chapter 1). Burgess's book is itself, then, part of the construction of the new father. Indeed, there is little evidence of a preoccupation with fathering as a social role in governmental and public discourses of masculinity before the 1980s. Perhaps it is safe to say that even if 'real' new fathers were both less engaged and more active than the popular image suggested, the emergence of such a cultural figure at this point is itself significant.

However, as Burgess's indifference suggests, important differentials of class as well as race and ethnicity have often either been reproduced or omitted in this process. As Lupton and Barclay observe,

> In contrast to this ideal of the 'new' father is that of the 'dangerous' father, the father who abuses and neglects his children, who has recently become a figure of moral panic. This father is frequently designated as poor, working-class or of non-European ethnicity, preserving the 'new' father image as predominantly white and middle class.
>
> (Lupton and Barclay 1997: 5)

The whiteness of the figure of the new father offers us a clue as to the ways in which he has worked ideologically, especially in media representations. Rather than transforming or radicalizing masculinity, the new dad effectively extended the realm of male domination and patriarchal power, appropriating domestic space and expertise while resisting changes in the workplace. The new focus on fathering was crucial to the project to modernize masculinity, by reworking aspects which had been problematized and appropriating elements traditionally associated with femininity. Bill Clinton was sometimes described – only half jokingly – as America's first black president, as though the appropriation of performative or expressive elements of black culture by a white man would be an effective substitute for the real extension of power to African-Americans. In a similar vein, the feminization both of the public sphere of politics and of the relationship which men have with their children cannot simply and uncritically be read as a triumph for women.

The 'new father' in film and television

Throughout the 1990s the reclamation of fathering took place in a wider range of cultural forms and discourses than that of political imagery and social criticism. Indeed, the number of films and television shows which took an increasingly serious interest in the dilemmas of fatherhood and in the significance of family relationships for men suggests that fathering had become widely recognized as a central component in contemporary discourses of masculinity. That this was done in often contradictory ways confirmed its problematic status. For many of these texts, the imperative that men – to be men – must be breadwinners was crucial, but it was supplemented by another which insisted on the importance of strong emotional bonds between fathers and their children. These bonds were often emphasized at the expense of those between mothers and children, so that in place of a balanced account of changing roles, two iconic figures began to appear in a weirdly anti-symbiotic relationship to each other: the 'good father' and the 'bad mother'. The good father became an important figure in a plethora of popular television narratives, in which he was invariably portrayed as struggling heroically and commendably with the task of raising the children who had been thrust upon him. In contrast, the figure of the 'bad mother' often drew on the demonized stereotype of the feckless welfare dependent that continued to circulate in popular accounts of the decline of the family.[5]

In the immensely popular British soap opera, *Coronation Street* (also discussed elsewhere in this book), throughout 1995 two parallel storylines were screened in which the contrast between different kinds of single parenting was played out. In one, the longest-serving character in the show, the middle-aged, well-educated, white and dependable – if somewhat boring – Ken Barlow, was represented as bravely and effectively taking on the role of single father to a newborn baby; in another, a much newer character, the stereotypical 'welfare mother', Tricia Rodgers, was shown struggling ineffectually to bring up a young son who repeatedly played truant and resisted discipline. The extraordinary ideological implications of these two narrative and representational strategies would be hard to overstate. Not only did the representation of Tricia mobilize every available stereotype of the single mother, with the character's dependence on benefits and evident inability to deal with everyday problems rendered a crucial feature of the stories woven around her, but the contrast with the programme's investment in the idea of fathering as a heroic project (certainly more heroic than mothering), through the figure of Ken Barlow, made the issue of patriarchal power – in the form of 'discipline' – absolutely central. Tricia's inability to be an effective parent was linked to her extreme passivity and the absence of a father figure for her son. In contrast, Ken's transformation into an effective new dad mobilized a range of ideas about the morality of fathering, which chimed with the newly modernized masculinity, in which the test of good fathering was not simply physical strength, but moral strength in the service of family.

A profoundly patriarchal dynamic around the reproduction of masculinity was therefore central to many of the narratives that made the issue of fathering a key topic. In popular drama, this testing of masculinity began to focus on men's relationships both with their children, especially sons, *and* with their own fathers, so that the problem of the reproduction of an appropriate patriarchy became central to the text. This is not to suggest that such dramas offered uncritical or uncomplex representations of fathering – many were at pains to do the opposite and managed to represent a whole range of versions that were nuanced and often highly appealing. It *is* to suggest, however, that in comparison with the popular drama of the 1970s, and also the 1980s, the social dimensions to fathering were interrogated much more fully and in greater depth.

In the American hospital drama *ER* (1994–), for example, masculine familialism was so central to the programme that the highly complex, often contradictory relationships with their own children or with ageing parents that characterized all the main male characters were a crucial element in the show's narrative dynamic. For example, in the 1998 season, Dr Benton, a character whose emotional repression and problematic cultural identity as an African-American had been used as a source of narrative tension, finally demonstrated that his was a properly modernized masculinity through his decision to take up paediatrics and through his tender relationship with his deaf son. A whole episode was devoted to the existential search for (real) fathers and the meaning of fatherhood by two other male characters, Dr Greene and Dr Ross; a search which was – appropriately – staged through the conventions of the road movie, a genre historically associated with a romanticized representation of the masculine search for identity. Indeed, throughout the show the continuing preoccupation with the relationship between an acceptably patriarchal masculinity in its political sense and the place of patriarchy in the private sense was a key theme. Central to this was the premise that in order for men to become proper fathers they must also learn to be good sons.

The British soap opera, *EastEnders,* also re-centred fathering in its narrative strands during the 1990s, although it did so through the conventions of social realism and 'kitchen sink' drama. The thuggish Mitchell brothers, a pair of cockney mechanics, who were conventionally represented as working only just within the law and who both had troubled histories of relationships with women, were recast through their roles as fathers. A masculinity which had been figured in terms of emotional incoherence was now shown transformed and redeemed by a child, who permitted the expression of repressed tenderness. In each of these cases, the child's masculine gender was particularly loaded, since the imperative to reproduce patriarchal power through a son was both acknowledged and defused by the characters' machismo. As Sarah Edge argues, the importance of the male child to such narratives suggests a powerful desire for 'the continuation of patriarchal society, which the demands of the feminist movement [have] clearly threatened' (1996: 78).

A complex example of this dynamic – together with a rejection of the idea of the new man and his willing forgoing of male privileges – can be found in the British film, *The Full Monty* (1997), which locates fathering at the centre of its narrative. The film offers an account of changes in male working-class identities that are explicitly linked with the decline of fatherhood as a social role. Indeed, the motivating force of the narrative is the desire of the main character, Gaz (Robert Carlyle), to *recover* his role as male breadwinner in order to sustain his relationship with his son, a project that is repeatedly blocked by his embittered ex-wife. In order for Gaz to do this, he must also rekindle his relationship with the boy. Power relations between child and father are presented as symptomatically reversed, with Gaz boyishly seeking his son's 'permission' to perform as a stripper and the child demonstrating a mature understanding of what is at stake.

This reversal of power seems to represent a vivid enactment of the 'crisis in masculinity', and especially of the profound disempowerment of working-class men who had little to claim in the first place. A kind of resolution is brought about, then, by the intervention of the male child, whose temporary appropriation of patriarchal control works to secure the partial recovery of adult masculinity. Yet *The Full Monty* actually represents *all* its male characters as childlike – offering their social incompetence as a consequence of their infantilization by redundancy. Indeed, this is addressed through the narrative's preoccupation with male sexuality, and especially sexual potency, in the final symbolic striptease.

The centrality of fathering to the narrative thus suggests that paternal identity is vital, not only to children but to men's sense of themselves. Yet there is no suggestion that it is Gaz's responsibility to do any of the nurturing, even though he clearly has the time to do so;

Figure 3.2 In *The Full Monty*, Gaz must rekindle his relationship with his son if he is also to recover his social place. In this still, the problematic relations of power between father and son are emphasized by the framing of the image. (Photo: Ronald Grant Archive)

indeed, he is spectacularly incompetent as a full-time parent (like so many of the reluctant dads discussed here). Rather, the reclamation of fathering which the film effects is one that seeks to assert men's rights and entitlements, especially within the context of a radically altered economic environment in which women are supposed to hold all the cards (Tincknell and Chambers 2002).

In this way, the possibility of nurturing for men was only problematically addressed by those films and television shows in the 1990s which took the project of fatherhood as their main theme. Mothering continued to be represented as a natural – and therefore unexciting – dimension of femininity, while fathering was represented both as a set of skills that had to be learned and as a heroic rediscovery of the self. Interestingly, truly bad fathers were relatively rare in popular drama and especially soap opera: they were either transformed by the cleansing punishment of loss or trauma, or evacuated from the story altogether, so that even the most morally dubious of characters was redeemed by his love for his children. Good fathers, however, were those who were prepared to undertake the great adventure.

The adventure of fatherhood: comic incompetence and the 'new dad'

During the 1990s the figure of the new dad also appeared in texts that featured the struggles of fatherhood as a form of humorous incompetence. Significantly, the specific genre which many of these narratives occupied was comedy – so often the site for the staging of cultural anxieties about gender and identity. Of course, plenty of comic texts, especially television sitcoms from the 1950s through to the 1990s (from *Leave it to Beaver* to *Father, Dear Father* and *Married . . . With Children*), have featured various combinations of fathers and children, as is explored in Chapter 5. The difference is that such texts, even when they subverted or sent up paternal authority, tended to represent fathering as an economic rather than a nurturing role within the family. There is little sense that such comedy fathers ever changed a nappy, even if it was only to demonstrate their natural incompetence at such a task.

In contrast, while continuing to operate through the comedic register, a number of popular television shows and films in the 1990s focused on new fathers in every sense: their dramatic emphasis was upon a man's relationship with infants and very young children, the groups most traditionally regarded as the domain of nurturing femininity, and it was this which emphatically marked the importance of fathering to the new masculinity. Where the drama or comedy of the past had largely revolved around father's relationship with teenage or pre-pubescent children, in the 1990s it was the brand new father's relationship with his infant that was the key site of modernized masculinity. Indeed, perhaps the cultural proximity of the new dad figure to adolescence, through some of the 'laddish' aspects identified earlier, made the possibility of a paternal relationship to teenagers more difficult to achieve (and the increased narrative centrality of the teenager rendered this even more problematic in terms of narrative address, as will be analysed in Chapter 5).

Yet there were also continuities between the conservatism of older sitcom and film representations of good fathers and modern television models. The nurturing new dads who began to appear so frequently were primarily white and middle class; their social status and racial identities both taken for granted and important markers of contemporary ideological currents. While their status as nurturing fathers was in some ways problematic, it could be recuperated by their closeness to a more familiar normative masculinity.

Holding the baby

This use of comedy to stage and therefore interrogate the idea of the new father can be explored by looking in detail at a couple of examples of popular texts. Importantly, many of these represented the new father as a reluctant or uncertain parent, whose emotional responsibility is only triggered by shock or loss. The British television sitcom, *Holding the Baby* (1996–98) was a good example of this. Starring the stand-up comedian, Nick Hancock, as a new single father, Gordon, the programme partly depended on the intertextual aspects of Hancock's existing 'new lad' persona as a way of coding the show's relationship to the new masculinity. Sometimes it did this by returning to essentialist or biological accounts in its insistence on male incompetence and female expertise with babies, and sometimes by laying claim to the new man territory of nurturing masculinity. The show's emphasis on Gordon's culinary skills prefigured the television appearance of Jamie Oliver, but worked in remarkably similar ways: it made him laddishly appealing while also portraying him as domesticated. But the programme also struggled with the idea of nurturing masculinity and its problematic status in relation to traditional gender roles. Interestingly, it dealt with this by contrasting

Gordon's new dad role with a secondary male character, his brother, whose 'man behaving badly' persona was permitted to say and do the things Gordon wouldn't. This worked to drive the comedy in ways that the characterization of Gordon made impossible, while simultaneously helping the text to operate a double discourse: that of the new man and that of the bad lad. Most noticeably, the baby itself was largely absent from the narrative.

What *Holding the Baby* mobilized most markedly, however, was a discourse which struggled to reconcile the contradictory elements central to the new masculinity: those of the father-as-little-boy with those of the father-as-nurturer. Gordon shifted constantly between loveable incompetence and expertise. He was both a reliable companion to the women he met at the mother-and-toddler group he attended and a new lad; but the impossibility of such a subject position was only problematically played out by the programme. *Holding the Baby* was also too confined by the conventions of the standard British sitcom either to develop the comic possibilities of its situation or to transgress boundaries. Its significance lay largely in its historical appearance and context.

Fathers on film

In cinema comedy the dilemma presented to and by the new father was largely organized around a drive towards the happy ending of the restoration of the nuclear family. The Hollywood comedy, *Nine Months* (1995), for example, starred Hugh Grant as the happily single Samuel who, when his girlfriend (Julianne Moore) announces that she is pregnant while they are driving along a mountain road, promptly swerves in front of an oncoming truck and crashes into roadworks. Fortunately, the pregnancy is unaffected by this extreme response. Samuel's consternation at impending fatherhood is, of course, eventually recuperated by the text's insistence on his innate empathy with children, an empathy which is signalled near the beginning of the film in a scene in which he effortlessly bonds with the little girls in his partner's ballet class.

Grant's star image of the likeably incompetent, vaguely public-school-educated Englishman had already worked to condense a range of meanings about a modernized masculinity in the earlier romantic comedy, *Four Weddings and a Funeral* (1994). In *Nine Months*, however, the combination of these elements and the additional anxieties about the responsibilities of fatherhood work together in complex and interesting ways. The equivocation about commitment that had seemed endearing in *Four Weddings* became here a device for the refusal of adult masculinity that paternity seems to require: Samuel is himself too childish to be able to accept the full meaning of adulthood. Just as *The Full Monty* figured its male characters as responding to an inability to come to terms with the consequences of economic change by returning to a childlike irresponsibility, so *Nine Months* suggests that becoming a father must be prefigured by a new maturity. Samuel has nine months in which to achieve this.

In another example, fatherhood itself, unlike mothering, is represented as an adventure, in which the necessity of nurturing in order for men to fully know and become themselves is presented as a series of escapades. The British romantic comedy-drama, *Jack and Sarah* (1995) circled around the dilemma faced by its main character, Jack (Richard E. Grant), when he is forced to care for his baby daughter, Sarah, after his wife has died in childbirth (a removal which provides the motive for the story and 'clears a space' for the narrative's preoccupation with fathering in much the way Harwood describes – by erasing the mother, 1997: 36). Jack has not *chosen* to nurture his daughter; it is forced upon him by circumstance, and for this reason he is shown as a more than usually ('loveably') incompetent father and one who attempts to solve his dilemma by hiring an American waitress, Amy (Samantha Mathis), to become Sarah's nanny. While Jack carries a number of new man traits – he is caring, emotionally complex, creative – and is represented as having high cultural capital, signified by his expensive and fashionably decorated house and bourgeois lifestyle, he is also an incompetent nurturer at the beginning of the film. Indeed, the point of the narrative is to trace Jack's growing confidence as a carer for his daughter, and his transformation from a playmate dad into a nurturing one. This is offered through many of the tropes of the masculine romance – the adventure story.

For example, in a scene set in a department store, the presence of a significantly signposted '*Mother* and Baby Room', but no 'Father and Baby Room', is used to highlight Jack's poignant struggle as a lone father – society makes no space for male nurturing – and his rebellion against social expectations. In a later scene, Jack is shown in the bath with baby Sarah: caring for her physically and playing with her as *both* a nurturing father and a playmate father in a utopian moment of togetherness. Yet this is hardly a consistently articulated theme, and at other points in the narrative Jack's struggle to be recognized as a nurturing father is displaced by the text's focus on other concerns, especially the various relationship complications. Indeed, while a marked contrast is produced around mothering and fathering, with Jack's own mother represented as a meddling snob who is contrasted unfavourably with his open, emotionally expansive and sympathetic father, this is not developed. But the film finds it difficult to reconcile these elements elsewhere and they are lost. Instead, *Jack and Sarah* suggests the *impossibility* of reconciling the role of male provider with that of nurturer – for bourgeois men.

Even more problematically, the responsibility for Jack's inability to combine the two roles is displaced on his female boss – a career bitch played by Cherie Lunghi, in the tradition of Sigourney Weaver in *Working Girl* (1988) – who is too concerned with her work to fulfil the properly feminine role of mother and is therefore also unsuitable as romantic partner. In contrast, Amy the nanny is emphatically *not* a career woman; and her early incompetence with the baby is transformed through love for Sarah into natural nurturing skills in a way that Jack's is not. By the end of the film it is Amy's love for the baby that marks the romantic turning point and prefigures the reconstruction of the nuclear family, indicated by the final tableau of Jack, Sarah and Amy. The key discourse of the film is thus one in which the dilemma of single fatherhood is resolved by a return to a traditional division of labour, in which women do the nurturing and men the playing.

The foregrounding of fathering as a transformative life project was thus both crucial to and problematically negotiated within these representations of a new masculinity. While many films and television narratives during the 1990s insisted upon paternity's existential centrality, they also returned it to more traditional models. It is significant, for example, that in each of the texts discussed above, nurturing fatherhood has been thrust upon the main character: none of these are stories about men who have chosen to become house-husbands. The comic play around incompetence therefore worked to emphasize that for men in the 1990s, looking after children could still just be a game.

Having it all: 'new lad/new dad' advice

The mid-1990s also saw the emergence of a relatively new genre of popular advice manuals and comic memoirs; the fatherhood advice narrative addressed directly to the new dad. Such books also represented the role of playmate as the dominant discourse of fatherhood, but they did so in contradictory and uncertain ways that seemed to be in conflicted negotiation with some of the incoherence and anxieties about adult responsibility that new laddism articulated. That is, such texts were marked by a jokey, euphemistic idiom, which intermittently emphasized, exaggerated, downgraded and celebrated fathering – an idiom that had clear continuities with the discourse of extended adolescence found in *Loaded*.

Just as the objectified female body, alternately leered over, managed and repudiated, structured the discursive register of the lads' magazine, so the 'problem' of women's bodies and their difference from those of men reappeared in the fathering manual. Pregnancy was represented as both profoundly natural and strangely unnatural – perhaps as a consequence of the dominance of a recreational model of sexuality – the mystified source of the confusion and uncertainty which such texts offered to dispel. The use of a comic register thus attempted to displace anxieties about the female body as a source of life and nurture:

> One increasingly obvious change you will notice is that the baby is getting bigger and bigger and bigger inside her. Using basic dimensional mathematics, it is easy to deduce that all your wife's other internal bits and pieces have less and less room. This causes decreased bladder size. In short, it means that your own lengthy interludes in the bathroom reading the local paper or the latest *Phantom* comic will have to be cut short. It also means that epic car journeys may need to be re-thought. And whatever you do, don't say, 'Can you just hang on for another half hour?' A woman with a bladder the size of a walnut should not be joked with.
>
> (Downey 1994: 56)

However, this uncertainty tended to re-mystify motherhood, precisely because it could not address it in other ways. Indeed, while the maternal body was the source of humorous confusion, that of the father was presented largely as a set of potential incompetences, especially around sexual behaviour. Indeed, the absence, or erasure, of the father's body and the insistence on the physicality of the mother's in these accounts effectively worked to reproduce the mind/body, nature/culture, male/female oppositions, which tend to structure western thought about gender.

The new dad books also promised both narrative and structural control to their readers; by locating the father, not the mother, at the centre of the narrative they offered discursive centrality and self-determination – to be a father is to be powerful. And their mobilization of a comic register was in marked contrast to the ways in which motherhood advice narratives tend to be offered. In mother and baby magazines, advice books and television programmes, the dominant discourse is one of passive wonder, 'scientific' seriousness and common-sense reassurance. In comparison, as Lupton and Barclay point out, the dominant discourse of the new dad books '[w]as that of fatherhood as an experience of personal growth for the *father*, a means to improve upon the self, a journey of self-discovery and fulfilment. It is assumed that the experience of fatherhood will lead invariably to a transformed, "better person"' (1997: 87).

The jokiness then, either masked discomfort and uncertainty or addressed it directly, reproducing assumptions that men's relationship to parenthood is, at best, a contradictory one. Peter Downey, for example, in *So You're Going To be A Dad* (1994) repeatedly makes uncomfortable reference to what he regards as unacceptable male behaviour, while insisting on the importance of care and love between prospective parents. This rhetorical insistence on a companionable, egalitarian relationship between men and women suggests that such relationships are more difficult to identify and sustain than might otherwise appear in an age of post-feminism.

Such books were also implicitly addressed to a white, middle-class readership, their authors identified as professional writers or thinkers or occupying creative cultural space through their work, or already established in another, appropriately configured role. The book by the comedian/actor, Nigel Planer, *A Good Enough Dad* (1994), is one example of this kind of new dad writing. His audience was likely to identify with his own white bourgeois subject position, and might be expected to empathize also with his personal journey from alternative comedian in the 1980s to responsible father, one whose mobilization of jokey seriousness in the book also spoke to the contradictions of masculinity during the 1990s.

Above all, the comic register worked to reproduce and consolidate the idea that male parenting is a form of work that is play, that the serious project of parenthood can only be mediated for men by lack of seriousness. Indeed, the contradictory concept of the adult male as simply another child, a little boy who also needs to be nurtured by the wife/mother was often reasserted in the very address of such texts, with their anxious insistence on the necessity of responsibility coupled with pleasure. And, as with the location of fathering narratives in the genre of comedy in film or television discussed above, the comic play helped to mask or displace some profound anxieties about male and female bodies, social roles and emotional dependency.

Fathers can be mothers, too: the 'reproductive' male body

If comedy remained one of the most important ways with which popular culture dealt with changing ideas about gender roles, conflicts over reproductive rights and claims and the impact of social and technological change during the 1990s, we can end by looking at a film comedy which articulated these concerns in quite explicit ways. In *Junior* (1994), Arnold Schwarzenegger plays an emotionally repressed but vocationally committed research scientist,

Dr Alexander Hess, who is persuaded by his machiavellian colleague, gynaecologist Dr Larry Arbogast (Danny de Vito), to test out on his own body the anti-miscarriage drug he has developed. In order to do this, Hess must become pregnant, and a donated egg belonging to an English rival, Dr Diana Reddin (Emma Thompson), is stolen by Arbogast and implanted in Hess's body. However, once he has been impregnated, Hess is reluctant to give up his baby, insisting on carrying it to term. The plot is further complicated when it is revealed that Arbogast's estranged wife is also pregnant (though not by him), as a consequence of which she attempts to rekindle their marriage.

In some respects, *Junior* may be read as a fantasy of male control over reproduction which clearly engages with the enormous changes in reproductive technology that were a feature of the 1990s. Importantly, Alexander can only 'give birth' at the end of the film with the help of male medical intervention in the form of a Caesarean. Yet while the film is both knowing and playful in its representation of gender difference, the central problematic of the story – should men be able to give birth? – is, in many respects, recuperated by the narrative structure and by the film's tendency to essentialize gendered behaviour.

For example, once he has become pregnant and his 'female hormones' take effect, the character of Hess undergoes a fundamental transformation; he shifts from a hyper-masculine position in which he is cold, unemotional and objective about the world and his relationship to it, to an emotional, feminized position. This change is rendered particularly absurd because of its contradictory relationship to Schwarzenegger's already established star persona as the epitome of machismo, and thus becomes a key source of much of the comedy. Hess begins to cook, empathize with women and indulge in physical displays of affection. All of this is deliberately underlined by the film's *mise-en-scène*, which moves with Hess's life change from the austerity of the campus apartment where he had lived as a research professor, to Arbogast's Victorian family home with its connotations of cosy domesticity. The bedroom décor, in particular, changes from the institutional grey walls and wooden furniture of the university to a riot of pink flowers, drapes and frills, all of which express Hess's personality change at the level of non-representational codes. Moreover, the feminization process makes him susceptible to romance and he falls in love with Diana. In other words, the character is humanized as well as feminized by his experience.

This humanization process seems also to incorporate some elements of *feminism* as well as femininity, in ways that powerfully suggest the former's centrality to contemporary discourses of womanhood, as Hollows has noted (2000). When Alexander is threatened with the possibility of the university appropriating his pregnancy for official research, he responds angrily with the feminist riposte, 'My body. My choice.' Later in the film, when he has been secretly transferred to a specialist clinic in the country, disguised as a woman, he is shown participating in the culture and activities enthusiastically, making friends with the other women and apparently committed (or resigned) to a new life as a woman. However, while the film offers some space for Schwarzenegger to claim ownership of feminist-inspired beliefs in freedom of choice about reproduction, there is very little given to women to express such views. Diana is represented as particularly anxious to reclaim her fertility before it is too late – that is why she donated the egg that becomes 'Junior'. In a scene in the garden of the clinic, a female obstetrician is shown addressing her audience of pregnant women about the myth of the maternal instinct; at precisely this moment, her image disappears from the screen and her voice fades from the soundtrack, to be replaced by Alexander's reverie about giving birth. Rather than confirming that caring for a baby may be done equally by men and women, *Junior* literally silences the expression of such an idea and replaces it with the image of a man whose nurturing desires are only triggered by the artificial presence of female hormones.

Junior is, therefore, ambivalent about the scenario it offers. On the one hand, it seems to open up the possibility of radically new forms of reproduction; on the other, it closes them off again. At the very end of the film Diana herself is shown as 'naturally' pregnant with Alexander's baby, her role as a mother and his as a father fully restored. And, as in *Jack and Sarah*, narrative closure is produced through ideological closure: the nuclear family and traditional gender roles are effectively reconstituted as the two new families, the Hesses and the Arbogasts are shown picnicking on a beach with their babies.

Conclusion

In many of these texts, the proper role for fathers remained problematic and contradictory. The possibility of simply playing dad – that is, playing at being an adult – was both pervasive and seductive, but it sat uneasily alongside political attempts to intervene in and reconstruct family structures. While new laddism promised a perennial adolescence in which adult responsibility was irreconcilable with pleasure, social movements such as The Promisekeepers and Families Need Fathers, in their different ways, seemed to be attempting to claim back a traditional model of fathering that feminism was supposed to have stolen. And while the equation of adult responsibility with femininity and a discomfiting domesticity is familiar from post war texts, which circle around the problem, it is also a feature of many of these narratives, with their incoherences and contradictions. The feminization of men has thus seemed to involve the idea of fathering as a 'life project', in which claims of a new kind of masculine identity were part of the development of the reflexive self of postmodern culture identified by Giddens (1992). However, the new masculinity has frequently sought to claim the space of femininity without relinquishing the power of the old, patriarchal masculinity. This has been both crucial and problematic to the idea of the family itself.

Notes

1 Judith Williamson helped to focus my attention on the powerful myth of feminism's moment of ascendancy (the 1970s? the 1980s?) and its relationship to the 'crisis in masculinity' in a paper delivered at the Women's Section of MECCSA, January 2004.

2 The use of a casualized misogyny and pleasure in the idea of sexual violence towards women in these magazines was one of their most disturbing aspects. Many dealt with this by 'returning' the violence to women themselves, who were frequently cast as explicitly masochistic. One 'correspondent' on the *FHM* letters page, for example, complained that his girlfriend was addicted to sadomasochism and wanted to know how to deal with this. Whether the letter was real or the concern true is hard to ascertain. What we can point to is the way in which the prominence this was given, allied to the

frequent suggestion that violent sex was perfectly normal, worked to legitimate an underlying implication that women not only wanted 'it', but that they wanted to be hurt.

3 This tradition of 'soft' journalism, with its emphasis on issues of personal morality and behaviour, while largely addressed to female readers, has also tended to be dominated by conservative and anti-feminist columnists, such as Jean Rook in the 1960s and 1970s and Lynda Lee-Potter in the 1980s and 1990s. The 'liberal' and 'liberal feminist' version, espoused by writers such as Katharine Whitehorn and Jill Tweedie during the 1980s, and by Catherine Bennett and Deborah Orr in the 1990s and 2000s, while politically more left-wing, tended to share the discursive focus on the personal as an appropriately 'feminine' sphere of writing. Now, however, a new strand of apparently home-based but anti-domestic male writers, such as Andrew Martin, Tim Lott and Nicholas Lezard, have emerged in the wake of Hornby. Such writers, while making personal life their subject matter, often manage to suggest not only that the domestic sphere is simply too irritatingly feminine for them to take seriously, but also that their efforts to be 'new men' are rarely appreciated by women.

4 Hillary Rodham Clinton and Cherie Booth continued to occupy the space reserved for presidential and prime ministerial spouses (that is, wives), visible largely to be looked at, with their clothes, hair and demeanour constantly scrutinized by the media, and made available for that scrutiny, and intermittently demonized when their economic and intellectual independence was recognized.

5 Such representations of bad mothers continued to be a feature of British newspapers and television documentaries and of American television exposés throughout the 1990s, as the panic about teenage motherhood grew. A *Sunday Times* editorial in September 1999, for example, attributed the rise in teenage pregnancies to the 'loss of parental authority, greater acceptance of young mothers, and financial rewards in the short term', without reflecting on the centrality of 'young mothers' to the myths of the happy nuclear family in the 1950s and 1960s.

chapter four

Lost innocents: childhood in contemporary media

Introduction

A central nodal point for much contemporary thinking about the family, both at the level of common sense and in academic research and writing, has been the relationship between children and the media. Television, in particular, has been the focus for a range of moral panics, primarily concerned with its supposed potential to incite children into mimetically violent or sexual behaviour, especially in the absence of appropriate parental guardianship. These concerns have clearly been shaped by television's distinctive role within the domestic sphere – as entertainer, 'babysitter' and educator – but they have also been marked by a relationship to a longer history of social fears about the family and about what and who children are supposed to be. 'Childhood' in these configurations is a natural realm untouched by knowledge of a world in which violence, sexuality, injustice and fear prevail, and children are constructed as in need of special protection, both from that reality and from their own immaturity.

In addition to these concerns, academic work around the relationship between the family and the media has also proliferated over the last 20 years, largely in the disciplines which have a specific investment in the conceptualization and re-presentation of childhood and 'the child', such as psychology, anthropology and education, as well as media and cultural studies. What seems to emerge out of any analysis of this wealth of material, however, is, as David Buckingham points out, a recognition of 'the sheer quantity of it' (1998: 131).

This chapter is not only concerned with the vexed question of children's relations with the media as audiences. It is also interested in the complex and changing ways in which childhood and children themselves have been mediated: in literature, Hollywood films, television, advertising and photographs. It therefore begins by locating such panics within the context of the problematic ideal of childhood innocence, which continues to shape many of the debates. In particular, the legacy of the Enlightenment has helped to structure contemporary western attitudes towards children, especially the development of an idea of childhood as a distinctive stage in human development requiring protection, and a rigid emphasis on the child as *either* innocent or knowing, natural or cultural, savage or savant. Such binaries remain important to the ways in which competing discourses of childhood intersect or come into conflict with each other at the level of representation. However, while the romantic ideal remains powerful, an emergent model of the child as citizen-consumer has begun to trouble its legitimacy during the last 30 years.

The invention of childhood
Cultural investments

Patricia Holland has observed that much contemporary writing about the relationship between the child and the media fundamentally confuses the two concepts of children and childhood. In an exploration of the moral panic over 'video nasties' that took place in the UK during the 1980s and 1990s, she points to the regular conflation made between film texts *about* children and those deliberately addressed to a youthful audience:

> Cinematic and video narratives of demonic childhood – from *The Exorcist, The Omen* (1976), *Carrie* (1976) through to the *Child's Play* films in the late 1980s – have become interwoven with those narratives in the tabloid press which envisage a child audience caught up in their demonising influence.
>
> (Holland 1997: 50)

Such conflations are partly linked to a lengthy history of moral panics about unruly or socially threatening children and 'inadequate' or 'feckless' families, discussed in greater detail below. However, they are also a component of a different but linked set of concerns, largely focused on the perceived 'loss of innocence' found in contemporary discourses around children, and the threat this is perceived to represent to the family. As Holland goes on to point out, these particular films use the complex and contradictory nature of childhood as a vehicle to stage the relationship between good and evil for an adult audience, and have little connection with children themselves. Yet they have frequently become intertwined with accounts of children's real behaviour, as though the relationship between representation and experience were transparent and self-evident. Adult outrage about the apparent moral decline of society or its incipient violence thus frequently focuses on the figure of the 'corrupted child' (to use Holland's phrase), whose violation stands for a larger web of fear and suspicion. These concerns are also frequently cast in nostalgic terms: 'children are growing up too fast these days', or 'there are no proper toys for children now, only electronic games'. For Holland, 'the two interacting sets of narratives both express a deep disappointment and cynicism at the disappearance of the figure of the romantic child' (1997: 50).

I will return to the figure of the demon child later. Suffice to say at this point that while much of this anxiety is undoubtedly linked to understandable hopes and fears for our own children or those to whom we are close, it also tends to be articulated in larger, more abstract terms, as a matter of social and cultural investment in an ideal. As Dorfman and Mattelart put it:

> [a]dults create for themselves a childhood embodying their own angelic aspirations, which offer consolation, hope and a guarantee of a 'better' but unchanging future . . . Adult values are projected onto the child, as if childhood was a special domain where these values could be protected uncritically.
>
> (Dorfman and Mattelart 1972: 30–1)

The valorization of childhood, then, is rarely itself an innocent activity; it always carries with it a set of values, goals and, indeed, political concerns, which shape and inform it. Furthermore, childhood as a social, cultural and developmental category is primarily the invention of an adult perspective on the world. It is therefore worth considering where, how and why the specific ideal of the 'romantic child' appeared, as well as the meanings attached to this powerful cultural figure.

In *Centuries of Childhood* (1962), the French historian Philippe Aries was perhaps the first to argue that childhood is an entirely social construct, claiming that its 'invention' was part of the development of modern western societies and the growth of individualized forms of social relations and what we might now call the privatization of the family. This process has, as Buckingham notes, 'been accompanied by a veritable explosion of discourses, both *about* childhood and directed *at* children themselves' (1998: 131). Two key discourses, medicine (especially psychology) and education, have been crucial sites for the construction of norms, pathologies and prescriptions about children, all of which have contributed to the construction of an ideal and the problematization of deviance. Childhood became, in Foucault's phrase, 'a regime of truth', subject to disciplinary interventions that effectively produced the child and its identity. In particular, the idea of childhood as a developmental 'process of becoming', as Nick Lee terms it (2001), in which the individual child moves from a position of lack to one of social agency as a human subject, has been central to educational principles.

Aries argues that the moment of modernity represented an important cultural break; before the seventeenth century, he observes, no clear categorical distinction was made between children and adults; nor were children deemed to occupy an entirely separate cultural sphere with its own codes and cultural expectations. From the late seventeenth century and on into the twentieth, however, an increasingly complex and elaborated construction of children and their world began to emerge, in which the developmental idea of childhood was central. This was closely bound up with the growth of the modern family as an economic structure within the nation state, in which the notion of childhood as a period of dependence was – increasingly during the nineteenth and twentieth centuries, as we have seen – defined and directed by the state. Indeed, the development and elaboration of the discourse of childhood as a condition of dependence was clearly not a simple matter of a natural weakness, even though it would be explained in these terms. As Lee observes,

> the apparent inevitability of childhood's dependency is neither the result of any simple fact of physical weakness nor the result of some simple error of over-generalization from ideas of personal physical dependency . . . rather, the various forms of children's contemporary dependency . . . are intimately connected with the form and functions of the modern state.
>
> (Lee 2001: 240)

The 'invention of childhood' was, then, closely linked to the invention of the state as an instrument of government, with 'childhood the most intensively governed sector of personal existence' (Rose 1989: 121). During the latter part of the twentieth century and into the twenty-first, however, further shifts in the power relations between adults and children, including new claims to children's rights and citizenship and the effective creation of children as a powerful consumer constituency, have increasingly destabilized the 'truth' of this particular regime. (The UN Convention on the Rights of the Child, adopted in 1989, is symptomatic of this process. On the one hand, it seeks to protect children from economic and other forms of exploitation; on the other, it asserts that children can claim rights as citizens, even though children's dependence is also assumed in the prior claim.) This has produced a new moment in which childhood is in the process of being reinvented or perhaps even uninvented – it is difficult to say which.

Such transformations are, of course, rarely complete or totalizing, and recent changes in discourses around children and childhood may be better understood in the terms of Williams' (1977) model of dominant, residual and emergent cultural formations than in those of a cultural revolution. The treatment of young children's sexuality as a symptom of a native immodesty that had to be disciplined by a particular educational apparatus, as described by Aries (1962: 106–16), is one example of the persistence of an earlier residual cultural formation well into modern twentieth-century educational structures, such as in schools run by the Catholic Church. The developmental discourse of childhood did not reach everywhere in the same way and at the same time, and it was always inflected with class, gender and culturally specific differentials. The emergence of the child as a consumer-citizen is similarly fraught with contradictions.

Indeed, Aries' book may itself be seen as part of a 'high moment' in the culture of childhood, appearing as it did in the period of the post-war years of the twentieth century. Its publication coincides with the hegemony of family values in popular culture, the ideology of maternal deprivation in medicine and psychology, and the growth of an extensive consumer market for child-focused products, but it pre-dates the hegemony of youth culture. In this context, then, Aries' work may be seen to be part of the *constructionist* project as well as prefiguring childhood's deconstruction.

The Enlightenment and the age of innocence

The idea that childhood is a distinctive category, predicated on innocence and a lack of adult (sexual) knowledge, has undoubtedly been a crucial strand in western culture, a strand whose primary philosophical cast can be traced back to the emergence of Romanticism as a feature of post-Enlightenment ideas during the eighteenth century. The Enlightenment rejection of orthodox religion in favour of a natural relationship to the world shaped the development of new attitudes to child-rearing and education and a new ideal, the 'romantic child'. In his philosophical novel, *Emile* (1762), Jean-Jacques Rousseau had argued that children had a 'natural goodness' that required only to be drawn out by a social education that was open to nature itself, in opposition to the Church's suspicion of the untutored self and tendency to impose Christian morality through a combination of physical and mental discipline – beatings and the catechism. The idea of childhood as an age of innocence, with the child innately connected to an idealized natural world, thus became increasingly central to modern thought and practice, as industrialization transformed earlier models of social relations and helped to produce a re-imagination of nature itself, and as the hegemonic power of organized religion began its long decline.

A structural opposition between the idea of the natural child and a precociously experienced and knowing (or cultural) child, who has been exposed to the corruption of urban life, can be most explicitly found in the work of Romantic poets such as William Blake (*Songs of Innocence*, 1789) and William Wordsworth (*Songs of Experience*, 1794), as well as influencing the early writing of Dickens, in novels such as *Oliver Twist* (1839), where the innocent, country-born Oliver is contrasted with the corrupted (but redeemable) city boy, the Artful Dodger. It even reappears in later cinematic representations of knowing and demonic children, as we will see. Childhood as a specific category of development, experience and consciousness was in some ways, then, an invention of Romantic thought. It also incorporated the assumption that children are, as David Buckingham argues, 'quintessentially "other"'(1997: 33). Such otherness is constructed in contrast to adult qualities which children are assumed to lack: knowledge, experience and the ability to exercise the intellectual abilities that would give them social power. Yet it also includes characteristics generally perceived to be positive, such as charm, the absence of guile and an energetic enthusiasm for life that adults are likely to cherish as evidence of children's delightful unknowingness about the world.

The very idea of a childhood that can be corrupted, as opposed to one that requires guidance towards adult moral clarity, is, then, a relatively modern construct and one directly linked to western economic and cultural conditions. Indeed, the differences between cultural models of the child and childhood are spatial as well as temporal. Western ideologies of childhood as a time of freedom from work or responsibility are as culturally specific as medieval ideologies of morality and education, and may also carry with them powerfully oppressive dimensions when they are imposed elsewhere, or are taken to be timeless and therefore natural.

Nostalgia and childhood

The contemporary (if increasingly fragile) insistence on childhood as a space of heightened and specific experience is often discursively linked to nostalgia for a 'safe' past in which the family was also more properly itself. This nostalgia is imbued with longing – not simply for one's own lost childhood, but for an impossible ideal: the notion of a separate space, of freedom from the rules of adulthood yet within the safe context of a stable family. The persistence of this idealization is often associated with an equally nostalgic politics of family values and the assertion that a pure version of childhood may be found in the security of earlier versions of the family. In the 1980s and 1990s, for example, conservative writers and politicians tended to represent the 1950s as a key moment, not only for the family but also for the ideal of childhood, despite plenty of evidence to suggest that during that earlier decade, social fears about children's loss of innocence, in the form of panics about juvenile delinquency and latchkey children, were equally prevalent (see Chapter 1).[1]

Nostalgia for a golden age of the family is perhaps most noticeably, and contradictorily, articulated via the emphasis on tradition in most Christmas celebrations in western societies. This is not just a matter of the claims to ancient provenance of yule logs, carols and snow; it is also about the way in which the various rituals, from the decorating of the tree to the exchange of gifts and the over-indulgence of appetites, are stitched into a narrative that links childhood, family and tradition. As Davidoff et al. observe, the increased privatization of such rituals in the twentieth century also intensified their symbolic importance to the family and to children's roles within it (1999: 220). Indeed, the commodification of Christmas in many western countries – and perhaps especially in the UK – is also naturalized, explained away as the indulgence of children. This charged mix of family nostalgia and consumerism appears in an aestheticized form in lifestyle and home decorating magazines, such as *House and Garden* or *America's Most Beautiful Homes*. While tending to emphasize consumer individualism throughout most of the year, such magazines almost invariably foreground a (romantically inflected) family ideal in their Christmas editions, with the country house or cottage dining room dressed with a gift-laden Christmas tree, a full-sized table set for dinner and a row of stockings hanging on the chimney breast as the necessary signifier of childhood.

Indeed, the invention of a culture of childhood has been especially noticeable in the UK, where the idealization of childhood was historically tied to the physical and emotional separation of children from their families in middle- and upper-class life, and in the USA, where individualized notions of human development were closely linked to political ideals of 'change and renewal' (Cogan Thacker and Webb 2002: 15). Children's status as other in these cultures led to the creation of a distinctive set of practices and meanings from which adults (in particular, adult men) were contingently excluded. In both societies, children's literature became an important cultural space for these ideas and developed rapidly into a relatively sophisticated form by the end of the nineteenth century. One way of tracing the development of the discursive framework of childhood, then, is by looking at the growth of a rich literature *for* children, as well as a range of novels about them, from the mid-nineteenth century onwards.

However, there are some odd and obvious contradictions here. First, the formal, published and canonical versions of this children's literature are almost exclusively conceived and executed by adults, and are therefore subject to adult approval, even if individual texts have been struggled over or contested. Second, the otherness of childhood and of children themselves informs both the ways in which being a child has been cast and literature's address to children as audiences, although frequently the two have been conflated, as I noted above. Moreover, the *specific* otherness of childhood has often worked to disguise the extent to which different kinds of otherness have been eclipsed by a relatively monolithic – and therefore masculine and white – humanistic conception of what 'the child' is. Representations of black children or of girls are rarely taken to stand for a general model of childhood – they are, instead, marked by their difference. Any consideration of the ways in which children have been represented, constructed, or hailed must, therefore, also take into account a simple problem: children themselves have had little control over such processes – and may refuse to recognize the subject positions they offer.

Secret gardens, private realms: children's literature and the idealization of childhood

Christian soldiers?

Folk and fairy tales are generally represented – and *re-presented* in modern illustrated or animated versions – as having been written especially for children, yet most emerged out of a cultural context in which childhood had not yet been invented and were only latterly recast as children's literature. Charles Perrault's fairy tales (1697) began as post-chivalric fantasies for adults in which the social entanglements of the French court, aristocracy and nobility were mythologized, while Grimm's stories (1812–22) were a collection of traditional folk narratives whose original audience would have been cross-generational. It is therefore only with the elaboration of childhood's difference and the relegation of fantasy to its realm that such material could, in effect, be reinvented as the preserve of those without a full adult subjectivity.

Unsurprisingly, much western writing expressly for children had its origins in the Christian tracts and improving didactic literature of the pre-childhood culture of the seventeenth and eighteenth centuries (such as Hannah More's *Cheap Repository Tracts*, 1795–98), aimed at children, but not particularly concerned to entertain or engage them as a distinctive cultural group. Even during the early and high Victorian periods – with the important exception of *Alice in Wonderland* (1865), which looked back to the fairy-tale tradition in its use of fantasy – realist novels written for children, such as Dean Farrar's *Eric, or Little by Little* (1858), were informed by a powerfully indoctrinatory approach to the child reader, and can seem intensely alien to contemporary eyes because of their high moral seriousness – about everything. Such books were popular with parents if not children.[2] Indeed, throughout the mid-Victorian period, Christian literature, or literature with a strongly moral theme, remained a dominant mode, with books such as Captain Marryat's *Children of the New Forest* (1847) and Thomas Hughes' *Tom Brown's School Days* (1857) becoming best-sellers. Well into the 1870s, books for children retained some elements of religiosity and didacticism (Louisa Alcott's *Little Women* even loosely follows the structure of John Bunyan's *Pilgrim's Progress*), while conceptualizing the inner self of the child, largely in terms of a receptacle awaiting moral guidance. At the same time, many of these novels helped to articulate emergent tensions around the contradictory relationship between nineteenth-century Christian virtues and the child's apprenticeship into bourgeois individualism, especially in their manifestations as manliness or womanliness, so that struggles over the adoption of an appropriately gendered adult identity becomes a central concern in such texts.

One complex example of this can be found in the tradition of North American novels written specifically for girls, by authors working within a liberal feminist strand of cultural politics, which emphasized the power of domestic virtues. Works such as Alcott's *Little Women*

(1869) and Susan Coolidge's *What Katy Did* (1872), as well as the later L. M. Montgomery's *Anne of Green Gables* (1908), Katė Douglas Wiggin's *Rebecca of Sunnybrook Farm* (1903) and Eleonor H. Porter's *Pollyanna* (1913), are all narratively structured by a range of tensions around the difficult move from child to woman. Each of these stories emphasizes female physical activity, practicality and the extension of domestic skills into the public world, as Lynne Vallone observes (1995: 114). They are also important for the way in which they attempt to make space for girls within the discourse of childhood. However, the main device available to resolve the contradictions this produces in the context of Victorian patriarchy is an uneasy compromise between individualism and self-abnegation, in which the main girl character must ultimately and willingly take on a properly compliant femininity. Jo in *Little Women* learns to abandon her writing career for marriage, eventually discovering a deeper happiness in caring for orphaned boys, while Coolidge's Katy is physically crippled because she disobeys an adult by playing on a damaged swing. The carefree attitude that is central to such female characters' initial appeal to readers is thus tamed into a domesticated adult sensibility by the end of the narrative, in a move that is clearly a form of ideological closure.

Furthermore, in every one of these stories, female independence is in part explained – or explained away – by paternal absence, parental death or the lack of patriarchal control. Family relations and networks are represented as a structuring absence as well as a presence, and it becomes clear that a return to the family and to domesticity, together with the reassertion of conventional familial power structures, is necessary for female social acceptance. The classic status of these novels and their continuing popularity suggests, moreover, that such themes retain the power to speak to contemporary readers, even if they do so in modified ways (*Little Women* has been adapted for film a number of times, most recently by Gillian Armstrong in 1994).

Magic and enchantment

By the 1880s, children's fiction was becoming a distinctive and popular genre with its own literary conventions, a readily identified market and the aim of entertaining as well as educating its readers. Formally, it frequently drew on and effectively reworked already existing adult genres (which were also explicitly gendered), including the domestic novel, as in the girls' stories discussed above, and the adventure story, such as Robert Louis Stevenson's yarn, *Treasure Island* (1881), which was told from the point of view of its boy hero, Jim. The Tractarian emphasis on the child's necessary acceptance of a particular set of adult (and religious) values began to disappear, replaced by a more complex exploration of 'the child's world' in which mystery and excitement were substituted for pious homilies. Many of E. Nesbit's novels, such as *The Story of the Treasure-Seekers* (1899) and *Five Children and It* (1902), not only reincorporated elements of magic and fantasy into otherwise realist narratives as if they were natural and intrinsic aspects of the childhood experience, but the former is also told in the voice of the main child character, Oswald Bastable, a boy whose attitude to religious self-improvement is, at best, one of amused suspicion. Childhood, in such novels, was thus increasingly constructed as a space of imagination, self-reliance and adventure, well away from adult surveillance and interference.

Peter Keating (1991: 222) claims that the establishment of this idea of childhood, as both distinct from the adult world and potentially carrying its own moral perspective, is most effectively staged and explored in F. Anstey's comic novel of father-son reversal, *Vice-Versa* (1882), which was pointedly subtitled 'a lesson to fathers'. Arguably, the idea that childhood has a set of rules, codes and morality that may be in some ways superior to (and certainly more fun than) those of the adult world continues to inform contemporary discourse: *Vice-Versa* was successfully turned into a Hollywood comedy in 1988. Yet Anstey's light-hearted romp also prefigured a range of darker, more serious explorations of children's lives in a way that refused the simple resolution of the restoration of conventional power relations. Frances Hodgson Burnett's *A Little Princess* (1905) and *The Secret Garden* (1911), for example, offer a fairly complex exploration of childhood loneliness and of children's rivalries and enmities in a world in which adults have abdicated their responsibilities. In both novels, a private children's space (a garden and a bedroom) stands for the psychological distance between children and adulthood, and in these stories the secret garden of childhood is both unavailable to adults and created by them.

Interestingly, the critical exploration of the interiority of childhood was also a powerful feature of the new 'serious' literature produced for an adult readership during the late nineteenth century. Henry James's *The Portrait of a Lady* (1881) and *What Maisie Knew* (1897) both contain disturbing dissections of a child's psychological state that link them to the cultural move also represented by psychoanalysis. By the 1920s and 1930s, children's literature had further developed this strongly interiorized and psychological focus, as well as a

Figure 4.1 In their different ways, the books of Louisa Alcott, E. Nesbit and C.S. Lewis offered a particular 'take' on the idea of childhood's separate realm. They combined fantasy, adventure and, in the case of Alcott and Lewis, an attempt to inculcate Christian beliefs in their young readers.

complex linguistic register that acutely articulated the idea of children's cultural distinctiveness and of childhood itself as a 'lost domain' (Alain-Fournier's *Le Grand Meulnes* – The Lost Domain, 1913 – expresses this beautifully, although it is by no means a 'children's book').

For Peter Hunt, this involved the 'filtering out' of threat and deprivation and the transposition of fear into fantasy (2001: 16). Often, too, it took the form of whimsy or a 'double voice' to both adults and children, as in the work of A. A. Milne. In its more sophisticated form, it also influenced the development of the sub-genre of children's fantasy, with books such as C. S. Lewis's *Narnia* chronicles and time-travel stories and ghost stories, which became an important cultural articulation of the special space of childhood during the post-war period. Lewis even insisted (misogynistically) on the necessity of his female child characters retaining a pre-pubescent purity if they were to remain in the magic kingdom of Narnia. In all of this, the romantic ideal of childhood was crucial.

The effective institutionalization of children's literature was cemented during the post-war period, with the growth of public library services, the establishment of literary prizes for children's authors, such as the Newbery and Carnegie medals (actually set up in 1922 and 1936, but only really acquiring cultural prestige in the post-war period), and the development of education towards a child-centred model; all of which helped to consolidate the idea of childhood as a distinctive cultural sphere with its own set of meanings. The writing for children that appeared during the 'golden age' between the 1950s and 1970s was, then, important not only as distinctive cultural practice in its own right, but also as part of the construction of childhood as a social identity. It was, however, often distinguished by its removal of children from a family context as a way of testing out and developing this emergent subjectivity. Indeed, it was only in nostalgic American children's fiction of the 1940s and 1950s, set 30 or 50 years earlier that the 'family story' predominated.

While writers such as Roald Dahl continued the tradition of fantasy throughout the 1960s and 1970s, children's stories began to be dominated by a new social realism in the 1970s, in a move which partially paralleled similar changes in film culture and which, oddly, returned to the family – albeit in a new way. The emergence of teen fiction exploring emergent youth cultures, sexual relationships and emotional conflicts by writers such as Anne Fine, Judy Blume and Robert Cormier, marked not only an important shift in the genre, but also a significant cultural move and a series of complications around the relationship between the way in which the child was imagined and family structures and emotions.

The global success of J. K. Rowling's *Harry Potter* series during the 1990s and 2000s seems to mark a number of further cultural shifts. One is a retreat from the social realism and family-centredness of much of the children's and teenage fiction of the 1960s through to the 1980s. The other is that Rowling's stories are saturated with a cultural nostalgia for old-fashioned yarns and even for an old-fashioned (and thoroughly middle-class) England of boarding schools and strict discipline, yet they are also absolutely contemporary in their use of grotesque elements drawn from the sub-Tolkienesque genre of fantasy. In this respect, the books may be part of a postmodern pleasure in a retro culture that manages to occupy both the past and the present simultaneously. They have also been central to the contemporary phenomenon of crossover reading in which children's books have been taken up by – and later deliberately marketed to – adults. While not completely unprecedented, the popularity of Harry Potter with adult readers seems to mark a new moment in which the cultural space of fantasy and playfulness that had, until recently, been ascribed almost exclusively to childhood has been reclaimed by grown-ups.

Childhood on screen: Hollywood and post-war cinema

Until the late 1930s, children in Hollywood films had tended to appear either in star vehicles, such as those made for Shirley Temple, where she played winsome 'little Miss Fix-It' characters, whose main function was to restore social order, or as loveable rogues with freckles and dirty knees. The idea of childhood as a lost domain or space of impossible freedom worthy of exploration only began to appear in cinema during the post-war years. One of the few canonical Hollywood films to make childhood central to its narrative thesis is *Citizen Kane* (1944), which represents childhood in terms that are both nostalgic and enigmatic, violently dramatizing the loss of family as an emotional trauma. Early on in the film, not only do we see the young Charles Foster Kane taken from his childhood home by Walter Thacker, in a poignant scene in which the child's freedom to play and exhilarated pleasure in an outdoors snowy landscape is deliberately framed by a dry contractual exchange between Thacker and Kane's mother taking place indoors (superbly realized by Welles' use of deep focus, which allows both indoors and outdoors to be clearly visible), but the sledge with which the boy is playing will also come to have a deeper resonance. 'Rosebud' is the last word uttered by the lonely and dying Kane and, as the final frame of the film reveals, it is the name of the sledge. Kane's loss of Rosebud is also the loss of his childhood and anything resembling a family, along with the possibilities it might have offered him.

This engagement with the threat/fear of loss of innocence also underpins one of the most celebrated 'children's films' to be made under the classical system, *The Wizard of Oz* (1939). Orphan Dorothy's (Judy Garland) search for happiness in the land of Oz is threatened by witches and by her own subliminal fears and anxieties, which the film, drawing on expressionist techniques as well as the tradition of fairy tale and fantasy, transforms into a spectacular evocation of a dreamworld in which an imagined family is reassembled out of the characters Dorothy meets.

Indeed, while it is tempting to dismiss much of Hollywood's output involving children as sentimental, there are many examples of films that genuinely offer an unexpectedly wry or edgy representation of a child. One such is Vincente Minelli's *Meet Me in St. Louis* (1944), which includes a remarkably complex portrait of the youngest Smith daughter, Tootie (Margaret O' Brien), who uses the backyard as a 'cemetery' for her dolls, and destroys the snow figures she has made at Christmas when she thinks the family must leave St Louis for good. *Meet Me in St Louis* undoubtedly affirms family values and represents patriarchal power in decidedly benign terms – father is eventually outvoted by his family, who refuse to be moved to New York – but it does not do this uncritically, and the space it clears for the exploration of children's emotions and perspectives is genuine.

During the early post-war period a relatively large number of films were made that featured children as major characters or were about childhood itself, such as *The Yearling* (1946), *Mandy* (1952) and *The Yellow Balloon* (1956) in the UK, and *The Window* (1949) in the USA, which offers a remarkably convincing account of a child's point of view of a murder. This was clearly related to the assertion of children's place within the family as central to post-war recovery, not in an economic sense, but at the level of emotional equanimity. Fantasy remained important to some cinematic representations of childhood, which figured it in spatial as well as cultural terms. One example of this is Carol Reed's *A Kid for Two Farthings* (1955), a film set in and around a romantically evoked East End of London, in which the relationship between desire and reality is focused on a goat that a boy believes to be a magic unicorn that will grant wishes. Often, however, such films figured the child or childhood itself as a problem or an enigma to be resolved by the adult characters. One exception to this is Vittorio de Sica's neo-realist *Bicycle Thieves* (1948), in which a man searching for the stolen bicycle on which his precarious job as a poster hanger depends is accompanied by his son. In some respects, it may be argued that it is the humanist impulse of de Sica's form of realism that compels the inclusion of the child as part of the narrative. More than this, however, it seems to articulate one of the central concerns of the post-war moment in powerfully convincing terms: that the future of post-war society depended on the inclusion of children within its conception of the social.

Childhood on screen: Reithianism, class and politics in the UK

The radio hearth

This desire to incorporate children into the social, while also retaining the ideal of childhood as a separate sphere, is especially noticeable if we consider the recent history of broadcasting for children and its curious status and functions. In the UK, the BBC has had a long history of producing radio and television programmes especially for a juvenile audience. It also has an equally long history of cultural paternalism and the attempted inculcation of (roughly) bourgeois values in which the importance of active social engagement has been part of the ideal of public service. The guiding principles of the organization, originally developed and institutionalized by the deeply puritanical first director-general, John Reith, were founded on the proposition that public service broadcasting had to educate and inform as well as entertain its listeners and viewers. This precept was applied as rigorously – perhaps more rigorously – to children's programming as it was to adult, precisely because of the underlying developmental discourse and the assumption that children were particularly open to the influence of the media. It was also articulated in conscious and deliberate contrast to the emergent American commercial model, which, for Reith, represented a distasteful, culturally impoverished approach to broadcasting. Under Reith, the BBC strove to produce what Wagg calls 'the ambience of the middle-class home' (1992: 153), wherein children were accorded a particular – if subordinate – place of their own. *Children's Hour*, the programme devised for this purpose in the 1920s, was presented by a thoroughly middle-class cast of 'aunties' and 'uncles', whose role was to inculcate this ambience. The particular kind of cultural capital available to the child listener was therefore wholly tied to the dominant values not only of the BBC, but also of the British establishment more generally.

While the 'radio hearth' tradition also encompassed fun, it came in the form of a record request programme, *Children's Favourites*, which helped to construct the idea of childhood as a separate sphere of innocent pleasure through novelty discs featuring anthropomorphic animals and machines, such as 'The Runaway Train', 'Nellie the Elephant', 'The Laughing Policeman' and (my own childhood favourite in the 1960s) 'Windmill in Old Amsterdam', on which clog-wearing mice sang the chorus. Children's broadcasting between the 1920s and 1970s was, then, very clearly part of the process of the invention of childhood rather than a transparent response to a prior need, and was dominated by the same very middle-class English desire to ascribe a special magic to the culture of the child that informed many of the books of the same period.

Despite the condescension that seems apparent to Wagg, however, the BBC was concerned *not* to patronize or talk down to its youthful audience in its output. Children were to be accorded a degree of respect as a way of apprenticing them into the BBC's own cultural values. Children's broadcasting thus became the site of a complex series of tensions around the innocence/knowledge dyad. On the one hand, (middle-class) children were entitled to access to knowledge about the world if they were to take up an active role within society; on the other, that knowledge was carefully presented as though it were value-free or politically neutral.

Resisting consumer culture

By the mid-1950s the radio hearth had been transferred to television, with the development of a new strand of children's programmes encompassing popular drama, variety shows and, most iconically, the magazine show in the form of the still-running *Blue Peter*. First broadcast in 1958, the latter was partly conceived as a bulwark against an emergent consumerism that, in the 1950s and 1960s, was perceived to be a socially damaging component of creeping Americanization. *Blue Peter* powerfully articulated a transitional ideology of childhood as a sphere that required protection from excessive consumerism, but also carefully exposed children to the idea of social engagement. Two elements expressed these twin values most clearly. The first was the show's tradition of make-do-and-mend, in which home-made versions of popular toys were demonstrated using little more than washing-up bottles, sticky tape and cardboard. The second was the annual Blue Peter Christmas Appeal, which collected not money but discarded yet recyclable commodities such as silver foil for a different 'good cause' each year. In both cases, a strong anti-consumerism was emphasized, with childhood itself allied not to consumption but to creativity and social awareness, as Wagg points out (1992: 164). Of course, *Blue Peter* was also imbued with an equally insistent emphasis on its own ideologically neutral status, so that the bourgeois values it espoused could be represented as a cultural norm, and any social issues it raised were consistently represented as somehow non-political – or as resolvable through individualized social engagement.

However, the desire to educate children and to encourage active engagement rather than passive listening was also complexly related to the rapid development of new cultural practices. By the early 1960s, for example, the 'pure' model of a children's world that had been constructed through *Children's Hour* on the radio and through children's shows on television, was already troubled by the presence and popularity of pop music and its stars. By the 1980s and 1990s, the *Blue Peter* model of childhood had become increasingly residualized in media representations, despite the programme's own survival. British television, in particular, struggled to sustain Reithian values in the face of Thatcherism and the expansion of consumer culture to embrace the discerning child buyer.

Aspiring to adulthood?

Recent shifts in the relationship between adulthood, social agency and identificatory processes have also changed the representation of childhood on television. Greater flexibility and uncertainty about gender roles and the emergence of postmodern 'confluent relationships' (Giddens 1992), together with the cultural extension of adolescence have not only worked to inform adult masculinity (as was explored in Chapter 2), but they have also shaped our expectations of childhood. To begin with, as Davies et al. put it in an analysis of children's television tastes, '[c]hildhood, it would seem, isn't just for children anymore' (2000: 22). Pleasure in childishness, in a refusal of adult responsibilities and nostalgia for a moment when sexual desire was rarely accompanied by disappointment (perhaps because it remained unconsummated), is both a feature of the laddism that developed during the 1990s and a curious feature of contemporary media culture *for* and about children. *The Wonder Years* (1988–92), for example, is one example of a situation comedy, focused on a child's incipient adolescence, whose retro-nostalgia for the late 1960s also expresses a resistance to growing up and having to deal with the adult disappointments represented by the 1970s.

Self-reflexivity about childhood and childishness informs both representations of childhood in the media and the ways in which children themselves make sense of their identities. Contemporary children's television presenters, for example – in contrast to the 'grown-ups' of the 1960s and 1970s who claimed the natural authority of maturity (even if it was spurious) – 'perform' youth by dressing, speaking and behaving in ways which mimic children, and thus destabilize their adult status. This practice is part of the larger cultural tendency to dissolve the traditional boundaries between childhood and maturity through the privileging of teenage cultural forms and styles, as well as being linked to the discursive elaboration of childhood itself as an increasingly privileged space beyond the comprehension of adults. Such moves are, however, very different from earlier forms of childhood romanticization.

The BBC drama, *The Story of Tracy Beaker*, for instance, both privileges the point of view of its eponymous heroine by showing us events from her perspective and represents the adults who surround her as well-meaning but poor in judgement. Such an account, far from representing childhood as a period of innocence, suggests instead that the child invariably knows more about the world than the adults who control it, and this knowledge is not simply a symptom of corruption; it is, rather, evidence of the child's identity as a more

Figure 4.2 Contemporary children's television presenters 'perform' youth in their dress and physical presentation.

complex subject in discourse. In these texts, the child protagonists are rarely represented as aspiring to be like the adults they are surrounded by ('loser' social workers and teachers); instead, they want to be cool, without being fully grown-up. Indeed, such motivations seem to articulate some of the desires of the audience. As Davies et al. go on to say, rather than aspiring to become adults, the children they interviewed about their television preferences simply wanted to be teenagers (2000: 15).

The development of children's television towards an emphasis on childhood as a fragmented psychological state, or as part of a new fluidity around the relationship between cultural identity, age and power, thus has important implications for the way in which the self, whether of child or adult, is culturally produced and developed, and for the child as citizen-consumer within postmodernity.

The vulnerable child: 'effects' debates and anxieties
Childhood, class and television

One of the most problematic and powerful ways in which the relationship between family structures, childhood and media forms has been explored is in the debates that have taken place around the supposed effects of films and television on viewers, as was suggested earlier in this chapter. Television, in particular, has been the locus of particularly conflicted and intensified concerns, precisely because of its domestic status – its position within the private space of the home. There can be little doubt that watching a television programme or an advertisement will affect us in some way or another, of course, and what we see may even profoundly move us or makes us angry or repelled. This is not the same thing as taking on the messages media texts are assumed to direct at us, however; nor is it the same thing as being influenced to copy the actions of fictional characters. Such an emphasis on a mimetic relationship between various texts and their audiences is grounded in a very simple model of the psyche and, indeed, of the production of meaning. Yet this is precisely what some commentators and child psychologists have argued to be the cultural consequences of television and cinema's power (see, for example, the Newson Report 1994).

Furthermore, despite its apparent contemporaneity, what has come to be called the Effects Debate has a long history that can be traced back well beyond the development of television to earlier panics about the imagined social consequences of popular culture. From the 1860s through to the 1960s, a series of remarkably similar moral panics continued to erupt around the supposed effects various kinds of popular texts and forms – from the 'penny dreadfuls' to the music hall, and from rock and roll to sci-fi comics – were supposed to have (Pearson 1983). In much of this, the special nature of childhood and children's culture was invoked and agonized over. Such panics nearly always focus on new or emergent cultural forms as the site of equally new and vicious kinds of images, which, it is argued, might deprave and corrupt readers or viewers by leading to copycat crimes or antisocial behaviour. They also tend to focus on the family as the site of such potential corruption and on its role as the guardian of childhood innocence. The work of sociologists such as Marie Winn (1984) and Neil Postman (1985), for instance, identifies television as the culprit, but draws on the same nostalgic discourse of childhood as an idealized yet lost state (presumably mislaid at some point in the 1950s) that informed earlier social commentary.

In the USA in particular, the discourse of media effects has been legitimated with a whole battery of psychological and behavioural experiments designed to test – and prove – a causal relationship between films containing violent imagery and violent behaviour. The assumption that there *is* a causal relationship between the two has also been central to critical perceptions of recent shifts in familial relations and power structures. Such 'evidence' has frequently been used within the media itself to support claims that television or films are responsible for an increase in crime, sexual promiscuity or simply behaviour that goes against the grain of bourgeois conventions. As Graham Murdock points out, the claim that violent films or video nasties can have measurable effects at all is linked to the ways in which empiricist science may be profoundly connected to the production of common sense as regards social interaction. 'The dominant research tradition adopted the definition of "the problem" already established in popular and political commentary. The result was banal science, which failed to ask awkward questions . . . or to place "effects" in their social context' (1997: 69). In other words, such experiments frequently 'found' what they were looking for by deploying scientific approaches and methods so narrowly or specifically formulated that they would always deliver the expected answer.

These approaches also tended explicitly to avoid research which situated the viewing of television or films within a cultural context, such as the fragmented domestic viewing experience observed by cultural studies researchers (Walkerdine 1997; Gray 1992). Indeed, this reductively 'scientific' insistence on the irrelevance of the social and cultural relations involved has been a central component of the way in which effects research has been taken up by the media itself as part of a process in which the solution to a moral crisis – whether it is over videos, rap music or obesity – must lie in apparently simple remedies. In particular, the media's circulation of moral panics around supposed effects has helped to reify its own power. As Ellen Seiter observes, 'When television is represented as all-powerful, all-determining, it directs attention away from more important factors such as schools, housing, transportation, money, and health care' (1996: 141).

Crucially, the idea that popular media has such effects at all is also linked to a very specific conceptualization of the family and family relationships. It is not, however, marked by a consistency in the conceptualization of the effects themselves, since these are held to occupy a remarkably wide-ranging spectrum; from producing the moribundly passive couch potato to shaping the proto-criminal child hooligan. Furthermore, social anxieties about class and class power have tended to powerfully inform the discourse of effects, albeit in sometimes unacknowledged ways. Working-class families – and more recently, an underclass of the feckless or criminal – have been represented as insufficiently grounded in the appropriate moral and social codes to police their children's television viewing, while working-class children are presumed to be particularly vulnerable to imitating what they see on television because of this lack of social capital. In contrast, the fears surrounding middle-class children focus on the media's power to persuade them to reject the bourgeois values of their parents in favour of the culturally impoverished (or depraved) meanings and practices supposedly saturating popular youth culture. In the aftermath of the tragic murders at Columbine High School, Littleton, Colorado, in 1999, for example, the music of the 'Goth rocker' Marilyn Manson was entirely spuriously identified as the catalyst for the behaviour of the two middle-class white teenage boys responsible, rather than their inhabitation of a culture in which gun ownership was presented as an essential human right, or their barely articulated sense of a masculine, white entitlement that wasn't being properly recognized (Consalvo 2003; see also Chapter 3).

The case of *Child's Play III*

Perhaps the best-known example of a moral panic about the supposed effects of media representations of violence upon working-class children's behaviour is the British case of the murder of James Bulger, a Liverpool toddler, who in 1993 was enticed away from his mother and later killed by two older boys, Jon Thompson and Robert Venables. Most media reports of the case suggested a direct link between the older boys' behaviour and scenes in a horror-comedy video, *Child's Play III*, which, it was claimed, had been viewed by the children before the murder took place. Martin Barker (1997: 13) points out that the *Child's Play* link actually began as a vague and (probably) inappropriate speculation by the judge at Thompson and Venables' trial, yet it was rapidly turned into certainty that the film had indirectly caused the death of James Bulger through widespread repetition in the British media. This then became the 'truth' about the case, despite a complete lack of evidence. The claim was sustainable partly because the effects argument had already become part of the media's common sense, and partly because a discursive apparatus to demonize working-class children as feral, uncontrollable and threatening was also becoming hegemonic, fuelled by class anxieties and by the shifts in adult–child relations already noted. The proposition that children might be in some ways instrumental in their own or others' abuse was thus intensified by the media sensationalization of the Bulger case.

As Sarah Harwood argues (1997: 179), the case also prompted a range of material and legislative responses in the UK that were remarkably punitive and misogynist, including even tighter restrictions on video distribution and a new series of media panics about 'bad' mothers who allowed their children to wander. Together, these responses seemed to articulate a condensed version of fears circulating about the family, gendered and generational relations and nostalgia for the loss of innocence. Interestingly, however, in his magisterial work, *The Victorians* (2002), A. N. Wilson draws attention to an extraordinarily and tragically similar case of murder that took place in Stockport in 1860, but points out that the media or its equivalent was not blamed for the events.

The idea that children constitute a particularly vulnerable audience for the media continues to resonate, despite the considerable work done by researchers in media and cultural studies to demonstrate its lack of a solid basis, such as David Buckingham's (1987) analysis of the relationship between the British soap opera, *EastEnders*, and its audience, which demonstrated children's acute critical engagement with television's conventions and a clear sense of the boundaries between fiction and reality.

Indeed, while researching this chapter I came across a characteristic example of the media's own recirculation of such fears in the form of an article by the British media psychologist, Dr Raj Persaud, 'Shhh! I'm watching . . . can toddlers be TV addicts?' in (paradoxically) the April 2004 edition of the *BBC Parenting magazine*. The piece made several unreferenced allusions to research that 'proved' television had a detrimental effect on children's acquisition of basic skills, claiming that 'psychologists find that TV has a surprisingly sinister effect on our minds' – without offering a single source for this assertion. In effect, the piece was little more than a reworking of the common sense about effects, yet it was lent authority by Persaud's medical qualifications.

Since the late 1990s, however, fears about media violence and its influence upon children have been displaced by a new bogeyman, the internet. Unlike television or video, it is argued, computer networks enable anyone to access anything at any time, and this includes children, who may either deliberately or accidentally find websites devoted to graphic images of sex and violence, as well as adults in search of the same thing. Such anxieties would, of course, be impossible without the effective democratization of the market for computer technologies and systems during the 1980s and 1990s, so that large numbers of children, in the west and throughout Asia have ready access to personal computers. The response, however, has been a new call for adult surveillance and supervision of children's access to and use of the media and of play itself as a leisure activity (it is possible to buy a device, advertised directly to parents, that restricts internet access).

Pleasure and play
Organized play: gender and consumption

The relationship between play, fantasy and children has, then, been a problematic and slippery dimension to the way in which the category of childhood has developed and been mediated, especially in the context of children's increased access to consumer culture. On the one hand, play is seen as an intrinsic and wholly natural part of children's experience; on the other, there is a long and complex history of adult intervention in play, either at the level of instrumental decision-making around what is appropriate for girls or boys, or in the form of products which are invented, patented and manufactured by adults but sold to children. Each of these relations also involves a series of discursive moves around gender expectations, issues of taste and questions of agency. Indeed, the contradictions around the dynamic between producing children as desiring consumers and adult anxieties about what children's desires might entail is explored by Heather Hendershot in an analysis of the development, marketing and consumption of the Strawberry Shortcake doll.

Explicitly developed as a toy for little girls, Strawberry Shortcake's unique selling point was her sickly sweet smell, which, as Hendershot notes, coded her as a girl's toy by embodying an 'ideal of "sweet femininity"' that was itself 'part of a gender discourse in which the production of a proper femininity depended on the cultivation of particular kinds of smell' (1996: 98). For Hendershot, the problem was not that little girls liked the decidedly artificial 'strawberry' odour attached to the doll, but rather that such pleasures were rigorously policed in highly gendered terms by the doll's manufacturers, who insisted that a preference for sweet smells was essentially and biologically determined; girls were only permitted pleasure in fruit and flower smells, in contrast to a masculine delight in 'nasty' odours.

Such assertions constitute a part of the larger cultural production and management of children's behaviour, pleasures and emergent subjectivities in very specifically gendered terms. Not only are little girls required to like the smell of 'sugar and spice and all things nice', they are also expected to be compliant and obedient, while also cultivating an incipient desire to be desired through regulation of the body. As Hendershot points out (1996: 99), this means managing their own body odours and ensuring that they are as sweet as Strawberry Shortcake. The doll's 'sweetness' was therefore intended to inform their own developing gendered identity, by preparing them for adult femininity and for motherhood.

For boys, however, acquiring a proper masculinity means learning to produce themselves as autonomous subjects able to master and manipulate the world. Gillian Skirrow (1990: 336) argues that computer games offer a way of moving between storytelling and participatory sport in which mastering unconscious anxieties about one's relationship to power may be played out and resolved. This is both a psychic process and a social one. Performing domination and destruction through games that simulate battles with aliens or fantasy creatures becomes a way of claiming one's place in the social relations of patriarchy. Indeed, the widespread availability of boys' games which depend on exercising technical and combative skills helps to reify these, not only as specifically masculine, but also as part of a natural dominance of the public sphere to which they refer.

Organized play: paramilitarism

Managing children's entry into adulthood has, then, been a continuing problem in the way in which adult social fears are articulated. The imperative to direct children towards 'healthy' – as opposed to 'unhealthy' or inappropriately sexual – interests and pastimes was a crucial feature of many of the movements and organizations for children that developed during the late nineteenth and early twentieth centuries. Such groups as the Boy Scouts, founded in 1908 (and later the Girl Guides), the Church Lads' Brigade and even the left-based Woodcraft Folk tended to equate good health with outdoor activity and with the acquisition of practical skills that would direct the (male) child's interest away from antisocial behaviour or a 'morbid' interest in masturbation.

This concern, together with the imperialist and militarist values embedded in their structures and hierarchies, meant that scouting and its kin groups were explicitly engaged in a form of social engineering, largely focused on urban and working-class boys who might otherwise be drawn to hooliganism. For Bill Schwarz, the panic over hooliganism that erupted in the 1890s, and which was very effectively amplified and intensified by the new popular press of the time, such as the *Daily Mail* (first published in 1896), was structured around the relationship between masculine citizenship, particularly in the context of modernity, and 'a carnivalesque refusal of external authority' (1996: 116). As Schwarz goes on to argue, 'the discursive connection to citizenship and constitutionalism . . . gives the idea of hooliganism its longevity . . . and fixes it so effectively in the popular imagination' (1996: 119). The fear that working-class boys were effectively determining their *own* conditions of entry as citizens to the modern 'public sphere' of city streets, shops and meeting places was what drove the desire to shape their behaviour (and, indeed, recast their production of a self – although it wasn't expressed in these terms) towards 'respectable' values. Middle-class boys could, it seems, be safely left to the strictures of the boarding school.

As Stephen Wagg points out, the idea that children might be directed towards appropriately improving activity was predicated on very similar assumptions to those underpinning the effects debate discussed above: 'passive and vulnerable creatures should be exhorted to activity, because the devil made work for idle hands' (1992: 152). The Boy Scout movement's desire to cultivate deference to class hierarchies was complemented by its emphasis on bodily discipline, in which a regulated, managed and regimented body was equated with health and happiness and linked to the acquisition of (a certain amount of) social capital.[3]

Childhood sexuality: panics and pathologies

Images of children: desire and deviation

The management of children's sexuality is one of the most controversial, morally conflicted and troubling arenas of popular culture. Although the recent moral panics over paedophilia have tended to represent the issue as symptomatic of a new social degeneracy, fears about the relationship between desire, innocence and childhood are not wholly contemporary – they have simply re-emerged in a new form. Foucault (1981) points to the ways in which children's sexuality was increasingly subjected to regulation and control through the development of medical discourse in the nineteenth century, and one material manifestation of this was Baden Powell's concern to ensure that the Boy Scout movement would deter masturbation through healthy outdoor pursuits. It is important to see, too, that contemporary social fears about child sexual abuse are part of an ongoing struggle around the status of children, either as citizens with claims to rights or as the dependants of their parents.

Tensions between these discourses of childhood have circulated and been represented in the contemporary media in a range of sites and locations. It is not simply a matter of tabloid newspaper reports and sensational journalism, although these have played a role in the intensification of the issues. There is a sense in which sexual relations, within the family especially, have become one of the defining issues of the new millennium. Examples of this are explored below.

In the weeks in which I write (May 2004), three significant cultural events have taken place, all of which feature child sexual abuse within the family. The first, *Festen*, is a London stage production of the 1998 Dogme film by Thomas Vinterberg, in which a family gathering to celebrate the 60th birthday of the clan patriarch, Helge, is disrupted when one of his children accuses him of rape and of effectively causing his daughter's eventual suicide. The second, an American film documentary, *Capturing the Friedmans* (2004), is an account of child abuse both within and outside an apparently ordinary middle-class American family that led to arrest and imprisonment. The third, the broadcast of an episode of the BBC television series, *Police Protecting Children*, featured, controversially, the arrest of the rock star Pete Townsend on charges of accessing child pornography via the internet which, he claimed, was linked to research he was undertaking around his own past experiences of abuse (Townsend was later given a conditional discharge).

In each case, the impact of the stories depended in part on the apparently impeccable bourgeois credentials of the protagonists, and on pre-existing anxieties about the dissolution of the family that gave the accounts their credibility. Each case might, on its own terms, represent a single instance of an emergent set of anxieties; taken together they suggest something more profound: a deep-seated crisis in the relationship between children, adults, family structures and sexuality.

The inviolability of childhood is constructed as a matter of both physical and psychological containment. Sexual contact between an adult and a child is thus understood not only as an invasion of the pure sphere of childhood by the pollution of adult sexuality, but as symptomatic of a wider social malaise in which children are no longer protected. The figure of the paedophile has become a modern folk-devil. He (and it is nearly always a 'he' who stalks the popular imagination) not only condenses complex anxieties about male sexuality as innately predatory and uncontainable, which shadow other representations of male desire, but he also carries traces of social anxieties about modernity itself and its production of fragmented, asocial human subjects.

The preoccupation with children's sexuality within modernity has tended to focus intensively on the relationship between innocence and experience alluded to throughout this chapter. Indeed, Anne Higonnet points out that child portraits of the late eighteenth and early nineteenth centuries, at precisely the moment of the construction of the romantic child, such as Joshua Reynolds' *The Age of Innocence* (1788), circled around this binary: effectively representing the child as 'desirable precisely to the extent that it does not understand desire' (1998: 28). Pictures of children who are coyly appealing underneath oversized clothing, or who are shown cuddling kittens or puppies (both stylistic conventions which began during the romantic period and which persist in popular art), speak very precisely to the ideal of a socially and sexually innocent subject. Yet as Higonnet goes on to explore, the contradictions that surface around this discourse have returned in an especially troubling form in recent scandals relating to family photographs of children who are naked or deemed to be posed in ways that invite or challenge the viewer. Sally Mann's work in particular, with its 'knowing' children looking into the camera's gaze, challenges all those assumptions about childhood innocence and about families and power that are so cherished. As Higonnet says, 'Mann's work flouts the sexual innocence that was at the core of the Romantic child ideal', but it also 'expands the definition of childhood and parenting . . . irrevocably beyond the sentimental' (1998: 206).

The historical conjunction between the widespread panic about paedophilia, the sexualization and commodification of young girls in the form of pre-teen magazines, make-up and fashions, and wider social fears about the relationship between innocence, sexuality, power and knowledge is, then, important, as Valerie Walkerdine (1997) powerfully explores. Yet childish or childlike purity remains a powerful symbol, not only in the way in which children themselves are represented, but also in a whole tradition of images of adult women.

The child-woman

The idea that children's – or rather girls' – unknowing/knowing sexuality, rather than being a dimension of the child's own emergent identity, is instead a form of invitation to an adult male has appeared (and been problematized) recurrently in western literature, art and cinema. Vladimir Nabokov's novel, *Lolita*, is perhaps better known as a film made by Stanley Kubrick in 1962, or as a still iconic image of Sue Lyon in heart-shaped sunglasses. The film musical, *Gigi* (1958), romanticized not only prostitution but also the figure of the child-woman. Maurice Chevalier's performance as an ageing roué and, in particular, his celebration of 'leetle girls' may be read in an age acutely sensitive to paedophilia as profoundly discomfiting. Yet the fact that at its time of production (and even now) *Gigi* could be presented as a work of frothy gaiety meant that the film's resistance to a critical examination of sexual politics – or rather its representation of differentials of sexual power as fundamentally benign – was evaded.

Interestingly, the contradictory figure of the child-woman also appeared in early cinema in the person of the popular silent film star, Mary Pickford, who played a series of 'growing girls' in films such as *Rebecca of Sunnybrook Farm* (1903), *Daddy-Long-Legs* (1912) and *Pollyanna* (1913), most of which were adaptations of the classic girls' stories examined earlier in this chapter. It must be evident, if only from the chronological span indicated by these titles' dates, that Pickford was well beyond the fictional age of most of these characters (and she also played a range of adult roles), yet her star image remained wedded to the ideal of the child-woman for much of her career. The image of Pickford with her hair in cascading ringlets, with flattened breasts and girlish floral frock, is, to contemporary eyes, a disturbing one because we are accustomed to girls who look like women rather than the reverse. It is important to remember, however, that these films are accounts of a transition from childhood to womanhood which involves being able to 'confront and cope with the adult world's miseries and inequities' (Tibbetts 2001: 51). Such films therefore worked to extend and popularize not only the ideal of childhood innocence as a part of common sense throughout the 1920s, but also the specific nature of the problem of femininity as an adult subjectivity. Paradoxically, while such films were based on sources written, in the main, by liberal feminists, the performance of Rebecca or Pollyanna by an adult woman dressed up as a child worked to infantilize rather than to empower her.

Higonnet argues convincingly that 'by the 1990s, the image of the child had become perhaps the most powerfully contradictory image in western consumer culture . . . trading on innocence but implying sexuality, simultaneously denying and arousing desire' (1998: 153). Certainly, that decade saw a proliferation of advertising images that deployed a range of increasingly ambiguous representations of the relationship between adult sexuality, adolescence and childhood purity, which also worked to produce 'trouble' within conventional discourses of the family. Higonnet cites the Calvin Klein jeans advertisements, photographed in 1980 and featuring a 15 year-old Brooke Shields, promising, 'Nothing comes between me and my Calvins', as an important prefigurative moment in this history.[4] The company returned to eroticized images of teenagers in a later and more overtly controversial advertising campaign during the mid-1990s, which was the subject of organized denunciation on the part of The American Family Association, whose objections were made explicitly in terms of the advertisements' 'threat' to the family, as though the jeans themselves might lead to divorce or teenage pregnancy (Higonnet 1998: 152).

The increased importance of teenage models – or models who looked as though they were teenage girls – to fashion during the 1990s and 2000s was both remarked and evaded. During that decade and in the wake of the Calvin Klein campaign, the 'waif', marked by her pubescent physique, childlike face and apparently unsophisticated manner, became a key icon of contemporary desirability. In contrast to the 1980s, which had seen the hegemony of the confident and athletic figure of the 'supermodel', such as Linda Evangelista and Cindy Crawford, the 1990s saw the emergence and growing dominance of a female ideal which fetishized juvenile sexuality and required adult women to present themselves in (impossibly) infantilized terms. Yet the real import of this, and its relationship both to women's greater economic power and to anxieties about male desire, was frequently displaced onto panics about permissive sexuality or the fashion industry's extravagance and absurdity.

For example, a controversy similar to the one around the Calvin Klein campaign focused on a series of fashion photographs taken of the model, Kate Moss, by Corinne Day for a British edition of *Vogue* in 1993, which featured Moss in what appeared to be a grubbily real bedsit, wearing singularly unglamorous underwear. Indeed, because the images mimicked the register of the candid or 'caught on camera' style of photo-realism, their deployment of the figure of the child-woman seemed to operate more powerfully than if Moss had been portrayed in a more conventional fashion photography style. They made the viewer feel like a voyeur. The shoot was accused of promoting 'heroin chic', in so far as its images of Moss presented her as reed-thin, gaunt and vulnerably desirable. This meant that the way in which these images also emphasized Moss's childlike appearance, especially through the apparently real location, was overshadowed by the spurious accusation that they promoted drug abuse. Indeed, the complex issues of desire, innocence and knowledge and their relationship to questions of gender and power were effectively displaced by the focus on drugs. As Higonnet observes, 'once adult women are infantilised, it becomes plausible to flip the equation and consider infants to be like adult women' (1998: 194).

Childhood and contemporary cinema
The demon child

At the beginning of this chapter I drew on Patricia Holland's work to consider the ways in which films about children have been blended with films *for* children as part of the circulation of social fears about children's innocence or vulnerability. However, it is important to reiterate that the idea of childhood innocence is linked to the production of children as other and also intimately related to its pair – that of childhood evil or possession – and that the particular films Holland cites depend on the operation of the binary to work as narratives. Furthermore, the science-fiction 'demon child' films produced during the 1970s, such as *Rosemary's Baby*, *The Omen* and *The Exorcist*, although treated as though they marked a violent shift in representations of childhood, were largely different because of the effective way in which graphic special effects expressed the horror they sought to portray. As expressions of a deep-seated anxiety about the relationship between knowledge and innocence, however, they are part of a long and continuing tradition in Hollywood cinema that, at a stretch, includes *The Village of the Damned* (1960) and even melodramas such as *Stella Dallas* (1937) and *Mildred Pierce* (1945), in which a child's filial ingratitude spills over into something more threatening and dangerous. In such films, the family, rather than being a site of safety, is represented as a space of conflict, repression and profound danger. The child is the carrier of these meanings but may not be their originating source. Crucially, however, whereas films such as *Psycho* identify the mother as the repressive or problematic source of conflict, the horror films of the 1970s offer a more ambivalent account.

It's all black and white

Chuck Jackson (2000) argues that whiteness as a racial and an aesthetic category is a central organizing metaphor of demon child narratives, precisely because it is usually deployed to signify purity. The golden-haired, blue-eyed, white child stands for the innocence of white culture more generally, so that when Shirley Temple dances with Bill 'Bojangles' Robinson in *The Little Colonel* (1935), a musical that celebrates the culture of the slave-owning ante-bellum Deep South, her blondeness and childlikeness become a way of displacing and reconfiguring the power relations of race. For Jackson, the whiteness of a Shirley Temple is constructed in such films in relation to a blackness that, as long as it is contained by white power, remains safe. However, in a film such as *The Bad Seed* (1956), the white-blondeness of little Rhoda Penmark, the bad seed of the title, signifies an inner corruption that leads her to cold-bloodedly murder other children while all the while maintaining an exterior of unperturbable sweetness. For Jackson, 'the 1920s and 1930s held up Shirley Temple as the good little white girl, and, to subvert this paradigm, Rhoda's image must sharply contrast with our assumptions about proper little white girls' (2000: 69).

This particular demon child's racial signification is even more interesting when we compare the ways in which black children – in stark contrast to black men – have been over-determined as cutely unthreatening in popular media. From advertising images that in some ways return us to the laughing picanniny of the nineteenth century to popular television sitcoms featuring African-American children who are safely contained by white families, such as *Diff'rent Strokes* and *Webster*, the black male child is represented as throroughly infantilized. Indeed, the physical smallness of Gary Coleman in *Diff'rent Strokes* was repeatedly used to express this, as though the programme's function, in a move not dissimilar to that operated through Bill Robinson's 'safe' relationship with the white Shirley Temple, was to play out over and over again the recuperation of white fears about the possibilities presented by the black male body. Mark Crispin Miller describes such moves as 'lunatic fantasies of containment' (1990: 308).

The demon child was threatening because he occupied a position of knowledge, and thus exposed the fantasy of childhood innocence. However, recent film versions of childhood have increasingly figured it as a time of knowing innocence, in which the relationship between adult responsibility and childhood freedom is recast. In films such as *Home Alone* (1990), for example, the ability of the child to defeat adult burglars is predicated both on their incompetence as adults and his precociousness as a child. An even more extreme example of this is the figure of Mikey in *Look Who's Talking* (1989), who exercises authorial control over the film's narrative from the beginning, despite being as yet unborn. In both cases, privileged access to knowledge and 'the truth' about the world is ascribed to the child rather than adults, much as it is in *The Story of Tracy Beaker*, thus destabilizing the relations of power involved (see also Chapter 2).

It's a family affair: the 1980s and 1990s adventure movie

During the 1980s and 1990s changes in the audience demographic, together with shifts in the global ownership, control and distribution of film, worked to significantly alter the kinds of films being made and the audiences being assembled. George Lucas's *Star Wars* (1977) and Steven Spielberg's *ET – The Extraterrestrial* (1982) brought the production values of the blockbuster to bear on what were, in many ways, film fables or fairy tales, deploying narrative conventions that were familiar from the children's films of the 1930s and 1940s, but using technical effects that were wholly contemporary, thus producing films that spoke to both childen and adults. Robin Wood argues that one of the most important consequences of the success of these movies in the 1970s was the development of 'children's films conceived and marketed largely for adults – films that construct the adult spectator as a child, or, more precisely, as a childish adult, an adult who would like to be a child' (1986: 162–3). Throughout the 1980s and 1990s a range of such films was produced, including *Ghostbusters* (1984), *Back to the Future* (1985), *Batman* (1990), *Jurassic Park* (1993), *The Lion King* (1994) and *Mulan* (1998).

Wood's decidely pejorative conclusions about this trajectory are based on the argument that childish pleasures in such films are innately regressive and that children themselves are in some ways neglected because their pleasures are incorporated into films for 'childish adults'. It might be better to see this development in rather different terms, however. If the high point of something called childhood appeared in the middle of the twentieth century, it is possible to think of the emergence of films that seem to be for both adults and children as part of a significant shift away from the ideal of separate cultural spheres. The family blockbuster movie, while being ruthlessly marketed to children through merchandising and cross-promotional deals with retailers already associated with a children's market, such as McDonald's, also sought to directly appeal to adults by combining the childish elements of visual spectacle with an adult ironic humour that added a new level to an apparently simplistic narrative, and even managed to address difficult emotional issues.

Indeed, Peter Kramer argues that what is remarkable about such films is the convergence of a range of contemporary anxieties about the family and children's relationships to parents within them:

> These films are imbued with sentimentality, spectacle and a sense of wonder, telling stories about the pain and longing caused by dysfunctional or incomplete families (usually with absent or dead fathers), about childish wishes and nightmares magically coming true and the responsibilities that go along with this ... and about the irrevocability of loss and separation.
>
> (Kramer 1998: 304)

However, one of the other cultural functions of such films, for Kramer, is their reassertion of the naturalness of the family and familial relations. In *Jurassic Park*, not only do the adult archaeologists come to form a strong emotional and quasi-familial bond with the two children they encounter in the theme park, but also the dinosaurs themselves are represented as spontaneously changing sex in order to reproduce 'naturally'. Such films therefore construct the family across a number of discursive formations. They do so in the sense that they assemble an audience that is imagined in terms of familialism, regardless of whether the real social relations of cinema-going are wholly bound by this; and they do so in the sense that an ideology of family values is reasserted in the texts themselves, either through the production of a 'family' by the end of the story or through an emphasis on inheritance, primogeniture and patriarchy as in some ways rooted in the natural world.

Indeed, with the exception of *Mulan* (and, more problematically, *The Lion King*), most of these films privilege the point of view and narrative position of male child characters – and white characters at that – and emphasize their acquisition of a properly masculine social agency, even where children of each sex are featured or where the characters concerned are animals. In *Jurassic Park*, for example, the film opens with a male child 'standing in' for the audience as a sceptical observer at a dig where the two main adult characters describe to him the likely consequences of an encounter with a real dinosaur. The male child's appropriation of knowledge is thus closely bound up with his ability to become a social agent in his own right, whether that is so he can fight dinosaurs or become a lion king – or simply take up an adult human masculinity. For Sarah Harwood, the differential in power between boy children and girl children is remarkable.

> Sons are far more powerful than daughters. They negotiate the symbolic realm and their own objectification and commodification within it, with greater ease and success. Daughters are more simply abandoned or victimized. Sons can actively construct new families for themselves – most literally in *Look Who's Talking* and *Back to the Future*.
>
> (Harwood 1997: 129)

Rather than being able to claim the social agency that enables them to act to restore the family, then, girls must depend on an adult female to help them.

Conclusion

As we have seen, in the 1990s the relatively rigid division between knowledge and innocence and between adulthood and childhood characteristics of modernity has undergone considerable destabilization. Yet if the tendency in recent media representations of children and childhood has been to affirm the cultural power of children and their right to act in an increasingly complex social realm, this has not been uncontested, nor has it ascribed such rights equally to male and female characters or black and white children. Perhaps most importantly, while the idea of something called 'childhood' has been problematized and the child's place within the family has become a source of uncertainty in these transformations, children themselves are increasingly produced not as in a process of becoming, but as already arrived: as newly empowered consumer-citizens.

Notes

1 In 1993, for example, the then British prime minister, John Major, launched his 'back to basics' campaign, which explicitly drew on a nostalgic evocation of English life in the 1950s as an ideal to be returned to.

2 *Eric, or Little by Little*, for example, contains a terrifying homily against masturbation, although this is written in such obscure language that its purpose may well be completely opaque to modern readers.

3 Clearly, because of their relationship to the cultural anxieties about the transition from child to adult that appeared in the late nineteenth century and became central to twentieth-century discourses about youth, some of the issues touched on here will be explored in more detail in Chapter 5. It is interesting to note, however, that the emergence of paramilitarist social movements, such as the Boy Scouts, which presented themselves primarily as children's organizations, were part of the moment in

which adolescence itself was beginning to be defined and taxonomized (Hall 1904). Their status is therefore ambivalent in some ways.

4   Sales of the jeans apparently rose by 300 per cent in the days after the poster first appeared, yet neither the photographer, Richard Avedon, nor the Calvin Klein company agreed to give Higonnet permission to reproduce the image (see Higonnet 1998: 154).

chapter five

Teenage kicks: constructing adolescence

Introduction

In this chapter I explore some of the meanings attached to the figure of the teenager in contemporary culture, especially in the context of the complex relationship twentieth-century youth cultures have had with the family. The current cultural dominance of youth is itself centrally and critically related to the fragmentation of a family ideal, to changes in sexual and gender identities and to material shifts in the family's real social formation. Paradoxically, the invention of the teenager in the post-war years was effectively part of a larger cultural modernization of social relations that also helped to produce the ideal of the nuclear family and the ideology of the companionate marriage, as was explored in Chapter 1. This chapter therefore considers the recent history of the teenager, and explores the ways in which cultural formations of many kinds, including academic interventions and critiques, have been part of the ongoing construction and management of youth as a subject position whose specific relationship to the family is at once antagonistic and oddly necessary.

Producing the 'teenager'
The psychosocial version

Despite the current ubiquity and cultural dominance of youth cultures and the representation of adolescence as a natural life-stage dominated by hormones, the teenager is effectively a cultural construct, a condition of existence that only really assumed significance around the middle of the twentieth century by a fortuitous combination of shifts in the capitalist economy, changes in socio-philosophical definitions of the self and a post-war baby boom, all of which helped to create the conditions for the emergence of a new cultural identity and new markets for goods. Indeed, the apparently neutral and scientific term, adolescence, was itself only coined in 1904 by an American psychologist, G. Stanley Hall, in a move that would both prefigure and help to shape the conceptual basis of the teenager's cultural identity. The development in the 1980s and 1990s of an enormously diverse range of texts and forms all addressed to a youth constituency that was increasingly loosely defined,

Figure 5.1 *The Partridge Family* television show, while working within the tradition of the American family drama, was one of the first to foreground teenage sensibility and the teenager's point of view as part of its narrative perspective. (Photo: © Bettman/CORBIS)

together with the blurring of the boundaries between adolescence and adulthood in the culture of the 'thirtysomething', is perhaps some indication of the contingency and cultural specificity of the category itself.

Before the latter part of the twentieth century, the place of the teenager within family structures was still that of a child (and childhood itself is a problematic category, as we have seen). Until the individual was able to earn a living, around the age of 16, or had reached the age of majority – around 21 – when he or she might inherit wealth, contemplate marriage and take on adult responsibilities, the teenager was at best an apprentice to adulthood, while the relatively brief period of adolescence was generally regarded as culturally insignificant. Youth as a recognized social category first appeared in the eighteenth century, alongside the invention of the steam engine and the ascendancy of industrial modernity, according to Frank Musgrove (1964). Even by the late nineteenth century, adolescence was only properly experienced by those who could afford it: the upper and middle classes (and even then the idea that specific cultural forms might address the condition of adolescence was barely imaginable). Its democratization in the twentieth century was entirely bound up with economic changes in western societies, as well as social and cultural transformations.

One example of this is the way in which, with the exception of the 'growing girl' films of the silent era (discussed in Chapter 4), adolescence was not regarded as very interesting cinematic subject matter until the post-war period. Although there had been a limited history of films produced by Warner Brothers in the 1920s and 1930s, which had exploited social fears about juvenile delinquency and moral deviance, and which were generically linked to gangster melodramas, the figure of the troubled and tormented adolescent as a central protagonist in serious drama was largely absent. Popular films in the 1940s occasionally focused on a moment of transformation when the child became an adult or, specifically, when the girl became a woman and therefore legitimately desirable (such as the appearance of Elizabeth Taylor as a young woman in *Father of the Bride*, 1950), but this was also explicitly linked to marriageability. Examples of texts in which the specific *experience* of youth is extensively explored, with the exception of MGM's comic *Andy Hardy* series, are scarce. By the 1970s, however, the teenager had become institutionalized as a pivotal figure in popular representations of family life, particularly in television sitcoms such as *The Brady Bunch* (1969–74) in the USA and *Butterflies* (1978–83) in the UK, and in shows which attempted to bring together the teenage and the family audience, such as *The Partridge Family* (1970–74).

In these texts, male teenage characters are important identificatory figures for the audience, their ambivalent attitude towards the family and transitional position within it becoming an important symbol in the production of shifting meanings about family life. In later television representations from the 1990s, such as *Absolutely Fabulous* (1992–) and *Roseanne* (1987–98), it is teenage *girls* who tend to occupy this narrative position, yet here they are cast as morally responsible figures, both within the family and in relation to its public mediation, culminating in Sarah Michelle Geller's double-edged role of *Buffy the Vampire Slayer* (1994–2003), discussed in more detail below.

The teenager's current dominance in western popular culture is therefore hinged upon two important, if divergent, factors that are linked to contemporary anxieties about the burden of adult responsibilities in an increasingly complex world and the competing tensions produced by the contradictions found in western forms of individualism. These are the apparently dual access to the 'innocent' world of childhood and to the knowing realm of adult maturity that the adolescent is supposed to enjoy; and the increasing centrality of identity politics and 'lifestyle' issues to western social models (Giddens 1992). The angst-ridden teenage boy has been figured as the main locus of these social transformations in textual representations, with his crisis of identity working as the symbolic staging of wider social fears and anxieties. J. D. Salinger's *The Catcher in the Rye* (1951), for example, is a text whose first-person narrative of adolescent confusion and longing captures both the conjunctural emergence of the teenager as a key cultural figure in the 1950s and a wider field of post-war existential anxiety.

Furthermore, as Ian MacDonald (1994) points out, the rapid development of pop music and youth culture during the 1960s, together with the formation of various counter-cultural movements, was part of a longer-term cultural shift in western societies from an emphasis on social to personal transformation: what he calls a 'revolution in the head'. Equally important was the social alienation expressed as teenage rebellion in the 1950s, and later given form in the 1960s and 1970s in political and counter-cultural groups, which saw itself as expressly oppositional – to a stiflingly conventional parent culture that suppressed individual creativity in favour of social status or material success. The conventional suburban middle-class family was, therefore, the primary object of hostility in these configurations; but it was also often perceived to be too powerful to resist completely. Julian Barnes' novel, *Metroland* (1981), for example, deftly evokes the way in which its main character is briefly seduced by the sexual and political ferment of Paris in the late 1960s, believing himself to have rejected the safe suburban values of 'metroland' where he grew up (the outer London suburbs reached by the railways), only to find himself returning there to settle happily with his wife and child in the 1970s.

Yet attachment to the idea of the creatively unique individual is itself a feature of western models of identity. Teenage rebellion may thus be understood as a necessary precursor of adult conformity – a testing of the boundaries rather than a revolutionary act in itself. Indeed, the widespread popularization of psychoanalytical explanatory frameworks for social behaviour during the post-war years helped to clear cultural space for the normalization of teenage rebellion as the enactment of a primal struggle between competing and predetermined 'drives' that must ultimately be mastered by the conscious self, or ego, so that the individual can safely 'return' to the family.

Representational strategies for the depiction of teenage experience and culture have been dominated by two crucial ideological positions, both of which identify adolescence as a period of intense, even epiphanous experience, and in which the site of this crisis is the family itself. The first, and older version, is the idea of the teenager and youth culture as a form of social deviance in which sexual desire, physical energy and resistance to parental pressures lead to criminality unless more fruitfully harnessed. The second draws on these models, but articulates a more positive version of the adolescent quest for meaningful identity, in which the energy and passion of rebellion is a necessary part of social change. In both cases, however, the relationship of the adolescent to the family structure and parental authority has been crucial. Until very recently, the teenager in such accounts was always a male subject who stood for a larger human experience, so that femininity was the troublesome other against which a proper and full human subjectivity was defined and then resolved. Teenage girls, it seems, were 'always already' part of the family. Indeed, adult heterosexual masculinity is produced *in opposition* to femininity: 'to be a man is to be not-woman, not-gay, not absorbed back into a mother–son relationship' (Holland et al. 1996: 251). It is these specifically masculine anxieties which have frequently shaped the mediation and cultural articulation of teenagerhood more generally, and have made it difficult for teenage girls to produce themselves as the proper subject of adolescence.

Cultural articulations

The word 'teenager' first appeared in the American popular press during the 1920s and 1930s – almost invariably applied to the scions of white, middle-class families. Its coinage was thus initially linked to the tentative production of a self-consciously separate subculture by members of a privileged class, rather than a widespread and rapid social transformation: the original model of the teenager was a white, middle-class boy rather than a black, working-class girl. The wider development of an emergent and distinctive teenage subculture during the 1940s was linked to changing social attitudes around sexuality and identity, facilitated by the growth and commodification of new forms of cultural expression, leisure and recreation, especially recorded music (Kett 1977).

Yet as Maltby points out (1989: 140), the development of a fully-fledged, commercialized and increasingly transnational version of teenage culture did not appear until the 1950s, when the combination of improved and extended educational opportunities, increases in disposable income and leisure time, and a higher number of young people as a proportion of the general population created significant new markets for goods and services. By 1959, Grace and Fred Hechinger claimed that the 'average' American teenager was spending $555 per annum on 'goods and services not including the necessities normally supplied by their parents' (1963: 54). The emergence of a set of distinctively teenage consumer practices, tastes, spaces, desires and aspirations was central to this, and was made sense of largely in identificatory terms. As Barbara Ehrenreich et al. observe, '[d]efined by its own products and advertising slogans, teenhood became more than a prelude to adulthood; it was a status to be proud of – emotionally and sexually complete unto itself' (1992: 98). The appearance of rock and roll as the definitive articulation of this identity in the mid-1950s, therefore, also marked a significant moment in the cultural history of the twentieth century in which the relationship between identity and consumption began to be thoroughly intertwined. By the 1960s, 'youth' was regularly connected with conspicuous and leisure-orientated consumption in the new consumer culture.

Panics and problems
The 'permissive moment'

The emergence and consolidation of youth culture in western popular culture and of the figure of the teenager as a contemporary icon was to some extent congruent with what Jeffrey Weeks has called 'the permissive moment'. By the early 1960s, shifting and increasingly critical social attitudes towards sexuality, the family and traditional, often authoritarian, models of morality had begun to figure in many western societies, especially in the USA and the UK, fuelled by the greater affluence and social stability achieved during the post-war years. The permissive moment centred upon this liberalization in attitudes, especially towards sex: prohibitions around premarital sex and homosexuality began to relax alongside changes in race relations and the 'rediscovery' of poverty as a social issue. As Weeks puts it, the 'official drift' during the 1960s was against legal prosecutions of 'obscenity' and towards sexual tolerance (1989: 250). In some respects, the figure of the teenager acted as a lightning conductor for the struggles over morality and social identity that were taking place during this period; identified as the natural locus of social change and of the new consumer culture, but ambivalently regarded because of this. These contrasting versions thus moved between what Dick Hebdige calls 'youth-as-fun' and 'youth-as-trouble' (1988).

The permissive moment – and subsequent decades in the twentieth century – was therefore marked by a wave of successive moral panics, focused on the sexual practices and subcultural pleasures of teenagers and young people. The idea of 'permissiveness' itself was similarly subjected to anxious, but not always very scrupulous, scrutiny. Such panics ranged from the concerns about juvenile delinquency and teenage gangs of the 1950s and early 1960s, through the anxieties generated about the corruptive power of television by Mary Whitehouse's National Viewers' and Listeners' Association in the early 1960s in the UK, to the concerns over rave culture and the menace of ecstasy in the 1990s. In each case, the idea that youth culture posed a special threat to the family was regularly mobilized. Yet the panics, like the youth cultures they demonized, were themselves highly mediated: often organized by sensationalist newspaper reports (as in the panic over mods and rockers in 1964) and exacerbated by political opportunism (Cohen 1972; Thompson 1998).

Stories about depraved youth thus made the imagined source of depravity, youth cultures of various kinds, doubly attractive for teenagers themselves and helped to turn those involved into sophisticated and inventive creators of media anxiety. Sarah Thornton gives an entertaining account of the way in which those involved in British rave culture in the 1980s and 1990s anticipated, exploited and therefore helped to shape the sensationalist reports about drug use in the tabloid press, by knowingly representing themselves in ways that would produce a suitably sensationalised response and further (useful) coverage in the media (1995: 129–37).

One example of a wholly unanticipated panic, however, was the wave of social fears focused on teenage girls' magazines that occurred in the UK during the late 1990s. Titles such as *J17*, *Bliss*, *Sugar* and *More* were identified as the main source of an excess of sexual knowledge among young women, a knowledge that was assumed – at least in the dominant conservative political discourses of the UK – to be linked to the proliferation of teenage pregnancies. Legislation proposed by the British Conservative MP, Peter Luff, in February 1996, for example, was intended to require publishers to place age suitability warnings on the covers of young women's magazines because of their use of 'sexually explicit' material. The naivety of this proposal and the likelihood that such warnings would effectively serve only to attract readers seemed not to have been considered initially, although it undoubtedly contributed to the bill's eventual defeat. Indeed, the dubiousness of the causal logic that was being applied also indicated the extent to which panics about teenage sexuality are always about young women's sexual agency and the threat this poses to patriarchal power. What emerged most forcefully out of this most recent struggle over moral authority versus sexuality was the symbolic importance of the figure of the teenager – or, more properly, the teenage girl – to debates about the future of the family.[1]

Aimless youth in the 1980s and 1990s

While the various panics about youth since the 1950s have frequently deployed the same concerns in new ways, anxieties about masculinity and crime resurfaced in a very specific form in the 1980s and 1990s in the USA, focusing not on youth as deviance, but on youth as aimless and apathetic. To some extent, these concerns overlapped with the fears about media effects and the power of popular culture to produce certain kinds of behaviour (explored in Chapter 4). They were also linked to competing social anxieties about the rise of yuppie culture in large cities, about the materialism it celebrated, and about the freedom which wealth and social and geographical mobility offered to young people. And, as Charles R. Acland observes, panics about youth are also always about other things too: 'the destruction of the nuclear family, the drug problem, the problems of "inner-city" (read: non-white) populations, the plethora of pornography, the failure of public education, and even . . . the popularity of satanism' (1995: 10). Indeed, the threat which male youth, in particular, supposedly presents to society is repeatedly cast as a threat to the family, not least because of its relationship to adolescent masculinity's problematic relationship with the feminine and with domesticity. The crisis in youth, then, is a crisis in family relations, and in power relations, too, as the restraints which a strong patriarchy is supposed to exercise are apparently loosened or challenged.

As Acland goes on to argue, the crisis is always *returned* to the family, too:

> . . . the crisis in the 'Teens in Crisis' episode of *Oprah* is not that of teens in general, but of youth in 'aberrant' family situations. The show documents the stories of 'teen victims' who consequently become involved in a broad range of other crimes. This social cycle of transgression is traced back to the family.
>
> (Acland 1995: 112)

For Acland, the rapid adoption of the concept of 'Generation X' (taken from Douglas Coupland's 1991 novel of the same name) into American popular culture marks the wider acceleration of fears about the place of teenagers within a consumer-driven society.

Throughout the 1980s and early 1990s a series of films focusing on an adolescent masculinity that was increasingly amoral, emotionally cold and socially disengaged appeared, all of which drew on the underlying discourse of a 'blank' generation (Generation X) without purpose or a clear identity. Films such as *The Boys Next Door* (1985), *River's Edge* (1986) and *Less Than Zero* (1987) all engaged with these concerns, and did so through the spectacularization of youth as deviance and the dissolution of family values. For Acland, *River's Edge* 'presents the complete carnage of the traditional family by creating two universes of the young and the adult, each unable to reach the other' (1995: 131). Indeed, the film circulates around the anomie of a culture in which the difference between the dead and the living has all but been abolished. Based on real events that had taken place in California in the early 1980s, it charts the experiences of a group of teenagers who cover up the murder of one of their number (a girl) by another (a boy), partly because they don't have the social or moral capital to make sense of the events that have taken place, and partly because it seems that the death has no real significance to them. The film was, briefly, a *cause célèbre*, and was widely received as a commentary on the contemporary alienation of wasted youth, according to Acland (1995: 123).

Yet this reading failed to pull out both the specifically gendered terms of the crime and its relationship to the wider culture – or, rather, it took as a given that the disaffection of youth will be played out on the bodies of deviant women. *River's Edge* thus 'depicts the young as the terrible products of a general disappearance of affect, of an order that rests on social atomization, and of a society whose patriarchal foundation requires the construction of the lifeless woman to assure its power' (1995: 132) . Indeed, Acland explicitly links the appearance of these films with a real-life sex crime in 1986, in New York's Central Park: what became known as 'the preppy murder' of Jennifer Levin by Robert Chambers. Both events were recast by the popular media in terms of young women's newly acquired sexual freedom, which, it was claimed made men the 'new victims'. The identification of young women's agency, both social and sexual, as the primary threat to the family thus appeared across a number of media panics during the 1980s and 1990s, as teenage girls themselves were struggling to claim the rights that were taken for granted by young males.

Resistance and rebellion: music, youth and authenticity

The definitive teenage cultural form, rock and pop music, and its attendant subcultural styles and practices, has invariably been produced in response to the conventions and inhibitions of family life. Youth culture vigorously defines itself against family values, and this resistance to adult authority and refusal of domesticity has been, since the 1950s, the most important creative force in the development of new cultural styles and new ways of conceptualizing the self. As Simon Frith observes:

> [B]ecause teenage experience is still grounded in the home, the boredom/excitement axis is focused, narcissistically, on the most immediate adolescent anxieties. Sexuality, for example, becomes the site of fantasies of going to extremes, and it is taken for granted that the most intense sensations (sex and drugs and rock and roll) are those enjoyed furtively, fearfully, kept hidden from the family.
>
> (Frith 1997: 277)

Yet pop music is actually marked by complex tensions that are not always explicable in terms of anti-familialism. Rock and roll's early emphasis on an aggressive masculine sexuality and hostility towards domesticity was balanced by the development of pop and its cultivation of the romantic ballad, and later by art-rock's hybrid and experimental style. While the excessive masculinity of rock's original idiom made it problematic for young women to identify or be accepted as performers – because they represented, in a diluted form, the ties of domesticity that rock music challenged and because they lacked the cultural autonomy that masculinity claimed as a right – some forms of pop were more open to feminine and feminized cultural values. At the same time, the structure of feeling that underpinned rock, and later rap music, offered a space of resistance to the family and to domesticity.

Rock and roll first emerged as a distinctive and specifically youth-oriented musical form in the USA during the early 1950s, and its combination of a driving rhythm and sexually suggestive lyrics – indicated by the appropriation of an African-American slang term for sexual intercourse as its generic title – initially represented a fundamental break with the dominant style of popular music. In place of the romantic commitment to the monogamous heterosexual couple articulated by older traditions of commercial popular song, rock and roll offered a differently romanticized celebration of male sexual performance and power. The music's success also helped to consolidate the economic power of young people by producing a realignment of the relations between the consumer and the market. Its unanticipated cultural impact and later refinement and redefinition as 'pop' music during the early 1960s also led, paradoxically, to its incorporation back into mainstream culture.

Rock and pop's history is, however, a complex narrative of cultural encounters, hybridities and struggles. The genre of rock and roll was itself the product of a fusion between white country music and black blues and gospel styles, and its appearance as a culturally distinctive form was prefigured by the growing accessibility of recorded black music to a traditionally segregated white audience via local (usually southern) American radio stations during the late 1940s (Mundy, 1999: 97). To white and suburban teenagers black music seemed to articulate the alienation from mainstream society that they aspired to but had no means of expressing. Indeed, rock and roll became, as Mundy observes, the cultural space in which the structural dichotomies around this desire to be *both* rebellious and conformist, to reject parental authority yet acquire material possessions, was 'given expression, explored and, symbolically at least, resolved' (1999: 99).

Yet while black experience was often privileged in the emergent discourse of rock and roll as more 'authentic' than white experience, perhaps because of the material exclusion from power of the African-American community, perhaps because of other – more essentialist – notions of race, black *performers* remained systematically marginalized from the music industry's mainstream. Indeed, the racist hostility of white producers meant that it was a white boy who 'sounded black' – Elvis Presley – who would become the first real star of rock and roll. Described as 'a guitar playing Marlon Brando', Presley's iconic significance to an emergent youth culture was crucial: here was a singer whose combination of sexual promise and rebellious disdain seemed to condense all its important elements. Presley's masculinity and his whiteness were thus essential to his stardom and to the meanings that circulated around him as a cultural icon; but so too was his exploitation of black styles of performance – a particularly pertinent irony given that one of his biggest hits, 'Hound Dog', had originally been written and performed by Bessie Smith, a middle-aged black woman. At the same time, the threat to family values that he seemed to pose was intensified by his early appearances on television in 1956: his 'obscene' performance style was beamed directly into the respectable sitting rooms of middle America via *The Ed Sullivan Show*.

Youth's growing cultural significance during the late 1950s and early 1960s seemed to be consolidated by the appearance of new television shows which were specifically geared to showcase the new performers and music styles (*Six-Five-Special*), as well as the transformation of older programmes into texts more clearly addressed to a youth audience (*American Bandstand*). Yet such shows also attempted to incorporate rock and roll back into family entertainment and the showbiz tradition; either through paternalistic presenters such as Ed Sullivan, whose benign approval defused the danger presented by groups such as the Rolling Stones or the Animals, or through a discursive link with romance and femininity produced by the presence of 'safer' female performers, such as Dusty Springfield or Cilla Black.

Throughout the subsequent decades of the twentieth century, the ideology of rock has been marked by these tensions. The fragmentation of pop music into chart-based, mainstream pop and progressive – later 'independent' – rock concretized the differences between rebelling and conforming, and also naturalized them. By the 1970s the antinomies around rock and pop had assumed a firmly gendered – and often class- and education-defined – character. The culturally devalued, commercial, melody-based and danceable pop was primarily figured as feminine, while (supposedly) uncommercial, experimental or alternative rock music was almost wholly identified as masculine and middle class. However, such over-determinations of gendered oppositions around authenticity are clearly disrupted by the creative centrality of black forms and styles to popular music. Soul and disco in the 1960s and 1970s, for example, although imbued with the supposedly authentic raw emotional power of black music, largely figured as singles-based, commercial genres of pop.

In the 1980s, and 1990s, the emergence of hip hop, rap and house music marked a further important shift in the ethnic configuration of pop and in the iconography of masculine cool. The contemporary dominance of youth cultures and styles by urban, African-American rap musicians, such as Ice-T and Puff Daddy, who reclaimed the power to control and define the meanings associated with blackness and especially black masculinity, represents a significant transformation in the music business and in the cultural economy of youth. However, commitment to the (private space of) the family is still figured as antithetical to a commitment to (masculine) authenticity – whether that is characterized as 'the street', 'the hood' or the open road.

Resistance and rebellion: adolescent masculinities on film

The growth in the cultural significance of youth in the post-war years was most spectacularly represented by the development of a new kind of (white) masculinity, which was increasingly sexualized as well as increasingly emotionally open. Central to this, as we have seen, was the iconic figure of the (male) teenage rebel, who both embodied the lived dimensions to social change and represented a powerful form of resistance. Richard Dyer notes (1979: 25) that the emergence of 'sensitive', angst-ridden young male film stars, such as James Dean, Montgomery Clift and Marlon Brando during the 1950s, who exhibited new kinds of emotional masculinity, represented a significant alteration in meanings around gender. Their identification as method actors helped to intensify this since, as Maltby observes, '[the method's] emphasis on emotional meaning over other aspects of character succeeded in investing male performance with a degree of emotional expressiveness not seen since silent melodrama' (2003: 398). This focus on the psychological dimensions to character and performance was symptomatic, too, of the dominance of psychoanalysis in post-war American culture, and its claim to reveal the truth about the self.

The appearance of such stars did not, however, enlarge the cultural space available to young women. While the meanings attached to Brando, Dean and Clift overlapped with those produced around Presley and the sexually and emotionally intense style of rock and roll, these 'sensitive' men were primarily figured as adolescent rather than adult, and their sensitivity was frequently articulated as a powerful and misogynistically violent response to the family and familial relationships – a response that was legitimated by the way in which the family itself was represented (see also Chapter 1). In *Rebel Without a Cause* (1955), for example, the teenage hero's emotional breakdown is represented as an incoherent but ultimately explicable response to the impossibility of his family relations. And, as Steve Neale (1999: 221) points out, in contrast to the youthful delinquents of earlier films, who had nearly always been represented as innately bad or as coming from a socially deprived background, James Dean's Jim Stark is an alienated *middle-class* boy from an affluent suburban home. His rebellion is therefore offered as a response to a crisis within the family rather than as the expression of a latent criminality. It is as though, by putting the teenager into the family narrative, the conflicts and tensions of family life can at last be represented.

Marlon Brando's resistance to the conventions of small-town life in *The Wild One* (1954) is also implicitly figured as a form of rebellion against domesticity and marriage. Interestingly, such 'social problem' films also suggest the extent to which masculine teenage rebellion in the 1950s was facilitated by a new mobility: motorbikes, cars and the road itself are crucial to the escape from social constraint and adult authority. The young rebel could simply drive away from his responsibilities and from the domestic constraints that older men were required to live within. Moreover, as John Mundy points out, in both *The Wild One* and *Rebel Without a Cause*, teenage rebellion is figured as an enigma – signified by the latter's title – to an older generation for whom 1950s suburban family life represented the achievement of the American dream (1999: 105).

The romanticized figure of the emotionally complex white male teenage rebel has remained a powerful cultural icon, in the persons of Kurt Cobain or Eminem, for example. As Doherty points out (1988: 234), even a film with the avant-garde pretensions of *Easy Rider* (1969), produced at the height of the counter-cultural moment, drew heavily on the conventions established by *The Wild One*. Far from offering a radically alternative form of social consciousness or organization that would make space for women, *Easy Rider* re-articulates the gendered antinomies in which the freedom of the road and freedom from emotional ties are wholly bound up with a specifically masculine identity.

The 'teenpic' and the pop musical: addressing and mediating youth from the 1950s to the 1980s

I don't want to be a juvenile delinquent

The emergence of films specifically addressed to and focused on teenagers themselves – teenpics – came about partly because the market for mainstream Hollywood films was already in decline in the post-war years. By 1957, only 35 cents out of every $5 spent on leisure consumption was being channelled towards cinema, compared with $1 out of every $5 in

1946 (Mundy 1999: 103). In addition, the American government's implementation of divorcement and divestiture in the film industry presented a problem for Hollywood's economic position. Threatened by the rapid development of film's competitor, television, as a successful and conveniently domestic form of popular entertainment, and by the suburbanization that was literally moving the family audience away from city-centre cinemas, the Hollywood studios began to focus on the teenage audience as a new and reliable source of revenue.

However, while such films occasionally crossed over into the serious-minded territory of *Rebel Without a Cause* discussed above, teenpics were frequently sensationalist and exploitational in their focus on juvenile delinquency and prurient fascination with adolescent sexuality. Titles such as *Teenage Crime Wave* (1955) and *Girls in Prison* (1956) articulated the same combination of fear and attraction mobilized by the newspaper panics over teen culture; and, while seeking to secure a teenage audience, uncritically represented teenagers themselves as a social problem.

Nonetheless, some examples, such as *I Was a Teenage Werewolf* (1957), *Dragstrip Riot* (1958) and the British *Beat Girl* (1959), demonstrated an energy and engagement with the affective pleasures of teenage culture (often despite themselves),[2] while also successfully drawing on and reworking a wider (but, it should be noted, wholly white) teenage culture that included horror and fantasy comics, drag racing and hot-rodding, as well as rock and roll. Indeed, the teenpic not only *solicited* a teenage audience, but it was also inevitably in the business of *representing* teenagers and teenage culture back to that audience, and this included partially shifting the focus of narratives from adult to adolescent experience.

However, while teen culture began to be the source of cinematic interest, most of the early 'respectable' films to feature rock and roll, including *Blackboard Jungle* (1955), *Rock Around the Clock* (1956) and *The Girl Can't Help It* (1956), managed to condescend both to the music and to teenagers, by juxtaposing moralistic narratives about wayward youth with a relatively cavalier treatment of the performances by musicians such as Little Richard or Bill Haley (Doherty 1988: 82). Teenagers in these films are secondary to characters played by middle-aged stars and the attitude to rock and roll itself is, at best, ambivalent.

The pop musical, like the teenpic, was originally conceived as an attempt to exploit the teenage market through the incorporation of a pop soundtrack and youthful characters into an already existing film genre, the musical. As Jane Feuer observes, '. . . [it] emerged as one of the first examples of the post-studio mode of production in which a precise audience, in this case the youth audience, was "targeted" for "exploitation"' (1993: 125). Later examples, particularly those starring Elvis Presley – with the possible exception of *Jailhouse Rock* (1957) – while better budgeted and with a greater respect for the audience, also drew on the established cinematic conventions of the film musical in order to incorporate – and recuperate – the stars and the music back into family values, often by literally relocating the performance of rock and roll away from the dangerous public sphere of the dance hall or cellar bar into the 'safe' domain of the family. Presley's performance of the title song of *Love Me Tender* (1956), for example, is contained by the fact that it is being done for his mother, while sitting in her rocking chair.

By the early 1960s, however, the genre was more fully established as a discursive space for the exploration of youth culture as a legitimate theme in itself, as well as the competing discourses around teenage sensibility and identity. Star vehicles such as *Summer Holiday* (1962), made with the British pop singer Cliff Richard, and the American 'beach party' and 'clean teen' films produced between 1962 and 1967, while relatively bland, were also marked by their filmic creation of a utopian world almost wholly inhabited by (white) teenagers, in which adults figured largely as an outside threat to youthful pleasures, whether these were the contemporary forms of surfing and beach dancing or flirtation and romance. Such films effectively acknowledged that youth culture and pop music was not a temporary fad but a distinctive and innovatory form of cultural production.

The stylistically radical films featuring the Beatles and directed by Richard Lester also suggested that the sub-genre could be genuinely innovatory. For example, in both *A Hard Day's Night* (1964) and *Help!* (1965) the musical's conventional narrative emphasis on heterosexual romance is wholly abandoned in favour of plots that revolved around the experience of 'being a Beatle' in the former and a comic mystery in the latter. The band's refusal to be incorporated into the pop musical's hackneyed conventions was even foregrounded by John Lennon's comments, a criticism that helped to mark the increasing confidence of youth culture in its own values:

> 'We weren't interested in being stuck in one of those typical nobody-understands-our-music plots where the local dignitaries are trying to ban something as terrible as the Saturday Night Hop. The kind of thing where we'd just pop up a couple of times between the action, all smiles and clean shirt-collars to sing our latest record.'
>
> (quoted in Carr 1996: 30)

A Hard Day's Night's quasi-documentary style also meant that its representation of Beatlemania and footage of real fans worked instead to produce a range of new meanings, about fandom, about the group and about youth culture itself: this, it seemed to suggest, was what it *meant* to be a teenager.

It makes me feel like dancin'

A Hard Day's Night was also pivotal in the further development of the youth market and youth culture through cross-promotional texts designed to consolidate the commercial potential of popular bands: it featured specially composed songs, which, for the first time, were also tied in to an album of the same name. Indeed, the film was made 'for the express purpose of having a soundtrack album' (Neaverson 1997: 12). Such scores were to become an important selling point in the wider distribution of films aimed at the youth market, and the further refinement of popular music into 'serious' rock linked the emergent counter-culture to the commercial mainstream. As Jeff Smith observes, the successful use of rock scores for *The Graduate* (1967) and *Easy Rider* (1969) marked the increasing maturity of the youth culture market and of the teenage audience (1998: 155). By the late 1970s and 1980s the soundtrack album had become a crucial feature of film promotion, as the success of *Saturday Night Fever* (1977) demonstrated.

These two decades also saw the development of an important strand of cultural nostalgia around the key originating moment of the teenager – the late 1950s and early 1960s – in the appearance of self-consciously 'retro' films and television shows, such as *American Graffiti* (1973), *American Hot Wax* (1977), *Happy Days* (1974–84) and *Back to the Future* (1985), all of which helped in the organization of a preferred version of the history of youth culture, as Shumway suggests (1999).

The appearance and influential power of these and other retro texts at this point seem to suggest two things. First, that as youth culture and pop music were maturing into a domination of mainstream culture in the 1970s, their authenticity – the expression of 'real' masculine rebellion – was perceived to have been lost or tainted by commercialism and the consolidation of the youth market. This authenticity could only be recaptured by revisiting the moment of youth culture's birth, and especially the moment of rock and roll's appearance. Second, that the tensions such texts clearly expressed about the relationship between the teenager and the family remained an important source of creative interest, but also a potential site of nostalgia. Ironically, by the 1970s and in the wake of significant changes relating to gender relations and social mores, the stable and apparently safe 1950s family, of breadwinner father, housewife mother and suburban-dwelling children, was already being mythologized – even in texts addressed to a teenage audience which also celebrated the adolescent male rebel. Yet the ways in which such texts sought to recover the moment of youth also differed markedly. Where *American Graffiti* is elegiac and politically serious about the past and about youth itself, *Happy Days* pastiches both 1950s norms and the figure of the cool rebel himself.

One retro text from this moment, the pop musical *Grease* (1978), powerfully articulates this cultural ambivalence by offering a pastiche (but *not* a satire) of the cultural codes of 1950s teenage life, while also settling for a conventional happy ending that can be explained away by reference to period expectations. Locating its story of teenage romance and small-town rebellion in a mythologized and, it should be emphasized, entirely white American past, in which teenage gangs are too busy posing with their leather jackets and metal combs to present much of a threat to social order, the film offers an affectionate account of the golden age of the teenager that also knowingly refers to the 'clean teen' movies discussed above. It casts the same Frankie Avalon who had been a teenage pin-up in the anodyne beach movies of the 1960s as a guardian angel. The continued success of *Grease* as a cultural artefact into the new century thus depends on the cultural competences of postmodern knowingness, in which familiarity with rock and roll as a *style* of rebellion (as opposed to a form of real social subversion) is crucial, and adolescent masculinity retains a privileged (if less certain) status.

By the 1980s the growing importance of cable television channels, such as MTV, helped to strengthen the cultural hegemony of pop music and of youth itself as a style of identity. As John Mundy points out, '[o]ne measure of the primacy of pop music across all media has been the growing use of a music bed for radio news, particularly prevalent in British commercial radio. In the screen media, this music video aesthetic has been increasingly evident in contemporary commercial cinema' (1999: 224). This tendency to use pop and rock as the 'soundtrack' to everything is perhaps symptomatic of the extent to which such music can no longer be read as a simple articulation of adolescent subjectivity; indeed, the simultaneous and continuing presence of performers from different moments within the history of pop and rock (from Mick Jagger through Elvis Costello to the Spice Girls), all of whom stand for an idea of youth, suggests that the relationship between the two is already being stretched. For Bill Osgerby, the logical consequence of this is that '"Youth" has simply become a mode of consumption' (1998: 332).

Subcultures, style and resistance: the academic celebration of youth

Sociological and cultural studies accounts of subcultures and styles of youthful rebellion are, of course, themselves mediations of the idea of youth (initially as a politics of resistance in the 1970s), and have been crucial to the ideological production of youth culture's larger social significance. Unsurprisingly, the development of social and cultural analyses of youth cultures paralleled their increasing visibility within popular culture more generally as well as responding to other mediations, especially the panics about youth crime in the early 1970s. Such work oddly reflected the journey from the margins to the centre that the figure of the teenager was taking, while also articulating this shift within the specialized register of academically approved knowledge. For example, in the 1940s and 1950s, the Chicago School sociologists were primarily interested in the relationship between deviance and cultural identities among the emergent jazz-focused 'beat' subcultures of Greenwich Village in New York; subcultures that, strictly speaking, actually prefigured the moment of youth culture. Later sociological studies of deviance and youth in Britain, such as Stanley Cohen's *Folk Devils and Moral Panics* (1972), concentrated on the fomentation of social fears about youth cultures by the mainstream press. Such cultural work, like the social problem films of the 1950s and 1960s, sometimes helped to reproduce and manage the very ideological assumptions it claimed to critique: especially around the threat of adolescent masculinity. By the mid-1970s, however, research into youth culture had shifted away from a criminology-informed focus on individual deviance to explore the way in which youth cultures collectively offered complex models of social identity.

In the UK in particular, the extraordinary richness of youth subcultural forms from the post-war period onwards – from Teddy boys in the 1950s to skinheads in the 1970s and new romantics in the 1980s – has been seen as symptomatic, not only of the increased cultural space claimed by teenagers throughout this period, but also of the specific experience of working-class youth within a profoundly class-ridden society. As Thornton, quoting Bourdieu, points out, 'British youth cultures exhibit that "stylization of life" or "systemic commitment which orients and organizes the most diverse practices" that develops as the objective distance from necessity grows' (1995: 103). Such subcultures are perhaps peculiarly symptomatic of a combination of relative affluence and freedom to experiment with identity that is only fleetingly available to working-class or lower middle-class adolescents. Their intensity and cultural complexity is thus part of this temporary creative moment.

British subcultures were also pivotal to the development of academic knowledge and critical frameworks about youth, identity and power within cultural studies. The body of subculture analysis that developed at the Birmingham Centre for Contemporary Cultural

Studies during the 1970s, for example, shared an interest in youth subcultural styles as a way of 'living' cultural meanings that refused or subverted middle-class expectations. The works of Phil Cohen, Stuart Hall and Tony Jefferson and Dick Hebdige, although sometimes theoretically and methodologically at variance with each other, were marked by a common (romantic, sometimes utopian) conviction that subcultures represented an important form of class struggle. For example, in Hall and Jefferson's influential edited collection, *Resistance Through Rituals*, the book's introduction offers a careful taxonomy of the specific ways in which working-class British youth subcultures, such as those of the mods, skinheads and Teddy boys (which were also primarily white and male), defined themselves through their own institutions, social relations and 'maps of meaning' (1976: 10).

Similarly, Dick Hebdige's *Subculture: the Meaning of Style*, perhaps the most influential – certainly the most evocative – study of this kind, represents the forms and relations of British punk culture in a way that emphasizes the complexity and resistant potential of *everything* involved, from the music to the safety pins. When Hebdige describes the characteristic punk dance style, the 'pogo', he thus emphasizes its subversiveness: 'the pogo was a caricature – a *reductio ad absurdum* of all the solo dance styles associated with rock music . . . the pogo made improvisation redundant: the only variations were imposed by changes in the tempo of the music' (1979: 108–9). However, as Graeme Turner points out, the underlying assumptions of his thesis ran the risk of 'simply equating the subordinate with the resistant' (1992: 117). In other words, producing oneself as a punk was frequently conflated with a more overtly political refusal of social norms.

Furthermore, much of the Birmingham work automatically and somewhat

Figure 5.2 The work of the Centre for Contemporary Cultural Studies on youth subcultures during the 1970s helped to secure the idea that punk was a form of political resistance to the restrictions of a stiflingly class-based and conventional society, in which the family was a primary site of tension. (Photo: Getty Images)

problematically set up subcultures as an authentic set of class-inflected practices that invariably worked in opposition to the mass media, as though the mediation of punk or mod music and styles on television or in the press represented a corruption of a finished, pure and organic cultural form, rather than a productive element in its development. Such a position failed to recognize the extent to which youth subcultures have always depended on a complex relationship between mediatory processes of various kinds, including the commodification of style itself, as discussed earlier. Jeremy Gilbert wittily observes that Hebdige's tendency to mythologize what he calls, 'punk's originary situation (presumably one of the "legendary" early Pistols gigs)' (1999: 32), excludes the possibility that it was only by watching the Sex Pistols *on television* that a provincial 16-year-old could acquire the necessary cultural capital to enable him to decide to become a punk. As Sarah Thornton points out, the assumption that subcultural forms are in some ways *always* resistant to dominant culture and therefore anti-capitalist (until, that is, they are incorporated into capitalism) is more difficult to support when looking at the self-consciously entrepreneurial and label-conscious club cultures of the 1980s and 1990s (1995: 165–6).

The strong emphasis on resistances linked to a (masculine) class identity found in the cultural studies analyses produced during the 1970s also worked to marginalize other, equally important formations, such as ethnicity and gender, and the sometimes fraught and contradictory relationship between young women and the family. Paul Willis's *Learning to Labour* (1977), for example, tended to ignore or repress the ways in which the working-class lads it was concerned with took the subordinated place of women and girls for granted. As McRobbie observes in *Settling Accounts with Subcultures: A Feminist Critique* (1981), subcultural studies of this kind were largely gender-blind or failed to address or, in fact, take very much interest in the specific forms teenage girls' subcultures took. Similarly, Hebdige's interest in the uses made by British punks of reggae music did not address the question of how and why punk itself was primarily a white subculture, nor what the implications for differing forms of subordination might be when a white working-class identity was explicitly produced in relation to black music (Jones 1988).

The fragmentation of music styles and forms in the 1980s and 1990s, together with the relative residualization of overtly oppositional subcultures and the development of forms of 'extended adolescence' noted above, helps to point up, then, the way in which the specific emphasis of subcultural theory and its investment in a politics of resistance also romanticized white working-class masculinity in ways that were not dissimilar to the teenpic or rock music itself.

Female fandom: teenage girls as audiences

Teen screams

McRobbie's critique and later work on the relationship between constructions of gender and identity points to the way in which girls have had a profoundly problematic status within youth cultures and in the cultural construction of 'teenagerness' more generally. They became most visible in pop culture during the late 1950s and early 1960s, largely as fans rather than performers (notwithstanding the presence of some powerful female singers), usually as the weeping, screaming or hysterical crowds beloved of news reports and tabloid horror stories. That is, they were overwhelmingly represented as the consumers rather than the producers of cultural forms, and this status was habitually treated with the same disdain (and often outright contempt) reserved for mass culture itself. As Andreas Huyssen observes, 'the fear of the masses . . . is also always a fear of woman, a fear of nature out of control, a fear of the unconsious, of sexuality, of the loss of identity and stable ego boundaries in the mass' (1986: 52).

This culturally subordinated – yet economically essential – position is linked to the difficulty women traditionally have had in claiming the right to produce culture, and to femininity's location within an 'unproductive' domestic sphere. While the consumption of pop has invariaby been unthinkingly associated with a devalued, feminine or feminized audience, the production of music (and especially innovatory styles or genres) has, with some exceptions, nearly always been implicitly associated with the possession of phallic power. Yet the cultural figure of the teenage consumer also condenses many myths and fears about consumer culture and about the desires of teenage girls themselves.

The desiring/consuming role of the female fan is necessary, but also potentially socially destabilizing, since the consumption of popular culture always threatens to spill over into a more active threat to existing power relations, and fandom itself seems to both stage and subvert acceptable models of femininity, with its excessive emotion. Indeed, the idea of the fan has been powerfully dominated by media images of 'threatening' hordes of teenage girls, from Beatlemania in the early 1960s through to the Spice Girls and the boy bands of the 1990s.[3]

Teenage girl fans are problematic precisely because they noisily claim public space in ways that are customarily masculine and because they have effectively refused to produce themselves as passively ladylike. Ehrenreich et al. suggest that their own experience of Beatlemania in 1964 prefigured the affective discourse of sexual liberation and feminism: '[t]o abandon control – to scream, faint, dash about in mobs – was, in form if not in conscious intent, to protest the sexual repressiveness, the rigid double standard of female teen culture. It was the first and most dramatic uprising of *women's* sexual revolution' (1992: 85). Similarly, Sheryl Garratt remembers a bus ride from her home on a Birmingham housing estate into the city centre to see a Bay City Rollers concert as being equally empowering, and as having, 'an atmosphere like a cup final coach, but with all of us on the same side and with one even more radical difference – there were no boys' (1990: 399). In both of these examples, the collective experience of female fandom seems to prevail over any pleasures produced by the stars themselves; it is as though becoming a fan offers the only (barely) legitimate mode of expression for young women to experience 'excessive' behaviour and the subversion of social norms.

The specific social fears aroused by such fans were effectively if incoherently articulated in the curious British film, *Privilege* (1967), made in the aftermath of the heights of Beatlemania and presumably inspired by it. In a parable of the dangers to public stability posed by fan hysteria, the film combines a number of contemporary anxieties, including those aroused by the development of the counter-culture. It narrates the destructive havoc

Figure 5.3 The figure of the screaming female fan, here represented by girls at the Beatles' Shea Stadium concert in August 1965, became a symbol both of pop music's power and of a pathological adolescent femininity during the early 1960s. (Photo: © Bettman/CORBIS)

produced by a movement led by adoring and increasingly hysterical female fans, who, in their desire to possess a male pop star, treat him as a messiah and ultimately destroy both him and society.

Privilege's ready conflation of fandom with a specifically feminine combination of bodily excess and cerebral lack – in which the fan expresses emotions that are irrational and is readily subject to manipulation – is a central component of wider discourses around female consumption practices, which are often linked to the improper channelling of 'maternal' desires. Crying at the Beatles' pop concerts in the early 1960s, for example, was linked by a psychologist writing in the British tabloid newspaper, *The News of the World*, to the expression of latent maternal feelings: 'The girls are subconsciously preparing for motherhood. Their frenzied screams are a rehearsal for that moment' (quoted in Norman 1981: 212). The erotomania frequently implicitly ascribed to female fans is also naturalized as a symptom of the pathology of femininity. As Joli Jensen observes, in such discourses, 'as a member of a crowd, the fan becomes irrational, and thus easily influenced. If she is female, the image includes sobbing and screaming and fainting, and assumes that an uncontrollable erotic energy is sparked by the chance to see or touch a male idol' (1992: 15).

Female fandom, therefore, has been subjected to a degree of pathologization in which it has been explained both in terms of a natural expression of pent-up and specifically feminine emotions (usually linked to women's reproductive capacities) *and* as a form of deviance from conventionally feminine behaviour. By recuperating female fandom back into an already pathologizing discourse of maternal femininity, however, the teenage girl can also be safely returned to the family.

During the early 1970s, the pop music business attempted to recover the success of Beatlemania with pop groups and performers such as the Bay City Rollers and David Cassidy, whose 'pretty boy' looks and upbeat love songs were designed to appeal specifically to teenage girls. Chart-based pop dominated the music business and teenage girls – teenyboppers – were its primary market. This approach was revived in the 1990s with the invention of the slick and streamlined boy band, Take That, and their many imitators, whose fan base began at pre-pubescence rather than adolescence. In this way, despite the social anxieties and occasional media panics that continued to circulate around teenage fans, the cultural practice of fandom was increasingly recuperated as a normal aspect of female adolescence during the 1980s and 1990s. It was also linked to the construction of the teenage girl as an expert consumer – which boy band do *you* prefer? – within an increasingly proliferating market of potential choices and pleasures.

Girl power?

That said, and while there is a continuing tendency in popular psychology, social comment and pop's own discourse of itself to associate teenage fandom with an innate and uncritical form of consumerism, it is important to reiterate that real female fans have always been extraordinarily active and productive in their fandom, from customizing their bedrooms or clothing in imitation of their favourite stars to effectively 'stalking' male pop singers as sexual prey. As John Fiske observes: '[b]eing a fan involves active, enthusiastic, partisan, participatory engagement with the text' (1989: 147). Fan knowledge is itself a form of cultural capital, although it is rarely officially acknowledged as such. Indeed, the production of a particular kind of self-identity as a fan may be linked to the complex ways in which, in Mike Featherstone's (1991) term, everyday life can be 'aestheticized'. It is also powerfully connected to a sense of self-empowerment.

This aspect of teenage girls' engagement with pop music and its self-empowering possibilities became most visible in the extraordinary success of the Spice Girls during the late 1990s. Appealing primarily to the pre-pubescent and early adolescent female fan base that had, throughout the early part of the decade, provided a market for the boy bands discussed above, the success of the Spice Girls marked a crucial break in the traditional relationship – the romance narrative – between male performers and female fans. Rather than being represented purely as objects of desire (although they may well have been consumed in this way by fans), they offered their fans the pleasures of identification. For the first time, a female pop group dominated popular media by promising teenage fans both a collective identity, 'girl power', and clearly delineated individual roles for each of its members – Ginger, Sporty, Scary, Posh and Baby – that represented various (if decidedly reductive) versions of contemporary femininity.

The Spice Girls' mobilization of an ideal of female solidarity was, however, also explicitly linked to consumption and commodification. As Jude Davies points out:

> What makes the Spice Girls interesting . . . is the reciprocity they set up between the articulation of an explicit ideology, so-called 'girl power', and mass consumption . . . From their first appearance, girl power helped to sell Spice Girl product, while at the same time consumption of the group put girl power on the lips and in the minds of female youth.
>
> (Davies 1999: 160)

It is important to say, then, that although girl power appeared to offer a newly emancipatory discourse to female fans, and one that drew quite self-consciously on the language of feminism while being itself only problematically feminist, the primary mode by which the fan was supposed to produce herself remained consumption[4] – unsurprising, perhaps, given that the Spice Girls were supposed to sell records and merchandise above anything else, but important to reiterate in the context of the excitement they generated.

The Spice Girls did, however, effect an important intervention in the history of pop music, since they helped to open up the space for what Davies calls 'a youth-orientated genre of (mostly) girl-centred fun pop which remain[ed] hegemonic in March 1999' (1999: 169). The subsequent success of girl groups such as All Saints and Destiny's Child, and the importance of female-orientated pop in contemporary popular culture, suggests that this has been a significant shift in some ways, although it has accompanied the growing fragmentation of pop music more generally. Indeed, while the feminization (and infantilization) of chart-based pop in the 1990s tended to consolidate rather than recast the cultural and gendered oppositions around commercial and authentic forms of popular music noted earlier, it was also crucial to the changing articulation of female identities in popular culture.

Living for romance? Teenage magazines and adolescent femininities

It is perhaps ironic, then, that the teen magazines that were so central, not only to the success of the Spice Girls in the late 1990s, but also to the temporary hegemony of something called girl power, were already under siege by 2004. *Smash Hits, J17, Bliss* and *More* had been part of an important moment in discourses of youth and femininity, especially in their articulation of an ideology of self-empowerment that was itself as incoherent as the Spice Girls' lyrics, but which appeared to mark a radical departure from earlier, romance-based magazines for girls. By the early twenty-first century, however, the market for such publications was becoming as fragmented as that for pop music, as the range of commodities, texts and products aimed at a youth constituency increased and the restrictions under which the teen magazines had to operate made it more difficult to compete.

The history of cultural research into teenage girls' magazines dates back to the second moment of youth culture, the 1970s, and to the ground-breaking work of Angela McRobbie (1978) on the British magazine *Jackie*. McRobbie's analysis explored the extent to which such magazines represented an 'acceptable femininity' structured around romance and the desire to be desired, and the emotional and physical labour women must undertake to sustain relationships. Indeed, while the idea of the teenage male in *Jackie* was in some ways a positive and culturally productive figure – an aspirant pop star or tortured genius – his female counterpart was primarily defined in terms of lack, waiting for romance and for her 'life' to begin through the empowering touch of male desire. This is not to suggest that *Jackie*'s readers either responded to or were unproblematically called on by the romance narrative they were offered. *Jackie*'s success, however, does point to the importance romance had as part of the culture of femininity.[5]

Throughout the 1970s and 1980s, newer magazines such as *Blue Jeans* and *Just Seventeen*, although technically modernized through the introduction of photo stories and colour pictures, and culturally modified through the changing array of beauty products and featured pop star pin-ups, continued to figure the teenage reader as primarily concerned with the search for romance or, at least, a passable boyfriend. Alongside this, feminist cultural research built on and extended McRobbie's early work by exploring the ways in which such magazines articulated, negotiated or subverted the culture of femininity (Hermes 1995; McRobbie 1991, 1996; Walkerdine 1997; Winship 1987, 1991; Ferguson 1983).

During the 1990s, however, the emergence of a new style of teenage magazine, including *More!*, *Mizz* and *Minx*, that seemed to articulate a more fully modernized, sexually confident femininity, in contrast to the romance-focused texts of the 1970s and 1980s, was initially identified by cultural critics as marking a potential break with older patterns and a welcome shift in discourses of gender (McRobbie 1996). Offering a more overtly sexualized (but consistently *hetero*sexual) account of teenage femininity, these magazines also recognized the complexities involved in negotiating contemporary western societies for young women, and – like the Spice Girls – offered a cheerily challenging assertion of girl power that seemed partly to bridge the relationship between femininity and feminism. Despite these shifts, however, such teen magazines continued to represent femininity as both contingent – requiring constant attention, renewal and concern, especially self-surveillance and risk-prevention – and defined primarily in terms of consumption. Perhaps even more importantly for us here, in their powerful emphasis on emotional labour as part of the necessary work of femininity, they continued to prepare girls for mothering and responsibility for the welfare of the family, together with the ongoing problem of how girls could produce an 'acceptable' femininity that would secure male approval. 'Girls, it seemed, still had to know how to decode, and then manage, masculinity in appropriate ways if they were to function effectively in a patriarchal society' (Tincknell et al. 2003: 60).

Such struggles around the definition of teenage femininity took place within the context of continued anxieties about young women's sexuality and social power. Indeed, moral panics occasionally focused – in erratic and incoherent ways – on teenage magazines, as we have seen, identifying them as the source of the same problem that was perceived to have produced other eruptions of inappropriate feminine behaviour, such as teenage motherhood: that is, the availability of an excessive sexual knowledge among young women.

Despite the important role played by teenage magazines in the articulation of girl power during the late 1990s and their emphasis on individualist (albeit consumerist) models of femininity, the absence of any credible equivalent texts explicitly addressed to teenage boys suggested that enormous divergences between the social expectations produced around femininity and masculinity remained (see Chapter 2). The crisis in the teenage magazine market of the early 2000s may therefore be symptomatic of the cultural shifts in the production of the self and the development of a new configuration around adolescence/adulthood that has underlain the discussion in this chapter – and throughout this book.

Teenage genres, retro pleasures
Horror and the high school

If the teenpics and pop musicals of the 1950s and 1960s represented an early example of the way in which teenage culture and identity has been produced and differentially mediated by film texts, the re-emergence of horror as a film genre newly and primarily addressed to a teenage audience during the late 1970s, with the appearance of what became known as the 'slasher' film (in which teenage victims are systematically stalked and 'slashed'), is particularly interesting. Such texts articulate a number of the tensions already circulating about the relationship of the teenager to the institution of the family, but do so in relatively allusive ways.

The first slasher movie to be recognized as such was *Halloween* (1978), a film that consolidated some of the major themes of the genre. It was, however, prefigured by a number of earlier and highly influential texts that contained some of the elements that would become crucial conventions, including the graphically horrific *The Texas Chainsaw Massacre* (1974), a film that located the horror at the very centre of the family. *Psycho* (1960) is also recognized as a seminal influence, largely because of its still terrifying shower scene and daring narrative shifts. The film's anti-hero, Norman Bates, is also a close relation to the troubled figure of the sensitive delinquent in the social problem film; his murderousness is a symptom of a quasi-incestuous relationship with his mother and the psychological disturbance provoked by desire (see Chapter 1). *Carrie* (1976) also offered a rehearsal of the slasher film's visual foregrounding of the bodily grotesque and a characterization of its habitual *mise-en-scène*, including the rituals and habits of teenage life: the small town, the high school, the summer camp and dating, babysitting and the school prom.

Halloween drew on all these elements and reconstituted them in ways that both reworked and directly addressed the underlying preoccupations and fears that circulated around adolescent desire, disgust and fear. Significantly, it represents the small-town community as dominated by the teenagers who are the main characters in the narrative; adult men, in particular, are almost wholly absent. The film also focuses on a central female character, Laurie, whom Carol Clover (1992) identifies as the 'final girl' of the nascent genre. Laurie, in contrast to the other teenagers in the story, is studious, watchful and, crucially, sexually inactive, although she is hardly a passively virginal heroine waiting to be rescued. Indeed, in *Halloween,* as in other slasher films made during the late 1970s and early 1980s – such as *Friday the 13ᵗʰ* (1979), *Prom Night* (1980), *Graduation Day* (1981) and *A Nightmare on Elm Street* (1984) – the 'final girl' functions as a female hero. Her active resistance to the monstrous stalker who threatens the teenage community, together with the absence of an equivalent male figure and her own masculine characteristics, render her an interestingly ambiguous figure. Clover argues that, for the mainly adolescent male audience,

> the final girl is . . . a congenial double for the adolescent male. She is feminine enough to act out in a gratifying way, a way unapproved for adult males, the terrors and masochistic pleasures of the underlying fantasy, but not so feminine as to disturb the structures of male competence and sexuality.
>
> (Clover 1992: 51)

Almost without exception, the teenage community is represented as sexualized, amoral and pleasure-seeking, careless of itself and others until it is confronted by the slasher himself, whose mission is punishment and revenge. Moreover, the dominant mode of address developed in the slasher film, the repeated and almost unbearably sustained device of suspense, and its deployment of the killer's point of view as an identificatory motif, make the narrative pleasures being offered to the teenage audience decidedly complex. In both *Halloween* and *Friday the 13th,* for example, active teenage sexuality is brutally punished by the killer, whose dispatch of copulating couples caught *in flagrante* is graphically and spectacularly staged for the camera. The significance of the slasher film as a genre addressed to a teenage audience, yet offering few of the conventional reassurances of the teenpic, is critical to the development of cultural configurations of adolescence. The films stage and spectacularize the punishment of teenage sexuality in an apparent nod to traditional morality, yet do so by isolating the teenage community from wider social relations.

Although the slasher movie had become largely residualized as a genre by the end of the 1980s, with a train of largely mechanistic sequels imitating what had been stylistically and narratively innovatory a decade earlier, it was recovered by postmodernism in the 1990s. A new wave of knowingly excessive horror films, including the *Scream* trilogy (1996–99) and *I Know What You Did Last Summer* (1997), successfully reinvigorated the genre by multiplying the elements to the point of parody. Interestingly, in postmodern texts of this kind, the teenage community is represented not simply as inevitable and unknowing victims but as sophisticated readers of horror itself. In a key scene in *Scream,* for example, the teenage 'experts' gather to watch *Halloween,* and argue over its generic codes and audience expectations – and are then duly dispatched by the killer in a moment of self-referential humour that is further compounded by our awareness that the real cinema audience for the series will be as knowing about the text as the characters who have just been murdered. By uncoupling knowledge from power in this way, however, postmodern slasher films have further problematized the desirability of adult status and social responsibility. If knowing about the world doesn't protect you from danger, then other kinds of social power also seem to be devalued.

Reunions and revivalism

The odd mix of cultural knowingness about film, fashion and performance and nostalgia for a past moment of youth that marked the postmodern slasher movie also appeared in the late 1990s in films that, in an intensive acceleration of revivalism, revisited 1980s youth culture. Films such as *Grosse Pointe Blank* (1997), *Romy and Michelle's High School Reunion* (1997) and *The Wedding Singer* (1998), while inflecting the theme of cultural nostalgia in different ways, all featured a return to the music, fashions and, most importantly, the 'affective moment' of the 1980s. Indeed, the main characters have never left youth behind: Robbie in *The Wedding Singer* spends his life as a cabaret artist performing covers of Culture Club numbers; Romy and Michelle share an apartment and an attachment to 'valley girl speak' that situates them as barely adult; and Martin Blank has never got over the loss of his high school girlfriend. In each of these texts, the years of adolescence represent unfulfilled longings that the narrative sets out to resolve by making its characters return to the locus of trauma: the high school. The metaphor of the school reunion is therefore one of the ways in which nostalgia for the moment of youth is not simply staged, but elaborately and lovingly narrated.

As Lesley Speed (29: 2000) argues, in such texts an extended youth is depicted as the solution to adult problems, since it is by refusing to abandon attachments to the cultural identities forged at school that the protagonists finally win through. The problematic relationship between knowledge, power and a fully adult subjectivity, also alluded to by postmodern slasher films, is therefore dealt with by magical resolutions that allow the main characters to enjoy adolescence indefinitely.

Teensoaps in the twenty-first century: cool conservatism?

This cultural ambivalence around adulthood was also important to the development in the 1990s and 2000s of a new kind of hybrid television drama – part soap opera, part horror – that solicited a culturally sophisticated teenage audience but was also watched by adult viewers. As Zoe Williams points out, *Buffy the Vampire Slayer* in particular, had a broad audience appeal that made its precise status difficult to determine, and an appropriate television slot hard to decide: 'Ever since *Buffy* started in the UK, there have been scheduling difficulties (teatime or post-pub?) that were ultimately resolved by showing it twice, the late show without the pre-watershed edits' (2001: 17).

The appearance of other compellingly watchable teen soaps, such as the Buffy spin-off, *Angel*, and *Smallville*, *Charmed* and *Dawson's Creek*, came in the wake of the international success of *Friends*, a sitcom that eschewed the tradition of the nuclear family as its conventional situation, in favour of a quasi-family of six twentysomethings, enjoying the kind of extended adolescence discussed above. *Friends* revolved around the deferral of family commitment in favour of the perpetuation of pre-familial ties, so that although its six main characters were in their late twenties, their preoccupations and habits seemed hardly to have changed since they were teenagers. The teen dramas take this tendency further by making teenagers themselves and, perhaps, the affective sensibility of teenagerdom – the emotional intensity and dramatic shifts from happiness to misery – their material.

Buffy, the Vampire Slayer draws on some of the elements found in the postmodern horror film, especially an ironic knowingness about adult society, but returns these to an older version of the genre, gothic horror, which is reshaped for a contemporary audience. In *Buffy* the threat of excessive, supernatural and murderous power is no longer located *outside* the community of teenagers, but within it, signified by the mutation of 'ordinary' teenage kids into vampires. Yet Buffy herself has even greater powers: although she is also a 'regular' kind of girl, she can slay vampires. And, although *Buffy*, like the slasher movie, is located in a small-town community, culturally dominated by teenagers, the final girl – Buffy herself – is empowered not only to defend herself but also to protect the family and the whole community. Her vampire-slaying is a duty to wider society rather than simply a form of extra personal protection. Buffy is helped in this apparently endless battle by the cultivated figure of her school librarian – a man whose Englishness codes him as having privileged access to the civilized, book-based knowledge (and the ego) that is represented as crucial to the defeat of evil, the id, represented by the vampires. This alliance between the virtuous Buffy and the forces of cultural authority thus suggests that the values being defended are themselves conservative. Paradoxically, at the beginning of the twenty-first century, one of the most powerful images of the teenager to appear on television is that of Buffy, the defender of social order.

The programme's most obviously radical move, then, is to make a teenage girl the hero, but Buffy herself is in other respects wholly unthreatening. She is small, slim, blonde and conventionally attractive, and the star, Sarah Michelle Gellar, has been successfully recovered as an object of desire as well as a post-feminist icon. Furthermore, *Buffy* is also resolutely monocultural. Where black characters appear, they are largely incorporated into the whiteness of small-town culture and their presence is, at best, gestural. This conservatism indicates the extent to which a text like *Buffy*, for all its apparent radicalism in terms of shifts in gender roles, is able to subvert some of the conventions around contemporary culture only by reasserting others.

Conclusion

In these texts, then, the responsibility for the continuation of social relations and what are profoundly conservative values is loaded onto the shoulders of the teenage characters who, in a significant cultural shift, are represented as both more reliable than their adult peers and certainly more pivotal to the future of the community. Like the emergent child consumer-citizen, the new teenager stands oddly (and permanently) poised between youth and adulthood. This 'cool conservatism' is a remarkable symptom of the cultural journey the teenager has taken, but it is also a sign of the extent to which a flight from adulthood, and certainly from conventional versions of the family, is a central component of contemporary culture.

Notes

1 A story in the *Daily Mail* of 4 November 1999, for example, used material from a report on teenage mothering by The Policy Studies Institute to make a clear, ideologically driven link between what it described as 'traditional values' in sexual behaviour (that is, marriage) and long-term health and happiness.

2 Andy Medhurst points out in his amusing account of the British film industry's frequently comically inept and ideologically incoherent attempts to make pop musicals, 'It Sort of Happened Here: the Strange, Brief Life of the British Pop Film', that in *Beat Girl*, 'the beat-crazy kids [are] evicted by David Farrar . . . with the treasurable line "Get out of my house, you jiving, drivelling scum"' (1995: 65). Obviously aiming to please the kids and their parents!

3 In fact, despite its mythologized status, Beatlemania was not wholly unprecedented, although its scale was what made it seem particularly threatening. Similar scenes of female public hysteria had marked the success of earlier music stars with sex appeal, such as Frank Sinatra and Johnny Ray, and, famously, had been part of the public mourning of the silent film star, Rudolph Valentino, in 1926. It was just that there were *more* Beatles fans and they were overwhelmingly teenage girls.

4 Jude Davies goes on to explore in some detail the highly slippery and incoherent character of the Spice Girls' politics and relationship to feminism in some detail, pointing out that they claimed that being a Spice Girl was 'like feminism – but you don't have to burn your bra', as well as asserting in an interview in the right-wing journal, *The Spectator*, that Lady Thatcher was 'the first Spice Girl', much to the delight of the British Conservative Party (1999: 167–9).

5 As someone who intermittently read but did not buy *Jackie* as a teenager, I can remember my own conflicted attitude to the magazine: engaged by but contemptuous of its insistence on romance because I had invested in other values (literary ones, mainly), but also fascinated by the problem pages and their dilemmas.

chapter six

Family pathologies and pluralities: reinventing the family from the 1970s to the 1990s

Introduction

The 1990s and 2000s have been interesting times for the family, marked by contradictory moves around its configuration and mediation. The radical pluralization of family structures and relationships has been accompanied by continued struggles over parenting and various attempts to return to debates about the value of the nuclear model. Conservative commentators and politicians (of both right and left), have argued that the family is under siege or is becoming inappropriately feminized through divorce and single parenting, and that it must not be allowed to change; even though, as we have seen, families have always been dynamic rather than static in structure, and the nuclear ideal is itself the product of a very specific moment in modernity (see, for example, the British columnist, Melanie Philips, in the *Daily Mail*, and Philips' book, *The Sex Change Society*, 1999).

The 1990s also saw further political intervention at the level of government policies intended to shore up the nuclear family in the face of these shifts in social relations and sexual identities, such as the UK government's 'Supporting Families' initiative in 1999. As Elizabeth B. Silva and Carol Smart point out, commenting on Tony Blair's first major conference speech as prime minister in 1997, which prefigured this, political rhetoric about the family tends to cast it, still, in singular, very particular, often nostalgic terms in which 'strong families are . . . seen as conjugal, heterosexual parents with an employed male breadwinner. Lone mothers and gay couples do not, by definition, constitute strong families in [Blair's] rhetoric. On the contrary, they are part of the problem' (1998: 3).

Yet politicians have also begun to recognize, somewhat tentatively, that a conservative rhetoric of family values and of a single, traditional version of the family cannot be very comfortably reconciled with the material social changes that are taking place around family relations, including perhaps within their own lives. Indeed, as heterosexual couples resist or defer marriage and lesbian and gay relationships become more socially embedded as part of the pluralization of society, the monolithic model of an ideal family becomes increasingly difficult to sustain ideologically (Weeks et al. 2000: 84). While the family has become increasingly feminized, alternative models of intimacy and sociality have also developed alongside it.

At the same time, as divorce has become more common and as families have been extended, redefined and rethought, the relationship between heterosexual individuals and parenting has become more fraught. As we saw in Chapter 3, men's rights to parent, to develop a nurturing relationship with their children and to engage with a more complex model of fathering have been important sites of struggle over the last two decades. All of these concerns have, in different ways, figured in the cultural work being carried out in relation to family relations. Indeed, while households built around looser networks of friendship, non-marital sexual relations and same-sex relationships continue to be treated as a social threat in some parts of the media, in many others the possibilities that such ties promise has been celebrated.

This chapter will consider the relationship between changing models of the family and the contradictory accounts of those changes in media representations. It will focus, in particular, on Hollywood's sometimes troubled charting of the family romance from the 1970s to the 1990s, and on television's equally complex representations of family relationships and its articulation of some important discursive shifts in the idea of the family.

Families of choice, friends and neighbours

The sheer range of representations of *non-familial* relationships in the media and on film is symptomatic of these cultural shifts, as are the contradictions we can find in familial narratives and in the attempts to hold in tension competing versions of family life. Indeed, the overwhelming popularity of media texts which feature – and celebrate – friendship and flexible networks of relationships as a legitimate alternative to the family suggests that these transformations have already been recognized as an enduring feature of contemporary life. One symptom of this is that the most memorable (and, significantly, globally successful) American sitcoms produced during the 1990s and into the early 2000s, such as *Friends*, *Seinfeld*, *Ellen*, *Sex and the City* and *Will and Grace*, while in many respects highly diverse in their take on American life, were united in their emphasis on an urban (rather than suburban) milieu, and in their celebration of friendship and plural sexualities rather than – or as well as – family ties.

Sociologists such as Anthony Giddens (1999) have been particularly interested in these transformations in private life, intimacy and gender relations, arguing that such changes represent a democratization of the emotions. For Giddens, 'chosen' relationships are in some ways superior to kinship structures because they operate through negotiation and personal values, offering what he calls a 'pure' relationship (1992), rather than one embedded in patriarchal familialism or in the social expectations of modernity. While it is important to note that this claim seems to uncritically endorse (rather than interrogate) emergent western relationship models that may seem rather less pure to other observers, there can be little doubt that this change is both real and culturally significant. The fluidity and contingency of such relationships thus articulates the increasing lack of fixity found in postmodern social relations. It is also linked to the development of postmodern models of sexuality and identity in which the self is no longer taken to be an essential and predetermined entity, but rather something that we continuously produce and perform, especially in the context of gendered subjectivities, as Judith Butler has argued (1990).

This shift within postmodernity, towards a *recognition* of contingency and performance in the production of gender (signified perhaps by the greater visibility of various forms of drag), has thus also informed the ways in which ideas about the family as a natural, timeless and exclusively heterosexual structure can be thought out. If the self is neither essential nor simply socially determined, our relationship to the institution of the family, which effectively mediates and manages the link between the personal and the social, becomes harder to fix, too.

At the same time, the powerful appeal of the idea of family has retained its allure, even when it has been considerably reconfigured. Far from disappearing or collapsing, the family is undergoing a further set of transformations produced by the shifts in expectations around intimacy and gender noted above. As Silva and Smart argue, 'families remain a crucial relational entity playing a fundamental part in the intimate life of and connections between individuals' (1998: 5). The right of same-sex couples to be recognized as families, and to bear or adopt children, is one of the ways in which the idea of the family has been recast in this way, and this claim has partly been enabled through the deployment of an extended discourse of individual choice, as well as by the further individualization of the language of rights.

One example of this was the high-profile case of a British gay couple, Tony Barlow and Barrie Drewitt, who, in 1999, paid an American surrogate mother to conceive twins for them. The British press and, in particular, the right-wing papers that had made the issue of the future of the family so central to their position, rushed to condemn the two men, as Deborah Chambers (2001) explores. The problems the couple encountered in adopting the twins and then bringing them to the UK were closely monitored, and indeed intensified and 'worked over', by the British media in various ways. Yet the underlying claim being made was a highly significant one: it was that 'families of choice', whatever their kinship structure or lack of it, were as legitimate as sites for the care and nurture of children as any other kind of family. Indeed, the case also importantly marked a moment in which, in a sense, the politics of homosexuality had publicly moved into the politics of marriage. The anxieties that surrounded the case and its centrality to a moral panic about same-sex marriages and parental rights were not simply evidence of a predictable backlash, or even of the continued dominance of conventionalized family models; instead, they seemed to suggest that these transformations in the family were already taking place and would continue to do so, in spite of the repressive apparatus of the state, and in resistance to the excesses of media hysteria.[1]

Crisis, what crisis? Hollywood and the family from the 1970s to the 1990s
Goodbye to all that

If the popular saga of the 1980s struggled to claim a space for maternal and family values, both in the capitalist project and within a masculine public sphere, as we have seen, it may be interesting to begin by considering the ways in which Hollywood films dealt with the critique of the family presented by feminism, and the changes taking place in sexual and gender relations during the same period. Up until the late 1960s, Hollywood had continued to make films that 'solved' the problem of desire through marriage, although these became fewer in the emergent context of youth culture's increasing dominance and the discourse of sexual liberation. Indeed, the relaxation of censorship in mainstream films, together with the reinvention of genres such as the gangster movie (*Bonnie and Clyde*, 1967) and, crucially, the loss of women as audiences for cinema, also led to the gradual disappearance of 'women's films'. Just as Hollywood 'discovered' the teenager in the 1950s, by the early 1970s it had concluded that its target audience was now mainly young and male (Maltby 2003: 21). Not only was this marked by the lack of films specifically addressed to female audiences, but it also informed the ways in which women were represented more generally – as sexual objects or abject victims – and the range of themes and ideas that were explored.

Yet, as with earlier cultural configurations of youth, childhood and marriage itself, the emergence of a new discourse was at least temporarily accompanied by the residual presence of an older emphasis on family values and sexual monogamy. For example, *Bob and Carol and Ted and Alice* (1969), which simultaneously parodied and celebrated the sexual freedoms of the Californian 'swinger' culture, and the paradigmatic buddy film, *Butch Cassidy and the Sundance Kid* (1969), both came just a year after Doris Day's last film, *With Six You Get Egg Roll* (1968), which was a fairly old-fashioned romantic comedy, even though the Day character was now widowed (not, of course, divorced) and the story revolved (fashionably) around the problem of uniting two existing families through remarriage.

However, romantic comedy more generally began a marked decline during this period, as its traditional preoccupation – the difficulty of desire – and solution – marriage – assumed a range of new articulations. The urbane yet troubled 'nervous romances' of the 1970s, such as *Semi-Tough* (1972) and *Annie Hall* (1977), were therefore faced with two difficulties. First, there was what Frank Krutnik calls the 'wrecked vessels of old romantic discourse' (1998: 18), which meant they were unable to call on the certainties of marriage and true love. Second, there was also a fresh candidness around sexuality, and an intensified pathologization of its nature, newly articulated by pornography. Furthermore, when these films attempted to portray the family at all, they tended to represent it in implicitly negative ways, as the site of a hopelessly unresolved primal trauma or as an institution in which youthful creativity and energy would inevitably become sapped, suppressed or stifled (see, for example, *The Graduate*, 1969 and *Annie Hall*). The idea that marriage and the reconstitution of the family in the form of a new pairing between lovers represented a satisfactory resolution to romance thus became increasingly difficult to sustain.

'Ordinary people'

While strong central roles for women tended to be scarce during the mid- and late 1970s because of the decline in the traditional woman's film, a few important films appeared that showcased in newly naturalistic ways the 'ordinary' lives of working-class women, as workers and as mothers. *Alice Doesn't Live Here Anymore* (1974), directed by Martin Scorsese (who has shown little interest in female characters since), *An Unmarried Woman* (1978) and *Norma Rae* (1979), all represented a significant attempt to address the space of women's experience – especially in the context of changing attitudes to divorce and feminist claims to sexuality – and to do so within the terms of a new cinematic realism. Yet the relative paucity of examples of such films (and of others made by female directors, in particular) is symptomatic of the way in which this brief, conjunctural moment of feminism (if it can be described as such) was produced by specific factors.

It happened largely because the economic, cultural and political shifts within American society that had enabled feminism, gay liberation, black power and the counter-culture to gather momentum also coincided with significant structural and economic changes within the Hollywood system, leading to the emergence of new styles of film-making, production and distribution. At such times, it is not unusual for new voices to be heard and new ways of telling stories to emerge, but such emergences are often brief and violently struggled over. The 'New Hollywood' that developed out of these conditions during the early 1970s expressed some of these counter-cultural ideals and also – for a time – drew on the aesthetic and political concerns of European art cinema, reframing these for an American context in order to re-imagine genre, narrative and, indeed, issues of heroic causality and meaning (Smith 1998).

Films such as *Five Easy Pieces* (1970) and *McCabe and Mrs Miller* (1971) deliberately eschewed the closure of happy endings, especially in the form of marriage, motherhood and suburban contentment. They also sometimes exacerbated the counter-culture's tendency towards misogynistic representation of women (especially mothers) as neurotic, possessive and unstable.[2] Indeed, by the early 1980s, the political emergence of neo-conservatism in the form of Reaganism coincided with a slew of 'boys own' stories and a return to genre cinema heralded by the success of George Lucas's *Star Wars* (1977) and Steven Spielberg's *Raiders of the Lost Ark* (1981), together with the advent of the action-adventure movie, in which muscled heroes played by Bruce Willis and Arnold Schwarzenegger dominated the available narrative and visual space. In all of these, the family was either an institution to be escaped from, an ideal to be rescued (but hardly explored) or an absence (see also Chapter 4, for a more detailed discussion of the family film in the 1990s).

Despite this, 1980 saw the release of a film that looked to classical Hollywood not only for its production values but also for its political and ideological account of the family. *Ordinary People* seemed to mark a return to the middle classes as Hollywood's *locus classicus* in its exploration of a family's emotional breakdown after the death by drowning of the eldest son, and was rewarded with four Oscars. As Richard Maltby observes, 'its thematic focus on the affluent but troubled was a marked change from Hollywood's representation of more working-class milieux in the 1970s, and its tightly constructed plot also signalled a shift away from the more expansive structures of that decade's road and odyssey pictures' (2003: 358–9). The film was therefore celebrated for its complex exploration of psychological trauma and what was taken as a return to the narrative values of the past. Yet, it not only effectively silences its main female character, the mother, Beth (Mary Tyler Moore), as its trajectory proceeds, but also locates her as spatially isolated in the way in which it frames and places her. Maltby points out that this 'registers Beth as the movie's persistent victim, deprived of the representational rights accorded to the rest of her family' (364). Indeed, the ideological emphasis of the film is to reinforce this isolation by showing Beth's refusal to come to terms with her responsibility for the family's dissolution. It ends with her leaving, while her husband and son are reconciled.

Ordinary People's success seemed to mark the reassertion of the domain of middle-class family life in a number of other films about other 'ordinary' people (that is, not black or gay or working class), such as *Table for Five* (1983) and even *Fatal Attraction* (1987). However, in contrast to earlier family dramas and comedies, the family stories of the late 1970s and early 1980s took the *breakdown* of the middle-class white family as a new given. These films also effectively linked that process to feminist-driven changes in society, such as new divorce rights and control over fertility. The decision to leave home that had been (tentatively) represented in earlier texts as the assertion of new and recognized rights for women was now transformed into a morally incriminating act. In *Kramer vs Kramer* (1979), for example, a bitter divorce and custody battle is explicitly offered as the consequence of a discontented (lesbian) wife's decision to leave, and the story is largely told from the point of view of the husband. For Andrew Britton, both *Ordinary People* and *Kramer vs Kramer* represented a tawdry apology for patriarchy: 'the woman, the value of whose independence has already been undermined, is denied as well even her traditional sphere of competence, and is left, as the endings of both films make very clear, with absolutely nowhere to go' (1986: 24). In such films, the 'crisis in the family' was clearly ascribed to changes in women's lives and behaviour.

'Ordinary people' II: subversions or affirmations?

Throughout the 1980s, the white, bourgeois nuclear family retained its discursive status as a cultural norm, however tarnished. By the late 1990s and into the early twenty-first century, however, this seemed to be much more precarious. *American Beauty* (2000), for example, was offered and largely read as a ruthless yet empathetic dissection of the emptiness at the heart of American family life and of middle-class values, perhaps even of the American Dream itself. It was also seen as a symptomatic text of the crisis in (bourgeois) masculinity. The film charts the emotional breakdown of its middle-aged and middle-class central character, Lester Burnham (Kevin Spacey), who, despised by his family, deliberately loses his job as an advertising executive and plunges into a series of lurching sexual misunderstandings and despair. Lester begins by lusting after his teenage daughter's friend, whom he fantasizes about in a sequence of surreal montages, and ends with a tragic encounter with his neighbour, a closet homosexual. As the film proceeds, we see his wife's obsessive materialism and concern for appearances precipitate into hatred for Lester, while his daughter conducts a clandestine relationship with a boyfriend whose own apparent emotional inscrutability is gradually revealed to be the consequence of a brutally excessive patriarchal power.

Throughout the film, the metaphor of the 'American Beauty', a deep, blowzily-red rose, stands for the surface brightness of American suburban life, and the rottenness at its core. Burnham dies because there is nothing to live for within the life he has. The film's centring of Lester, including the use of his voice-over at the beginning, in a credit sequence that pans over leafy suburban streets while on the soundtrack he matter-of-factly informs us that he will be dead by the following year, is reminiscent of *Sunset Boulevard*'s (1950) audacious deployment of a 'dead' man to frame its story. And Lester's reliability as a narrator is similarly untrustworthy. Yet *American Beauty*'s demonization of the suburbs is hardly original (we can find such fears as far back as John Buchan's novel, *The 39 Steps*, in 1918); nor is its implicit conflation of the suburban with a culturally devalued feminine (Carolyn, Lester's wife, exchanges tips on gardening with the Burnhams' domestically content gay next-door neighbours) and its suggestion that Lester has somehow become trapped in a way of life that is beyond his intervention.

Furthermore, not only is Carolyn (Annette Bening) represented in the depressingly familiar terms of the neurotically controlling middle-aged wife, but Lester's sexual fantasies about the child-woman teenager who is his daughter's best friend, Angela (Mena Suvari), although presented as the product of his own frustrations, are so lyrical in their visual evocation that we may forget to consider the problematic gender politics involved. Lester's desire is, it seems, symptomatic of his age (and perhaps his own anxiety about this in a youth-dominated culture) and therefore explicable, or at least understandable. Lester even abandons his 'grown-up' job and goes to work in a drive-in burger bar, alongside the teenagers and gap-year adolescents with whom he identifies.

Indeed, even before the credits begin, the film opens with a scene that is not only deliberately placed out of sequence in order to establish an enigma but also intimates the text's underlying ideological tendency, by privileging the perspective of teenage characters: a lovers' conversation and apparent murder plan between two young people, whom we only later come to know as Lester's daughter, Jane (Thora Birch), and the neighbour, Ricky Fitt (Wes Bentley). By the end of the film it has become clear that this takes place towards the end, not the beginning of the story, and is a key moment in which moral seriousness is being explored and tested rather than abandoned. If anything, *American Beauty*'s moral centre thus lies with Ricky rather than with Lester or any other of the adults, as his confident dismissal of Angela's empty valley-girl desirability indicates.

The film's complex narrative layering also obscures the extent to which it privileges a masculine viewpoint and, indeed, a male gaze. Ricky's possession of a digital camera through which he (and the audience) observes and records his neighbours – and Jane in particular – is a device that by the end of the film has come to stand for the text's own preferred perspective, as well as naturalizing Ricky's ownership of the powerfully controlling and voyeuristic gaze. It ensures that, although the failed patriarchs, Lester and Colonel Fitts, are dead or defeated, Ricky is licenced to appropriate the power that patriarchy confers. In this way, *American Beauty*, like other recent texts about the family, partially decentres adult consciousness and subjectivity, replacing it with the privileged perspective of the teenager, while also shifting – and redefining – the terms of masculine ownership of discourse.

American Beauty's elegiac reflection on the pathology of the white middle-class family is therefore not quite an obituary. While the materialistic values and pointless ambitions of the suburban bourgeoisie are relentlessly exposed, Ricky's own ingenuity as an entrepreneur – he is a very wealthy drug-dealer – together with the way in which Jane readily agrees to leave with him for New York, suggest that the film actually does not want to abandon individualism or even the conventionalized heterosexual couple as its central focus. Jane's rebellion does not take her much beyond Angela's despised desire to be desired in the end, while Ricky has the makings of a young Bill Gates, if only he can get into something legal. Indeed, the critical success of the film, like that of *Ordinary People* 20 years before, suggests that the discursively privileged status of the bourgeois family and its representation as somehow 'standing for' the culture more generally has not entirely disappeared.

'New' Hollywood: decentring the family?

During the early 1990s, a 'new' New Hollywood, largely consisting of film-makers operating outside the conventional economic structures and playing with traditional narrative and stylistic conventions, such as Quentin Tarantino, Greg Araki and the Coen brothers, emerged. Such directors (with the occasional exception of the Coens) continued the tendency, found in mainstream 1970s cinema, to marginalize women, producing films that, through their exploration of bonds between men within work or criminal networks, managed the problem of men's relations with women and with the family by evading a direct exploration of the latter or by privileging it as a site of homosocial relationships, as in the long cycle of gangster movies that appeared throughout the 1990s (including *Goodfellas*, 1990, *Reservoir Dogs*, 1992 and *Casino*, 1995).

It is, of course, possible to identify in such texts a relationship to the complex working through of the claims and disavowals surrounding fatherhood (noted in Chapter 3), particularly in their elaborate over-determination of phallic patriarchy. However, Sharon Willis argues that *Pulp Fiction* (1994), which engages with the gangster genre while not wholly being part of it, is overshadowed throughout by an authoritative but unseen 'mother' in the form of Bonnie, the black woman whose house must be cleaned of blood by the inept hit men, Jules and Vincent, who have accidently killed their accomplice. For Willis, the scene 'discloses a central motivation for the film's excesses, playing with what you wouldn't want Mom to see or hear: shit, genitals, and obscene language. Such a reading is consistent with the status of feminine authority in the Bonnie situation' (2000: 289). Yet even if this ascribes power to a black mother figure, it cannot adequately represent her, nor does it seek to do so.

In some films produced under the independent rubric, female characters have been located at a distance from or placed only contingently within family structures, so that the woman's relationship to patriarchy – if not overtly challenging – was at least critical. One of the most interesting examples of this appears in the Coen brothers' *Fargo* (1996), in which

Frances McDormand plays the role of Marge Gunderson, the chief of police in the small, snowbound town where a series of murders are being committed. Crucially, Marge's pregnancy is foregrounded throughout the film. As Hilary Radner says, 'her body makes demands – she constantly eats – she vomits – she sleeps – she dresses; this body is obtrusive and conspicuous' (1998: 254). But it is not conspicuous in the way that female bodies are generally required to be in Hollywood cinema, that is, as an object of desire. As Radner goes on to point out, Marge represents the law, not desire, and it is her job to make sense of what has taken place and to restore order. The location of a woman within such a position in a relatively mainstream text is itself unusual. Even where female police officers feature or are permitted some degree of agency, their ability to act is often undercut or framed by the more powerful agency of men in conventional film narratives. But Marge works against this and 'takes the [frontier] legend into custody in order to institute the law of women' (1998: 257). In addition, here, Marge's autonomy is in some ways emphasized by her pregnancy and by its signification of her body as something other than an object of desire. Although the film ends with Marge at home in bed, with her dull, endearing but undoubtedly unassertive husband, Norm, there is a sense that, rather than being simply returned to the family, Marge's right and ability to operate in the public sphere has been affirmed. Even so, *Fargo* depends on a particular and deliberate claim to public space being made that partly calls attention to the extent to which women's relationship to the familial and to paid work continues to be cast as a problem.

A more radical, if in some ways submerged, destabilization and reworking of sexuality and identity appeared in *Being John Malkovich* (1999), although this was not emphasized in its critical reception. The film's representation of gender, and indeed identity in its wider sense, not only subverted the idea of an essential self, through its conceit that its characters might temporarily occupy (and 'peform') Malkovich's body by accessing him through a portal in an office wall, but it also overturned conventional representations of the relationship between sex and desire. The two main female characters discover their own desire for each other by inhabiting 'Malkovich's' desire, and by enacting it in making love. Whether in so doing they are expressing something called lesbian desire or a fundamental bisexuality the film doesn't tell us and it doesn't seem to matter. The women abandon the nervous and conflicted male puppeteer who initially brought them together, in order to set up home as a couple and raise a daughter, as the final scenes of the film reveal. This coda seems to suggest that forming a happy family has little to do with the assertion of male desire or even heteronormativity. Instead, the fluidity of contemporary family relations is beautifully suggested by the rippling images of water and of the delighted cries of the child as she splashes in a swimming pool.

Thus, while the New Hollywood of the 1990s was very far from representing women in ways that might be seen to be unproblematically feminist, the opening up of some of its structures and, in particular, the emergence of independent films (however difficult these are to define) made some space for representations of femininity that resisted conformity and even began to explore the possibilities of unconventional parenthood and new styles of family.

Mainstream Hollywood: problematising the family
Absent mothers and bad nannies

Anxieties about the family resurfaced, however, in some examples of mainstream cinema in a new form during the 1990s, one that drew in part on the tradition of the melodrama, in part on the thriller and at crucial moments on the gothic horror film (prefigured, perhaps, by *Rosemary's Baby* (1968), which articulates profound anxieties about the maternal body). Lucy Fischer points to the way in which, in the early part of the decade, a range of scare stories about 'killer nannies' appeared in the American tabloid newspapers and elsewhere, many of which implicitly blamed women with 'careers' for abandoning their traditional duties and endangering their children. As Fischer observes, 'one is reminded that in *Mary Poppins* the demand for a nanny was spurred by Mrs. Banks's feminist activities. Hence women's rights have always been seen to imperil children' (1996: 134). Indeed, the conflicted relationship between the demand for women's and children's rights may be seen to be central to contemporary panics about the family, and especially about its perceived dysfunctionality.

Fischer goes on to identify some of the films that appeared in the context of the panic about the nanny (as well as other carers, such as babysitters and minders), all of which played with the possibility that children were constantly and inherently at risk – even if this was registered in comic terms. Both *Home Alone* (1990) and *Don't Tell Mom the Babysitter's Dead* (1991), for example, imply that mothers are, ultimately, more responsible for children than fathers (and this despite the claims to new fathering that were repeatedly made during the same decade).

Social fears about the danger of allowing another woman into the marital home as a carer for your child because you are a 'working mother' were most powerfully and threateningly articulated in the thriller, *The Hand That Rocks the Cradle* (1992). In this film, a well-off middle-class couple, Claire and Michael Bartel (Annabella Sciorra and Matt McCoy), are deceived into employing 'Peyton Flanders' (Rebecca DeMornay) as the nanny for their newborn son, unaware that she is out for revenge on the woman who reported her gynaecologist husband for sexual misconduct during a physical examination. The film presents the two women as parallels: both are pregnant at the same time, but Peyton, or Mrs Mott as she is properly called, miscarries as a result of the shock of her husband's disgrace and later suicide. Determined to destroy Claire for what she has done, Peyton insinuates herself into the family, and into the confidence not only of Claire but of Michael, too, whom she attempts to seduce. Perhaps most disturbingly for a contemporary audience, she also nurses Claire's child from her own breasts (full of milk for the lost child) in order to steal him from his mother.

In all of this, once Peyton is installed in the family home, only Claire's older child, Emma, and the black handyman, Solomon (Ernie Hudson), seem to sense that she is potentially dangerous, and respond to her with apprehension, but their lack of power within the family makes it impossible for them to intervene. The film stages these encounters through a series of tropes drawn from the gothic thriller – shadows, night-time encounters, even the house itself where the Bartels live – that heighten the tension, and the intensity, of the situation. Indeed, by offering mothering through the dual figures of the good and bad mother, it also reworks the gothic model of a split feminine self or subjectivity.

As Fischer points out, the responsibility for Peyton's deception is entirely loaded onto Claire, who is represented as weak, and therefore an inadequate mother in several ways, subject to fits of asthma that make it difficult for her to care for her children and unable to judge Peyton's true character. This weakness climaxes in Peyton's attempts to wrest Claire's children and husband away from her, having already murdered the one person with enough influence to alter Claire's attitude, her astute and suspicious best friend, Marlene. For Fischer, 'Peyton is every woman's nightmare babysitter – a phantom figure that fuels maternal guilt for the sin of independence' (1996: 140). It is only by recovering her strength as a mother – both morally and literally in a fight with Peyton – that Claire can claim her family back.

The figure of the working mother thus remained as problematic to much mainstream cinema during the 1980s and 1990s as she had been in earlier moments in cultural history. Perhaps the main difference was the way in which the narrative space to explore this was expanded; but occupation of narrative centrality was often accompanied by a renewed emphasis on female neurosis, albeit in a modified form. For example, *Baby Boom* (1988) begins with its female yuppie heroine, J. C. Wiatt, played by Diane Keaton, as a neurotic, driven, high-powered advertising executive, whose resistance to domesticity is expressed by her dependence on takeaway food. However, this is not her 'true' self – signified by the neurosis it provokes – which is latently maternal, although this is not initially apparent. Having 'inherited' a baby, the Keaton character moves out to the country where, after a series of disasters and mayhem caused by her inadequacy as a mother, she eventually settles down to family life with the local vet. Importantly, however, this is not a simple return to full time motherhood. Like the heroines of the family saga, J. C. has to show that she can 'juggle' work and motherhood successfully, and this is achieved by rejecting the excessively masculine career she enjoyed in New York and replacing it with domestic entrepreneurship: she begins to bottle and sell her home-made baby apple sauce, thus bringing together the skills of the public world of work and those of the private world of the home in a nicely sentimental conclusion. E. Ann Kaplan goes further than this, arguing that films like *Baby Boom* 'play out unconscious fantasies of abandonment (the bad mothers . . . who drop off their babies) . . . and end with the old values, in that the mother has to be re-inserted at the end, even if we are left with a slightly "unconventional" family' (1992: 198). *Baby Boom* was, then, in many ways a very conventional comedy drama about motherhood, one that would not have looked out of place 50 years before, despite its overt preoccupation with the problem of yuppie values.

The return of the 'romcom': love without marriage? marriage without sex?

The late 1980s and 1990s also saw the resurfacing of romantic comedy as a popular film genre, but in a markedly changed, 'post-AIDS' and postmodern version. For Steve Neale

(1992), 1987 marked an important moment, with films such as *Moonstruck* and *Roxanne*. Later examples, such as *Pretty Woman* (1990), *Green Card* (1992) and *Housesitter* (1992), further reworked the conflicted strands of romance found in the 'nervous' comedies of the 1970s in order to put 'the more unambigious project of a lasting monogamous heterosexual relationship . . . in inverted commas', as Evans and Deleyto characterize it (1998: 7). By ironizing the conventions of romance (as in *Pretty Woman's* framing commentary, which situates the film within a fairy-tale tradition and mocks its wish-fulfilment ending) or by overturning them, postmodern romantic comedies attempted to distance themselves from the closure of the marriage ending and the return to the family that this promised.

There is, then, a profound self-consciousness about matrimony and emotional commitment in these films. Often, while they call on nostalgia as a way of reaffirming the value of romance through an appeal to its power in the past, they do so through an ironic or parodic register that undermines the possibility of sincerity. The ur-text of these comedies, *When Harry Met Sally* (1989), even explicitly deploys popular ballads from the 1950s as part of its soundtrack, in order both to invoke the ideal of the heterosexual couple and to draw attention to that ideal's 'pastness'. The possibility of modern marriage lasting is thus a hopeful wish rather than a certainty – or, perhaps, simply a necessity. For Maria Lauret, the film's nostalgia articulates profound anxieties about the freedoms brought about by the sexual revolution, but also disquiet about the alternatives.

> Our ideological adherence to the idea of romantic, enduring monogamous marriage is purchased at the price of the utopia of the sexual revolution . . . it seems that *When Harry Met Sally* offers, in Jameson's terms, 'mere gratification in return for submission to passivity' in the comfort of knowing that there is no alternative: it had to be you, you, nobody else but you.
>
> (Lauret 1998: 28)

Oddly, while the possibility of marriage as a lasting solution to the problem of desire is repeatedly problematized in these films, the romantic comedy in the 1990s was also the site of a renewed emphasis on the rituals and practices of weddings themselves. From *Four Weddings and a Funeral* (1994), through The *Wedding Singer* (1998), *My Best Friend's Wedding* (1997), *The Runaway Bride* (1999) and *The Wedding Planner* (2002) (and perhaps even *Muriel's Wedding*, 1994), the focus moved to an emphasis on what might be called the ritual labour of the marriage ceremony. In their different ways these films frequently drew on different aspects of consumer discourses, with their pictorialism, their heavy emphasis on the female body as visual object and their exploration of the backstage elements to the staging of the ceremony. Equally importantly, this also involved a critical interrogation of the whole business of weddings and the ideological function they play. The plot of *Four Weddings and a Funeral*, for example, entirely revolves around the uncertainty of romantic love and of finding the 'right' person – and the possibility of not being able to do so.

Yet the focus on the ceremonial aspects in this and other films also seemed to partially decentre (or perhaps simply destabilize) the romance narrative and the possibility of permanent heterosexual love for women. *My Best Friend's Wedding*, for example, implies that its main character, Julianne (Julia Roberts), must settle for love – of a sort – with her gay friend, George (Rupert Everett), and the promise of 'plenty of dancing', instead of marriage to the man she has always loved, Michael (Dermot Mulroney). Yet, as Baz Dreisinger argues, 'the final dancing in the film is a visual affirmation of what the film has asserted all along: that the George–Jules relationship is far better than any heterosexual union' (2000: 7). Indeed, the fact that the version of the film that was eventually circulated differed in emphasis from an earlier incarnation, with the Everett character being given a much larger role, not only works to unbalance the premise of the plot, since the relationship between Julianne and George is given much more narrative space and is both more credible and more entertaining than the original love story, it even begs the question implied by the film's title: who exactly is the real 'best friend'? As Dreisinger points out, the film's emphasis on Julianne and George's musical empathy in the final scene's shared dance suggests not only that their relationship is at least quasi-erotic in its sensuality, but also that this may be worth holding on to in place of a reductively sexual heterosexual relationship.

Just as significant for us here, explorations of the possibility of intimacy and parenting between a heterosexual woman and a gay man reappeared in a number of films during the late 1990s and early 2000s, drawing on similar themes exploring sensuality versus sexuality, while also positing the possibilities inherent in producing this new kind of family. The complex relationship between the shifts in the politics of the family, signalled by the struggles over fathers' rights and the new visibility of gay parenting, symbolized by the Tony Barlow and Barrie Drewitt case, was therefore – however problematically – beginning to be staged in romantic comedy, the genre apparently most explicitly wedded (forgive the pun) to perpetuating the myth of the heterosexual happy ending.

For example, in *The Object of My Affection* (1998), Jennifer Aniston plays a single woman, Nina, who, having discovered she is pregnant by a boyfriend she isn't sure about, turns to her new lodger, George, an attractive but gay male teacher, for comfort and support and falls in love with him. Their attempts to live as a family are an interesting example of the playing out and 'queering' of contemporary uncertainties and emergent cultural attitudes around sexual desire. The film seems to want to suggest that Nina, George and baby Molly really are the 'perfect family', and even ends on a scene in which the three of them walk down the street together, yet this is problematized by the character of Nina's ex-boyfriend, Vince, whose recurrent appearances and insistence that she really belongs with him is never properly addressed. In the very similar *The Next Best Thing* (2000), Everett reprised his role as the gay best friend, this time one who agrees to have a baby with a heterosexual woman (played by Madonna) who has not yet found the right man. While the first half of the film works hard to suggest that their 'new family' is quite as good as a traditional one, especially when it comes to the sharing of parenting roles (indeed, this is tediously overemphasized), the situation is disrupted when Madonna meets the handsome heterosexual banker who is the man of her dreams. By resolving the narrative through the restoration of the conventional, hetero-normative family at the end of the story, *The Next Best Thing*, perhaps like the ideology of the family itself, seems to be struggling with too many contradictory strands.

Parenthood and pratfalls

From the late 1980s through to the early 2000s, Hollywood's limited engagement with the family seems to have been largely clustered in comedy of various kinds. *Parenthood* (1989) featured Steve Martin as a fun-loving suburban dad, struggling with a range of family troubles and crises, but the film's foregrounding of fathering and relative marginalization of its female characters seemed to prefigure the emergence of the fathering-focused films of the 1990s (discussed in Chapter 3). In contrast, the retro-pleasures of *The Flintstones* (1994) offered a kind of double reading of family values. The film was an expensively produced, effects-laden live version of a fairly cheaply made, if popular, television cartoon series from the early 1960s. The cartoon original, produced at the high point of 'the age of marriage' (see Chapter 1), effectively represented stone-age life as an amusingly primitive precursor of middle-American suburbia *circa* 1960, with in-jokes about a stone-age technology that prefigured the techno-futurism of the 1960s, and the nuclear family as its social norm, together with a host of highly specific assumptions about gender roles and power relations within the family. Thus, Fred Flintstone and Barney Rubble set off for their 'stone-age' office jobs in 'stone-age' cars every morning while Betty and Wilma stay home and bake stone-age cookies. In the 'live' version, these conventions are assumed to have a quaintly charming archaism that both locates them within the early 1960s and can be recovered as postmodern irony in the 1990s. The film thus plays with its levels of referentiality and, as a comedy, is able to distance itself from them at the same time.

The Birdcage (1995) is in some ways a more interesting, if deeply contradictory, text: a mainstream comedy (adapted from an earlier French version, *La Cage Aux Folles*, 1978, and ultimately from a play, which explains its farcical aspects and restricted *mise-en-scène*) in which the family is very far from conventional. The film's main characters, Armand (Robin Williams) and Albert (Nathan Lane), are a long-term gay couple living in Miami where they own a cabaret theatre in which Albert performs his regular drag act. Armand's son by an earlier liaison has decided to get married and wants to introduce Albert and Armand to his fiancée and her parents, a terrifyingly right-wing Republican senator and a family-values matriarch.

Afraid to reveal that they are a gay couple, the two men decide to 'play straight' for the night, with Armand as a patriarch with the firmest handshake in Florida and Albert as an absurdly primly feminine mother, flirting with the unwitting senator. The film's emphasis on performance and on the possibility that Albert is a 'better', more feminine, certainly immediately more desirable woman than any of the biological females in the film, is, of course, reminiscent of a long tradition of Hollywood drag comedy, including *Some Like It Hot* (1959), in which the fragility of gender identity is explored and exposed. Indeed, the film's centring of a gay couple, whose relationship, however stormy, is clearly as stable as that of the straight couples in the film, against a right-wing senator whose family values are revealed to be paper-thin, suggests some important moves away from a heteronormative representation of intimate and domestic relations in mainstream film. *The Birdcage* was, in some ways, part of the 'queering' of the mainstream that took place during the 1990s, in which gay characters and a more fluid model of sexuality began to appear (Tincknell and Chambers 2002).

However, these tentative acknowledgements of sexual pluralism are offset by *The Birdcage*'s emphasis on youthful heterosexual desire as the plot motor, by its dependence on camp caricature for much of the humour, and by its liberal conscience. Armand and Albert may be an affectionate couple, but their sexuality is largely figured through coded forms of representation rather than scenes of sexual activity. And 'acceptable' homosexuality must mimic straight relationships. Furthermore, homophobia is largely represented as the prerogative of right-wing (and hypocritical) Republicans, rather than an intrinsic aspect of contemporary social values. *The Birdcage* makes the gay family cosy, but it does so by evading the problematic questions of sexuality and desire.

Television, comedy and the family
Mad housewives, good patriarchs, unruly women

These shifts in relations of familial power and in social and cultural attitudes around class and gender have, in some respects, been more complexly dealt with by television, perhaps because of its status as a domestic medium which depends on securing and retaining an audience that is both diverse but also numerically dominated by female viewers. As a consequence, it has developed a range of genres which are either overtly feminine, such as soap opera, or domestically located, such as the sitcom. It must therefore attempt to speak to a range of possible subject positions or articulations.

Indeed, the history of the family-based sitcom is one in which patriarchal power and authority is repeatedly ridiculed and rendered absurd, either by junior members of the family or by equally subordinate outsiders, who are shown to be more astute, cunning or capable than the father figure. In the 1950s, for example, early television sitcoms, such as *The Burns and Allen Show* and *The Adventures of Ozzie and Harriet*, both depended on this simple device, although they also mobilized the stereotype of the mad, unpredictable (and neurotically unstable) housewife in ways that reasserted the importance of patriarchal power as a signifier of safety and stability. Allison McCracken points to the way in which in *The Burns and Allen Show*, the character of Gracie not only worked by mobilizing a kind of verbal reverse-logic, but also that this legitimated the terms on which the comedy operated:

> [George] both protects her and exhibits her, thus demonstrating traditional middle-class gender roles (wives are to be protected and displayed), but also directly linking this kind of marriage display with the freak show. Grace is the idiot savant and the promise of her idiot-savant freakiness is what draws audiences to the show.
>
> (McCracken 2002: 57)

This process is clearly linked to Bakhtin's (1984) principle of the carnivalesque, in which the conventional forms of power are temporarily turned upside down for the duration of the carnival, or in this case the half-hour of comedy. The comedy works largely because the audience knows that this is not a permanent disruption of power structures, simply a brief and pleasurable overturning of them. Moreover, as Mark Crispin Miller observes,

> shows featuring Dad's wife or kids were also tellingly named, with half titles that took Dad's point of view, expressing his permanent exasperation at the foibles of his underlings: *Leave It to Beaver* (to Screw Things Up), *My Little Margie* (Needs a Punch in the Mouth), and *I Love Lucy* (in Spite of Everything).
>
> (Miller 1990: 298)

For Miller, the reassertion of patriarchal power meant that 'Dad didn't have to raise a fist, but could restore conformity just by manifesting his supreme Dadhood' (1990: 298).

The social and cultural transformations of the 1960s had a significant impact, both on the way in which the family could be represented and on the specific figuring of the power relations involved, especially around class. During the late 1960s and 1970s, for example, a number of sitcoms were based around working-class or blue-collar families, including *Till Death Us Do Part* (1965–75) in the UK and its American equivalent, *All in the Family* (1971–79), both of which constructed the ageing male patriarch as a racist bigot, trapped by the limits of his class position and by his resistance to the cultural transformations being wrought. Such programmes were clearly informed by the counter-cultural values that privileged youthful idealism against the imaginary other of a failed patriarchy. Yet while both shows featured conflict between the sexes, and even foregrounded the condescension shading into contempt that these battered old patriarchs expressed for their wives (as in Alf Garnett's 'silly moo'), neither represented issues of gendered power relations as their primary critical terrain. The real battle was always between younger and older men. And, as Miller sharply points out, Archie Bunker's lack of social enlightenment was effectively conflated with his class position: he was a butt for jokes because he was an uneducated 'prole' (1990: 302).

By the 1980s, too, the increased space available to credible black characters in television, together with emergence of the figure of the new man, had begun to change the *style* in which fathers were represented in sitcoms, although it barely altered their ascribed power. The pipe-smoking, elbow-patched (white) authoritarian was replaced by a post-hippie, cool dad in shows such as *Family Ties* and *Silver Spoons*, while African-American families were beginning to appear, albeit in highly specific terms. For example, the globally successful *Cosby Show* (1984–92) featured the firmly middle-class Huxtable family, educationally ambitious and clean-living, inhabiting an equally middle-class (and therefore implicitly unthreatening to white cultural values) part of Harlem. Arguably, without its African-American characters and context, and despite its references to the liberal tradition of black politics in America, the programme would be readily identifiable as deeply conservative. In its assertion of patriarchal values, in its resistance to addressing issues of systematic racial prejudice that face many African Americans, and in its 'safe' humour, *The Cosby Show* rarely crossed further boundaries. Indeed, Clarence Lusane argues that,

> in terms of cultural values, *The Cosby Show*, with its professional, black middle-class ethos and flavor, was not different from *Good Times, Sanford and Son*,[3] or

Roc, shows that featured black working-class and poor families, but whose value systems were wholly middle class. Those shows emphasized strong family and educational attainment, questioned materialism, emphasized racial pride, and promoted individual responsibility.

(Lusane 1999: 15)

The show's explicit avowal of respectable values, and especially its familialism, was, then, a conscious intervention in the representational process. It deliberately sought to avoid the familiar black stereotypes by making its family professional, middle class and culturally aspirational. Yet the version of the family it offered was not only thoroughly bourgeois, but also neatly and patriarchally nuclear, with little suggestion of the wider kinship network available to many African-American families and no recognition of the matriarchal values that African-American culture encompasses.

As Timothy Havens points out, in a discussion of the programme's global popularity, this emphasis on the nuclear family has a powerful hegemonic dimension precisely because it is a black family that is being shown: 'the Huxtables' blackness plays an integral role in disseminating the "universality" of this particular family unit' (2004: 454). Ellen Seiter even concludes, having interviewed a range of audiences for the show from various social and ethnic backgrounds, that, '[f]or black viewers, *Cosby* is pernicious . . . because it forces African Americans to accept the television industry's position that normalcy means upper-middle-class status' (2004: 466–7).

Indeed, *The Cosby Show's* attempt to be both *about* black American life and politically neutral in its representation of their experience meant that it offered a reassuring account of the world – and of family relations – to white viewers, who could safely enjoy the Huxtables' similarity to themselves while combining 'an impeccably liberal attitude toward race with a deep-rooted suspicion of black people' (Jhally and Lewis 1992: 110, quoted in Seiter 2004: 466). At the same time, the show's avoidance of specifically American concerns meant it could, as Havens claims, 'gesture at a transnational black community, bound by similar political goals' (2004: 451).

For Miller, such goals disappear beneath *The Cosby Show's* relentless consumerism, which not only valorizes American corporate culture, but is also bound up with a representation of the family as a social formation whose primary purpose is consumption: 'each week, the happy Huxtables nearly vanish amid the porcelain, stainless steel, mahogany, and fabric of their lives. And . . . the plots and subplots . . . reflect in some way on consumption as a way of life' (1990: 305). In this respect, *The Cosby Show*, not unlike the family sagas discussed in Chapter 2, was part of the negotiations taking place around the cultural articulation of capitalism of the 1980s. It attempted to claim space for black aspirations and consumer values by allying them to the 'safe' institution of the nuclear family.

In contrast, the very different sitcom, *Roseanne*, matched *The Cosby Show's* global hegemony during the late 1980s by articulating what might be called counter-hegemonic family values, in which the mother was the dominant figure within the family, and the family itself was blue-collar and based unfashionably far from New York City, in Lanford, Illinois. Not only was Roseanne Connor represented as a credible working-class woman (including, significantly, her unruly size, hot temper and refusal of conventional femininity), but also the situation which she and her husband, Dan, were faced with was vastly different from the Cosbys' minor misunderstandings and wholly eschewed the easy homilies of self-improvement. Indeed, Roseanne Barr was herself a figure around whom extreme responses were produced, precisely because of the contradictions she seemed to express in terms of both class and gender conflicts. The show's emphasis on the Connor family's 'ordinariness' – especially their precarious finances and uncertain employment prospects in the era of Reaganomics – together with its exploration of the fragility of family bonds when put under pressure, marked an important move in the sitcom's history and in its representation of the family.

If *The Cosby Show* managed to claim the space and formal attributes that had hitherto been owned by white families on American television, and if *Roseanne* managed to suggest that the authentic values of the working-class family were worth preserving, then this was partly because of the ongoing pathologization of the middle classes throughout the 1980s and 1990s (discussed below in more detail). However, the BBC show, *My Family* (2000–), a programme whose genesis lay in the deliberate imitation of the production mode and televisual address of successful American family sitcoms – with their teams of writers, thoroughly bourgeois locations and patriarchal family values – seems to represent a remarkably successful exception to this long-term tendency.

Ostensibly about a white middle-class family living in modern-day Britain, *My Family*'s cultural values would hardly be out of place in the 1950s. Not only does the 'my' of *My Family* – as in the titular conventions of early sitcoms – clearly naturalize the paternal authority of the central adult male character (a well-meaning but permanently exasperated dentist), while simultaneously inviting the viewer to share his point of view, but his wife, a Lucy-like, wacky housewife, is both economically dependent and loveably incompetent, while the children are safely rebellious spendthrifts.

While this might have been played for irony or pastiche, there is little sense that *My Family* is intended as either. Indeed, the programme functions largely in nostalgic terms, not for the real old-fashioned family, but rather for what family sitcoms used to be like and what they seemed to represent: safety, security, patriarchal certainty. Despite this, and notwithstanding the show's success as a mainstream comedy, it is interesting that *My Family* looks like little more than a throwback to an earlier moment in television history rather than a credible account of contemporary family dynamics.

Dysfunctional is fun!

Importantly, the recent history of the family sitcom suggests that, while such conservative versions of the family and the comedy show retained some popularity throughout the 1980s, it was during the 1990s that television which represented the family as intrinsically pathological – or dysfunctional – spoke to audiences even more powerfully. Perhaps the most remarkable example of this is the continuing success of the cartoon series, *The Simpsons*, which, having started out as a form of low-level subversion of conventional family values in 1992, has acquired the global status of everyone's favourite family comedy show, with its characters and tag lines (Bart's 'eat my shorts' and Homer's 'Doh!') now firmly embedded in global popular culture.

The celebrated 'dysfunctionality' of *The Simpsons* made the show controversial when it started, but the programme is actually all about the family's *functionality* – however unconventionally this is achieved. Indeed, one of the unanticipated consequences of the programme must be its contribution to problematizing the functional/dysfunctional dyad. Moreover, as with many of the texts discussed here, one thing to emerge out of the success of *The Simpsons* is a reminder of the importance of the sitcom (even in a cartoon format) as a site for the testing out of new versions of the family, changing familial relations and shifts in the power dynamics involved. *The Simpsons*, like many other shows produced during the 1990s, offers a much extended narrative space to its child characters, Lisa and Bart, and also tends to privilege their point of view (just as a very different type of text, *American Beauty*, ultimately does).

A further example of this testing process is the American show, *Married . . . With Children* (1992–), which features the parodically lumpen, certainly 'white trash', under-educated and non-achieving Bundy family, Al, Peggy, Bud and Kelly. In contrast to the normative values that tend to saturate even non-familial American sitcoms, *Married . . . With Children* deliberately subverts bourgeois conventions and expectations. The Bundys not only occupy a space in the economy that is just above welfare and barely at the minimum wage, but they also have no qualms about pulling scams on their neighbours or cheating the boss or, indeed, the state. They are thoroughly alienated from the aspirational values expressed by the Cosbys and thoroughly dominated by their basest desires, for sex, consumer goods and cheap burgers. All of this comes as a refreshing and often brilliantly funny alternative to the feel-good values and tendency to preachiness of mainstream American sitcoms.

For Lusane, *Married . . . With Children* sets up the white American nuclear family in order to subvert it: 'it decentre[s] the nuclear family as the site for the transmission of traditional and conservative values . . . the nuclear family is not privileged, cynicism is celebrated, class oppression is omnipresent' (1999: 15). He goes on to suggest that, in the absence of a credible black sitcom that can do this, the Bundys effectively offer 'black' street or resistant values in their refusal to conform.[4] However, it is important not to read *Married . . . With Children* as a political critique of family values, however tempting this may be. As Lusane himself points out, the show is made by Fox Television, which is hardly in the business of undermining American society. More than this, the programme is, at heart, thoroughly cynical. It is as happy to ridicule the mendacity of the Bundys, and to caricature them, as it is to make fun of their neighbours' yuppy values. Furthermore, while the programme satirizes the family sitcom, it does not move very far from its basic conventions, not least in its characterization of the typical nuclear family, however dysfunctional, as the cultural centre of American life. The Bundys are themselves a barely concealed nod to the tradition of the patriarchal nuclear family.

Interestingly, what might at first look like a British version of *Married . . . With Children*, *The Royle Family* (1997–2002) is in many respects more genuinely innovatory, both in terms of form and in its testing of the audience's sympathies. Drawing heavily on the increased television naturalism prefigured by the growing success of reality shows (discussed in more

Figure 6.1 The ultra-naturalism of *The Royle Family's* televisual style and the show's celebration of a cosy slobbishness marked a larger shift in media representations towards an idea that all families were in some ways 'dysfunctional'.

detail below), *The Royle Family* took some of the family sitcom's familiar elements – the nuclear family structure, the opposed personalities and positions and even that hallowed piece of property, the sitcom sofa – and reworked them. The characterization avoids stereotyping largely through the nuances its naturalism permits. Jim Royle (Ricky Tomlinson) may be a work-shy grumbler, but he is also a sentimentalist. Barbara (Sue Johnston), his wife, is a well-meaning, if not very bright, eternal optimist, who puts in the emotional labour of holding the family together. Their daughter, Denise (Caroline Aherne), is a spoiled grown-up brat, whose idea of noble motherhood is to spend her child's post office savings on an expensive Christmas 'present' for herself, but she is also – occasionally – considerate to her 'nana' and her husband.

Furthermore, in contrast to the theatrical staginess of *Married . . . With Children's* comedy (and of the sitcom more generally), *The Royle Family* drew on the specifically televisual codes of British soap opera, not only in its use of close-ups and tight framing, but also in its detailed use of social observation and its valorization of working-class culture and community. Where *Married . . . With Children* cast the Bundys as cynical losers, *The Royle Family* took a similar range of characteristics and produced a profoundly uncynical, if sometimes sentimental, version of contemporary family life. What this difference suggests, moreover, is that in contemporary American popular culture, family dysfunctionality must first be defined, then taxonomized, then recuperated in some way, either by reasserting aspirational values or by caricaturing the dysfunctional family in such extreme terms that it ceases to address the audience meaningfully – perhaps because it seems to present too great a threat to social order. In the British version, however, family relations are less readily reduced to their pathology.

Struggling with difference: British soaps

Extending the family

In the UK, popular soap opera has a long tradition of exploring family relationships and kinship, although the way in which it has done this is rather different to the approach of the glossier American serials, whose milieu is primarily that of the sphere of business and wealthy suburbs (as was explored in Chapter 2). British soaps have their formal origins in the conventions of social realism; the first properly successful programme of this kind being *Coronation Street*, which appeared in 1960 as part of the same cultural moment of kitchen-sink drama that produced films about working-class life, such as *Saturday Night and Sunday Morning* (1960). However, their cultural importance and centrality increased dramatically during the 1980s and 1990s, especially with the introduction of the BBC's *EastEnders* in 1985. Popular soaps became a prime space for the exploration of contemporary meanings and values around identity, gender, sexuality and, most importantly, family life.

The family unit in soaps is represented both in terms of its internal relations and in its engagement with a wider community, whether on 'the street' or 'the square', and drama is produced out of the differing and potentially conflicted relationships which this engagement produces. Interestingly, while soap opera tends to privilege the family ideal, and perhaps especially the nuclear family, in its rhetorical and ideological emphases, the textual structure of soaps frequently works against a too reductive version of this. The continuing story model adopted by most soaps, together with their dependence on a cast of characters that works synchronically rather than diachronically (that is, their relations with each other are fixed at a given moment in time rather than during a long historical period), means that contemporary 'soap families' are remarkably fluid, flexible and divorce-extended. It is not unusual for a single 'family' over a ten-year period in a soap to begin with one set of characters and end up with an entirely different group of members, while maintaining the rhetorical attachment to a specific family allegiance or even changing that allegiance while claiming fidelity to the idea of family.

In *EastEnders*, for example, Sonia Jackson (Natalie Cassidy) first appeared as the nine-year-old daughter of a mother, Carol, who had had four children by different fathers, all of whom were important characters in the show. Sonia was thus identified as part of a Jackson family that already had a complex reproductive history. In subsequent years, Sonia's mother and all her 'brothers' and 'sisters' left the programme, Sonia had a child of her own, as well as a series of traumatic relationships, and a 'grandfather', Jim Branning (John Bardon), was introduced, married to a longstanding character, Dot Cotton (June Brown), and moved back into the Jackson family house. Sonia is thus now part of the Branning family and, with the short-term memory characteristic of soap's dramatic conventions, Jim and Dot are represented as though their relationship with Sonia has 'always already' been that of grandparents.

This kind of complex personal history is typical (and probably inevitable) of all long-running dramas, as cast members leave or new characters appear. What is particularly interesting for us here, though, is the relatively straightforward way in which the family is extended, transformed and redefined as these changes take place. Of course, to some extent, the ideological attachment to the family articulated by *EastEnders* (and by *Neighbours*, *Dallas* and many other serials) works to contain and manage the acceptability of particular relationships and sexual identities. Gay male characters tend to be cast as solitary outsiders with few discernible friendship networks, or as only problematically brought into the family – under certain conditions and through recuperative devices that render them safely unthreatening by removing the possibility of their sexuality being visible. Lesbian characters, when they appear, are too often treated as exotic or potentially titillating, with their sexuality the primary (or only) characteristic to be foregrounded (as was the case with the first lesbian kiss (1993) in another British soap opera, *Brookside* – much to the excitement of the tabloid press).

Despite this, the flexibility of the family in such shows in some ways prefigures contemporary attitudes and formations, as well as looking back to a pre-nuclear model in which aunts, uncles and cousins are as important as more immediate family members. *Coronation Street* has even made some explicit attempts to take on board the changes in family structure, gender roles and sexual identities that have been a significant feature of contemporary culture, by introducing a story built around a 'family of choice'. In the early 2000s it introduced a transsexual character, Hayley Patterson (Julie Hesmondhalgh), whose struggles to claim and remake a differently gendered identity became an important part of the ongoing narrative, even though this also worked to normalize the character. Disappointingly, her sexual and gendered identity was largely produced in the familiar quasi-essentialized terms of common sense rather than those of social or discursive construction: she was 'living in the wrong body', as though the corporeal and identificatory aspects of the self were wholly separate.

The relative success of the character meant that during 2003–4 the programme developed its tentative engagement with sexual plurality by marrying Hayley to another *Coronation Street* stalwart, Roy Cropper, and introducing a story about the couple's desire for a child, which culminated in their attempts to adopt a baby from a young unmarried mother (also conveniently living in 'the street', as these characters in soaps so often do!). However, *Coronation Street*'s attempts to normalize both Hayley's gender identity and her relationship with Roy through its emphasis on her 'natural' desire for a child thoroughly undercut any radical aspects to the characters and their relationship. It also simultaneously demonized the young mother whose baby the couple wanted, effectively trading a pathologization of Hayley's sexuality for that of the young woman. *Coronation Street*'s reluctance to disaggregate gender from sexuality and coupledom from reproduction thus makes it difficult to read the show in very radical terms. It also suggests that, following Raymond Williams, we can see that a text's relationship to dominant social relations – which remain those of heterosexual marriage even if that is changing – will help to shape its articulation of dissident or oppositional values. *Coronation Street*'s moral and sexual conservatism is not a reflection of social reality, but it may well be a negotiation of the ideas and values implicit in its history, the expectations of its audience and its relationship to the public realm.

Ethnicity and cultural norms

Because of this, both *Coronation Street* and *EastEnders* have a troubled history of attempting to include – and perhaps incorporate – ethnic diversity in their stories, and especially struggling to emphasize family structures and networks which are not conventionally part of the dominant white culture. While both programmes articulate a degree of nostalgia for an imagined past in which the extended family was a central link to the wider community, neither has successfully made space for contemporary non-white family forms which continue this model. *Coronation Street* has included black or Afro-Caribbean characters from the very beginning, yet they have rarely been situated within a convincing network of family relations, and are asked instead to 'stand for' blackness or Asianness, which, in turn, positions them as disruptive figures. As Christine Geraghty observes, 'in such a situation, the black character as an individual disappears under the responsibility of carrying the "race" issue and is used largely to demonstrate the notional tolerance of the largely white community' (1991: 142). *EastEnders* has a similar tradition of liberal attempts to include non-white characters and to gesture to cultural difference: from the beginnings of the show in 1985, black, Asian, Jewish and Turkish-Cypriot families were featured in a clear attempt to be fully representative of the range of ethnicities populating London in the late twentieth century. Too often, though, such characters have been so decontextualized from a recognizable British-Asian or British-Caribbean context that they are implausible or wholly tokenistic.

These efforts, then, have frequently been rendered incoherent. The dominant values of *EastEnders* are an uneasy compromise between liberal individualism and nostalgia for the white working-class extended family. Difference is thus brought into focus through characters from ethnic minority backgrounds, only to be erased and ultimately disavowed through the show's liberal-humanist desire to demonstrate that we're all the same under the skin. The process of including non-white (or non-Anglo) families thus becomes one of incorporation rather than a genuine recognition of the value of diversity: the rubric of 'East Enderness' eventually marginalizes alternative positions and subjectivities – of class as well as ethnicity. In this way, characters that are represented as *culturally* integrated can also be more effectively narratively integrated, because they do not 'disrupt' the text in the ways suggested by Geraghty.

For example, during the 1980s and early 1990s, Dr Legg (Leonard Fenton) was the programme's Jewish GP, but it was quite possible to be wholly unaware of his ethnic background, which was rarely emphasized (with the exception of a moving storyline in which he revisited his family's holocaust experiences in 1997), and there was certainly little textual emphasis on how his cultural identity might give him a different perspective on the life of 'the square'. Indeed, the character also always hovered on the 'margins of marginality' because, despite the story described above, he was also largely represented as outside the institution of the family (as well as being middle class). He was thus narratively integrated, but the possibility of exploring the differences that being Jewish entailed in a productive way was silenced by the programme's emphasis on cultural cohesion.

The tensions between different *kinds* of difference may also be articulated through the dramatization of subject positions or power structures that a programme finds problematic.

One example of this was the introduction of a new Asian family during 2003, the Ferreiras. Evidently coming originally from an Indian Catholic, but apparently relatively secularized background (which therefore avoided troubling Muslim sensibilities), the culturally complex and therefore potentially interesting positionality of the family's relationship to the East End of the show seemed to promise much. The programme even set up the issue of the family's religious and cultural origins as something of a narrative enigma, by having various white characters speculate (in a somewhat gratuitous fashion) on their likely food tastes. While much of this seemed lumberingly didactic, it also opened up the possibility that difference might contribute to the show's dynamic, by foregrounding debates about religious and cultural identities perhaps, or at least by taking them seriously. Furthermore, by giving the Ferreiras an Asian Christian background, the programme seemed to be attempting to manage some of these issues in a new way; the family was culturally aligned to the white characters yet also not 'the same'. Yet the stories featuring the Ferreiras have, instead, featured that favourite monster of the liberal west, the tyrannical Asian father who wants to control his daughter's sexuality (as if the control of women's sexuality had not also always been part of western family discourse).[5] Indeed, this focus has also returned the representation of Asian characters to the realm of an exoticized sexuality – to orientalism even. Instead of exploring the contrast between family structures, entitlements and expectations in Asian and white British families, the show attempted both to normalize the Ferreiras as British, by making the parents divorced, and to normalize them as Asian, by centring stories on the figure of the abusive father. In this way, the centrality of the family to the dramatic structure of the programme was maintained, but its veracity – as a representation of real life – was rendered improbable.

One further difficulty that such television fictional dramas now face in their efforts to represent reality is the plethora of so-called reality television shows, which have proved to be almost as popular with audiences (certainly as talked about at the water-cooler, as *Big Brother* demonstrated) as the soaps, although they are considerably cheaper to produce and are frequently saleable globally as 'formats' (and are therefore doubly attractive to television companies). Perhaps equally importantly for a cultural analysis, reality shows are frequently structured around, and therefore clear analytical space for, a whole range of diverse social relations that are not linked to the blood ties of family (see Tincknell and Raghuram 2002 for a more detailed discussion of these aspects). Instead, just as the 'biological' family has become increasingly pathologized, alternative models of households, social relations and sexuality have begun to be both more visible and more legitimately 'real'. Where reality television has taken on the family, then, it has tended to do so in ways that intensify and extend the discourse of pathological dysfunctionality. For such programmes, the family that fights is much more interesting than nuclear harmony.

Reality television and the pathologized family

While the term 'reality television' is relatively new and has only recently come into general circulation, the history of documentaries focused on private life and shot in real time goes back to the 1970s at least, and family relationships were originally central to the genre's discursive development. One of the earliest and most controversial examples of such a show, for example, was the fly-on-the-wall television series made by Paul Watson in 1978, simply called *The Family*, which tracked the lives, relationships and often heated emotional entanglements of the working-class Wilkins family of Reading in the UK. *The Family* was highly controversial, partly because the effing and blinding that was clearly intrinsic to the Wilkins family's daily verbal exchanges (and is central to British demotic speech in its uncensored form) had never been heard on British television before; perhaps also because of the way in which it brought into the public sphere the complex power relations and struggles that even the most realist of dramas had hitherto failed to represent. Most importantly, it showed the extent to which the private sphere was dominated by the strong figure of Mrs Wilkins, in ways that disrupted and disturbed common-sense models of the patriarchal family.

A different series made in Australia more than ten years later, in 1992, by Watson, which was partially modelled on *The Family* and called (after its location in a wealthy Sydney suburb) *Sylvania Waters*, produced similar controversy around its assertive middle-aged matriarch, Noelene Donaher, whose 'unconventional' lifestyle (living with a man she was not married to in a divorce-extended family) and materialistic values were gleefully demonized in the British press and struggled over in the Australian media, as Catherine Lumby points out (www.museum.tv/archives/etv/s/html/sylvaniawaters). Graeme Turner called the programme 'Suburbia verite', describing its exposure of private forms of racism, xenophobia and sexism, which strongly resembled the Wilkins' apparently casual inscription of anti-liberal ideas, as 'ugly' (1992).

These programmes clearly prefigured the explosion in what would come to be called 'docusoaps' during the 1990s, and their emphasis on the personal sphere and use of apparently unmediated filming techniques would later become the standard conventions of one strand of reality television. Central, too, was the way in which the role, status and 'peformance' of the women involved would be scrutinized as part of the reception of the programmes more generally.

Woman trouble

The over-determination of women, particularly mothers, as the site of trouble within the family continues to be part of reality television's discourse. In 2003, a show that combined the fly-on-the-wall filming tradition with a competitive element that, classically, pitched one woman directly against another and asked them to compare their domestic arrangements, was an unexpected success in the UK. *Wife Swap* took two families of roughly the same size and age group, but with radically different lifestyles, and asked the wives to change places for two weeks, during which they would be asked to play by the 'house rules' in the first week and then might impose their own rules in the second. By deliberately pairing the unlikeliest couples, the programme inevitably managed to generate drama out of the confrontation it had engineered between two sets of values, expectations and (rarely recognized overtly) class positions. Furthermore, the footage that was used to make up the hour-long television show was edited to foreground such differences. Rather than exploring differentials of class, social and educational expectations or (more problematically) the enormous gap between the work done in the home by the women involved and the men they lived with in any detail, the programme chose to emphasize an individualized and entirely feminized account of domestic competence in which the women competed with each other.

Of course, all of this was done with a knowing smile and a nod to postmodern irony. Each programme concluded with a face-to-face 'catfight' between the women, which was highly entertaining and patently intended to produce hurled insults and barely concealed slurs on each other's hygiene standards, much in the style of *The Jerry Springer Show*. But it also worked to underline the extent to which the day-to-day management of the family and the household remained women's responsibility, regardless of other demands. Indeed, even in those episodes where shared responsibility for childcare and household tasks between husband and wife appeared to be a norm, the programme's prior discursive framework made this impossible to explore in any meaningful sense.

In this way, while *Wife Swap* seemed overtly to present the audience with an account of the family that suggested their was no 'norm', only a plurality of competing versions, none of which was necessarily superior, its inability to frame the issue of housework and domesticity in anything other than individualized terms made it deeply problematic. Housework was unavoidably emphasized, but largely in terms of drudgery and obligation. Not only was there no explicit expression of a politics of the domestic sphere, but neither was there much sense that domestic tasks might have their pleasurable aspects either (in contrast to the cookery shows that became equally popular in the 1990s).

Not so much a wild man of rock, more a responsible father

Reality television's focus on the domestic sphere has, then, largely worked to develop and mobilize the discourse of the family as inherently unstable. Far from offering idealized representations of family life, the genre has deliberately sought out the monstrous and disgustingly diverting and has reframed them as entertainment. The MTV show, *The Osbournes* (2002–), for example, explicitly and knowingly draws on the conventions of 'monster-coms' (Marc 1992), such as *The Munsters* and *The Addams Family*, especially in its credit sequence, precisely in order to name and then defuse the 'threat' that seems to be on offer: that of pathological dysfunctionality. And, as Jennifer Gillan points out, like much reality television, *The Osbournes* works by offering '[the] melodrama of a soap opera, the real time footage of a documentary, the voyeuristic snooping of the celebrity house tour, the interaction of incompatible and competing personalities . . . all combined with the themes, issues and framing of a sitcom' (2004: 57).

As Gillan goes on to argue, however, just as with the ghoulish families depicted in *The Munsters* and *The Addams Family, The Osbournes* turns out to be about an 'entire famil[y] of innocent monsters trying to live their deviant lives among hostile, intolerant "normal" people' (2004: 58) . The trajectory of the show is in the direction of reaffirming the *normality* of their social relations with each other. As Gillan says, 'The Osbournes might be "creepy" and "kooky" . . . but they are also nice people' (2004: 56–7). The dysfunctionality of the family is therefore not only tempered – and perhaps also explained – by their wealthy lifestyle, but it is also made safe by Ozzie Osbourne's evident dependence on his wife, concern for his children and apparent bafflement at the world. This has enabled the programme to re-present its hero as a loveable national treasure rather than the 'wild man of rock'. Ozzie's recuperation as a shamblingly unthreatening but caring paternal figure is, perhaps, symptomatic of the larger implications of reality television's incursion into family life. On the one hand, every family and every individual is in some way abnormal; on the other, there can be no normal family if every one is strange. And, if the nuclear family is as odd, as diverse and as unsettling as these shows suggest, its status as a privileged space for childcare and for hetero-normativity becomes difficult to defend.

The death of the family

Like many predicted demises, the imminent death of the family has been exaggerated, often by those with a vested interest in retaining it in a form that benefits particular groups or individuals who are naturally resistant to changes in the power relations involved. Yet, as we have seen, while the ways in which the idea of the family has been mediated continue to diversify, the family itself has not entirely disappeared from the realm of representation. Instead, it has been reworked, recast and renegotiated.

At the time of writing, one of the most successful British television dramas with both critics and audiences has been Channel 4's *Shameless* (2004), a serial focused on the tangled lives of the Gallaghers, a family whose variously complex emotional, sexual and economic involvements would, it seems, provide enough material for a year's worth of social work case conferences. The Gallagher family live constantly on the wrong side of the law, they are sexually promiscuous, the father is a drunk and the mother has run off with a trucker girlfriend, leaving her eldest daughter to look after everyone else. Far from representing the Gallaghers in the moralistic, reductive or sensationalized terms that remain common for such characters in British popular drama, however, or making their troubles the subject of issue-driven writing that addresses an assumed public realm in which the social relations they stand for can be resolved, *Shameless* does something very different. It manages to suggest that 'the family', whatever it is and whoever belongs to it, exceeds conventional representational meanings and that emotional ties and commitment to an investment in the private sphere remain crucial.

Of course, the programme may be criticized for its refusal to present the Gallaghers as a problem, its tendency to romanticize (or evade) the issues of power between Frank Gallagher and his children and its wryly unjudgemental exploration of the polysexual. Set against those concerns must be the programme's resistance to simplification and its sense of fun. In all of this, the programme takes as its material the 'pathological' elements of the 'problem' family and defuses them. *Shameless* takes the family seriously, but it refuses to impose a conservative version of what the family should be. That seems like a good enough prescription to me.

Notes

1 A further example of new claims to the family being made by same-sex couples was the decision by the State of Massachusetts in May 2004 that same-sex marriages would be recognized as legal. Thousands of gay couples congregated in various locations throughout the state to celebrate by getting married.

2 In Robert Altman's *M*A*S*H* (1970), for example, the only significant female character, the career military nurse, Major 'Hotlips' Hoolihan, is represented as neurotically obsessed with the niceties of military authority (in contrast to the laid-back counter-cultural attitudes of the heroes) and is punished for this (and perhaps for her sexual unavailability) in a variety of humiliating scenes that put her back into 'her place' as a woman.

3 Given that *Sanford and Son* was originally based on a British sitcom about the working-class rag-and-bone trade, *Steptoe and Son*, that in many ways sought to subvert conventional family values through the sharp yet poignant relationship between father and son, it seems particularly ironic that the transformation to an American context also involved pulling its critical teeth. In the British version, the younger Harold Steptoe's cultural aspirations and despair at his father's unsavoury habits were a regular source of comedy, and there was little sense that his attempts to escape the business or his father would produce anything but comic failure (indeed, the show depended on this).

4 As I noted in Chapter 3, however, claims that 'black' values can be adequately expressed by white people (whether real or fictional) seem to me to require serious interrogation.

5 See also *East is East* (1998), which is a curious mixture of some radically new and inventive ideas and some terrible (and often misogynistic) stereotypes. Here, again, the Asian father is a tyrant, although his tyranny is resisted by his family and the complicated relationships involved are the source of much of the comedy.

Bibliography

Acland, C. R., 1995, *Youth, Murder, Spectacle: The Cultural Politics of 'Youth in Crisis'*. Boulder, CO, San Francisco, CA and Oxford: Westview Press.

Althusser, L. and Balibar, E., 1979, *Reading Capital*, London: Verso.

Amis, K., 1992, *Lucky Jim*, Harmondsworth: Penguin.

Andrews, M. and Talbot, M. M. (eds), 2000, *All the World and her Husband: Women in Twentieth-Century Consumer Culture*, London and New York: Cassell.

The Annan Committee Report on the Future of Broadcasting, 1977, London: HMSO.

Aries, P., 1962, *Centuries of Childhood*, London: Jonathan Cape.

Attfield, J., 1995, 'Inside Pram Town: A Case Study of Harlow House Interiors, 1951–61', in Attfield, J. and Kirkham, P. (eds), *A View from the Interior: Women and Design*, London: Women's Press.

Bakhtin, M., 1984 (originally published 1968), *Rabelais and his World*, Bloomington, IN: University of Indiana Press.

Barker, M. and Petley, J. (eds), 1997, *Ill Effects: The Media/Violence Debate*, London and New York: Routledge.

Barnes, J., 1980, *Metroland*, Bedford: St Martin's Press.

Barrett, M. and McIntosh, M., 1982, *The Anti-social Family*, London: Verso.

Barstow, S., 1962, *A Kind of Loving*, Harmondsworth: Penguin.

Beck, U., 1992, *Risk Society: Towards a New Modernity*, London: Sage.

Bernardes, J., 1997, *Family Studies*, London: Routledge.

Beveridge, W., 1942, *Social Insurance and Allied Services*, London: HMSO.

Blackford, C., 1995, 'Wives and Citizens and Watchdogs of Equality: Post-war British Feminism', in Fyrth, J. (ed.), *Labour's Promised Land: Culture and Society in Labour Britain 1945–51*, London: Lawrence and Wishart.

Bland, L., 1995, *Banishing the Beast: English Feminism and Sexual Morality, 1885–1914*, Harmondsworth: Penguin.

Bly, R., 1990, *Iron John: A Book About Men*, New York: Addison-Wesley.

Bourdieu, P., 1984, *Distinction: A Social Critique of the Judgement of Taste*, Cambridge, MA: Harvard University Press.

Bowlby, J., 1953, *Childcare and the Growth of Love*, Harmondsworth: Penguin.

Bowlby, R., 1985, *Just Looking: Consumer Culture in Dreiser, Gissing and Zola*, London: Methuen.

Bradford, B. T., 1979, *A Woman of Substance*, New York: Doubleday.

Bridgewood, C., 1986, 'Family Romances: The Contemporary Popular Family Saga', in Radford, J. (ed.), *The Progress of Romance: The Politics of Popular Fiction*, London and New York: Routledge and Kegan Paul, 167–94.

Britton, A., 1986, 'Blissing Out: The Politics of Reaganite Entertainment', *Movie* 31/32, winter, 1–42.

Bromley, R., 1978, 'Natural Boundaries: The Social Function of Popular Fiction', *Red Letters* 7, 34–60.

Browne, J., 2000, 'Decisions in DIY: Women, Home Improvements and Advertising in Post-war Britain', in Andrews, M. and Talbot, M. M. (eds), *All the World and her Husband: Women in Twentieth-Century Consumer Culture*, London and New York: Cassell.

Brunt, R., 1982, '"An Immense Verbosity": Permissive Sexual Advice in the 1970s', in Brunt, R. and Rowan, C. (eds), *Feminism, Culture and Politics*, London: Lawrence and Wishart.

Buckingham, D., 1987, *Public Secrets:* EastEnders *and its Audience*, London: BFI Publishing.

Buckingham, D., 1997, 'Electronic Child Abuse? Rethinking the Media's Effects on Children', in Barker, M. and Petley, J. (eds), *Ill Effects: The Media/Violence Debate*, London and New York: Routledge, 32–47.

Buckingham, D., 1998, 'Children and Television: A Critical Overview of the Research', in Dickinson, R., Harindranath, R. and Linne, O. (eds) *Approaches to Audiences: A Reader*, London, New York, Sydney and Auckland: Arnold.

Burgess, A., 1997, *Fatherhood Reclaimed: The Making of the Modern Father*, London: Vermilion.

Butler, J., 1990, *Gender Trouble*, London: Routledge.

Carr, R., 1996, *Beatles at the Movies*, New York: HarperCollins.

Chambers, D., 2001, *Representing the Family*, London: Sage Publications.

Chaney, D., 1983, 'The Department Store as Cultural Form', *Theory, Culture and Society* 1 (3), 22–31.

Chapman, R., 1988, 'The Great Pretender: Variations on the New Man Theme', in Chapman, R. and Rutherford, J. (eds), *Male Order: Unwrapping Masculinity*, London: Lawrence and Wishart.

Clover, C., 1992, *Men, Women and Chain Saws*, London: BFI Publishing.

Cogan Thacker, D. and Webb, J., 2002, *Introducing Children's Literature: From Romanticism to Postmodernism*, London and New York: Routledge.

Cohen, S., 1972, *Folk Devils and Moral Panics: The Creation of the Mods and Rockers*, London: Macgibbon and Kew.

Consalvo, M., 2003, 'The Monsters Next Door: Media Constructions of Boys and Masculinity', *Feminist Media Studies* 3 (1), 27–46.

Coontz, S., 1992, *The Way We Never Were: American Families and the Nostalgia Trap*, New York: Basic Books.

Crouch, M., 1962, *Treasure Seekers and Borrowers: Children's Books in Britain 1900–1960*, London: The Library Association.

Davidoff, L. and Hall, C., 1987, *Family Fortunes: Men and Women of the English Middle Class 1780–1850*, London: Hutchinson.

Davidoff, L., Doolittle, M., Fink, J. and Holden, K., 1999, *The Family Story: Blood, Contract and Intimacy, 1830–1960*, London and New York: Longman.

Davies, J., 1999, '"It's like feminism, but you don't have to burn your bra": girl power and the Spice Girls' breakthrough, 1996–7', in Blake, A. (ed.), *Living Through Pop*, London and New York: Routledge, 159–173.

Davies, H., Buckingham, D. and Kelley, P., 2000, 'In the Worst Possible Taste: Children, Television and Cultural Value', *European Journal of Cultural Studies*, 3 (1), 5–25.

Delafield, E. M., 1930, *Diary of a Provincial Lady*, London: Virago.

Doherty, T., 1988, *Teenagers and Teenpics: The Juvenilization of American Movies in the 1950s*, Boston: Unwin Hyman.

Donzelot, J., 1980, *The Policing of Families*, New York: Random House.

Dorfman, A. and Mattelart, A., 1972, *How to Read Donald Duck: Imperialist Ideology in the Disney Comic*, New York: International General.

Downey, P., 1994, *So You're Going To Be a Dad*, Sydney, New York, London, Toronto, Tokyo and Singapore: Viacom International.

Dreisinger, B., 2000, 'The Queen in Shining Armor: Safe Eroticism and the Gay Friend', *Journal of Popular Film and Television*, 28 (1) 2–9.

Dudovitz, R. L., 1990, *The Myth of Superwoman: Women's Bestsellers in France and the United States*, London and New York: Routledge.

Dyer, R., 1979, *Stars*, London: BFI Publishing.

Dyer, R., 1986, *Heavenly Bodies: Film Stars and Society*, London: Routledge.

Edge, S., 1996, 'When Did You Last See Your Father? The Bad Mother and the Good Father in Some Contemporary Hollywood Films', *Irish Journal of Feminist Studies* 1 (2).

Ehrenreich, B., Hess, E. and Jacobs, G., 1992, 'Beatlemania: Girls Just Want To Have Fun', in Lewis, L. A. (ed.), *The Adoring Audience: Fan Culture and Popular Media*, London: Routledge.

Engels, F., 1972 (originally published 1884), *The Origin of the Family, Private Property and the State*, London: Lawrence and Wishart.

Evans, P. W. and Deleyto, C. (eds), 1998a, *Terms of Endearment: Hollywood Romantic Comedy of the 1980s and 1990s*, Edinburgh: Edinburgh University Press.

Evans, P. W. and Deleyto, C., 1998b, 'Introduction: Surviving Love', in Evans, P. W. and Deleyto, C. (eds), *Terms of Endearment: Hollywood Romantic Comedy of the 1980s and 1990s*, Edinburgh: Edinburgh University Press.

Featherstone, M., 1991, *Consumer Culture and Postmodernism*, London: Sage.

Ferguson, M., 1983, *Forever Feminine: Women's Magazines and the Cult of Femininity*, London: Heinemann.

Feuer, J., 1984, 'Melodrama, Serial Form and Television Today', *Screen* 25 (1), 4–16.

Feuer, J., 1993, *The Hollywood Musical*, 2nd edn, London: Macmillan.

Finch, M., 1990, 'Sex and Address in *Dynasty*', in Alvarado, M. and Thompson, J. O. (eds), *The Media Reader*, London: BFI Publishing.

Firestone, S., 1979 (originally published 1971), *The Dialectic of Sex: The Case for Feminist Revolution*, London: The Women's Press.

Fischer, L., 1996, *Cinematernity: Film, Motherhood, Genre*, Princeton, NJ: Princeton University Press.

Fiske, J., 1989, *Understanding Popular Culture*, London: Routledge.

Foucault, M., 1981, *The History of Sexuality: Volume One: An Introduction*, London: Pelican.

Fowler, B., 1991, *The Alienated Reader: Women and Popular Romantic Literature*, Hemel Hempstead: Harvester Wheatsheaf.

Fox Harding, L., 1996, *Family, State and Social Policy*, London: Macmillan.

Franklin, S., Lury, C. and Stacey, J. (eds), 1991, *Off-Centre: Feminism and Cultural Studies*, London and New York: Harper Collins Academic.

Friedan, B., 1963, *The Feminine Mystique*, New York: Dell.

Friedan, B., 1981, *The Second Stage*, New York: Summit.

Frith, S., 1983, 'The Pleasures of the Hearth', in Donald, J. (ed.), *Formations of Pleasure*, London: Routledge.

Frith, S., 1997, 'The Suburban Sensibility in British Rock and Pop', in Silverstone, R. (ed.), *Visions of Suburbia*, London: Routledge.

Garratt, S., 1990, 'Teenage Dreams', in Frith, S. and Goodwin, A. (eds), *On Record*, London: Routledge, 394–421.

Geraghty, C., 1991, *Women in Soap Opera*, Cambridge: Polity.

Geraghty, C., 2000, *British Cinema in the Fifties: Gender, Genre and the 'New Look'*, London and New York: Routledge.

Giddens, A., 1992, *The Transformation of Intimacy*, Cambridge: Polity.

Giddens, A., 1999, *Runaway World: How Globalisation Is Shaping Our Lives*, London: Profile Books.

Gilbert, J., 1999, 'White Light/White Heat: *Jouissance* Beyond Gender in the Velvet Underground', in Blake, A. (ed.), *Living Through Pop*, London and New York: Routledge, 31–48.

Giles, J., 1995, '"You Meet 'em and That's It": Working-Class Women's Refusal of Romance Between the Wars in Britain', in Pearce, L. and Stacey, J. (eds), *Romance Revisited*, London: Lawrence and Wishart, 279–92.

Gillan, J., 2004, 'From Ozzie Nelson to Ozzy Osbourne: The Genesis and Development of the Reality (Star) Sitcom', In Allen, R. C. and Hill, A. (eds), *The Television Studies Reader*, London and New York: Routledge, 56–7.

Gittins, D., 1993, *The Family in Question: Changing Households and Familial Ideologies*, London: Macmillan.

Gordon, L., 1994, *Pitied But Not Entitled: Single Mothers and the History of Welfare, 1890–1935*, New York: The Free Press.

Grant, N., 1984, 'Citizen Soldiers: Army Education in World War II', in Formations Editorial Board (ed.), *Formations of Nation and People*, London, Boston, Melbourne and Henley: Routledge and Kegan Paul, 171–87.

Gray, A., 1992, *Video Replay: The Gendering of a Leisure Technology*, London: Routledge.

Greer, G., 1971, *The Female Eunuch*, London: Flamingo.

Hall, G. S., 1904, *Adolescence and its Psychology and its Relations to Physiology, Anthropology, Sociology, Sex, Crime, Religion, and Education*, New York: D. Appleton.

Hall, S. and Jefferson, T., 1976, *Resistance Through Rituals*, London: Hutchinson.

Hall, S. and Jacques, M., 1983, *The Politics of Thatcherism*, London: Lawrence and Wishart.

Harwood, S., 1997, *Family Fictions: Representations of the Family in 1980s Hollywood Cinema*, Basingstoke: Macmillan.

Hatch, K., 2002, 'Selling Soap: Post-war Television Soap Opera and the American Housewife', in Thumin, J. (ed.), *Small Screens, Big Ideas: Television in the 1950s*, London and New York: I.B. Tauris.

Havens, T., 2004, 'Race and the Global Popularity of *The Cosby Show*', in Allen, R. C. and Hill, A. (eds), *The Television Studies Reader*, London and New York: Routledge, 442–56.

Hebdige, D., 1979, *Subculture: The Meaning of Style*, London: Methuen.

Hebdige, D., 1988, 'Hiding in the Light: Youth Surveillance and Display', in Hebdige, D. (ed.), *Hiding in the Light: On Images and Things*, London: Routledge.

Hechinger, G. and Hechinger, F., 1963, *Teen-Age Tyranny*, New York: William Morrow.

Hendershot, H., 1996, 'Dolls: Odour, Disgust, Femininity and Toy Design', in Kirkham, P. (ed.), *The Gendered Object*, Manchester and New York: Manchester University Press.

Henessey, P., 1993, *Never Again: Britain, 1945–1951*, New York: Pantheon Books.

Hermes, J., 1995, *Reading Women's Magazines: An Analysis of Everyday Media Use*, London: Polity.

Higonnet, A., 1998, *Pictures of Innocence: The History and Crisis of Ideal Childhood*, London: Thames and Hudson.

Hoggart, R., 1957, *Uses of Literacy*, London: Penguin.

Holland, P., 1997, 'Living for Libido; or, *Child's Play IV*: The Imagery of Childhood and the Call for Censorship', in Barker, M. and Petley, J. (eds), *Ill-Effects: The Media/Violence Debate*, London and New York: Routledge, 48–56.

Holland, J., Ramazanoglu, C., Sharpe, S. and Thomson, R., 1996, 'Reputations: Journeying into Gendered Power Relations', in Weeks, J. and Holland, J. (eds), *Sexual Cultures: Communities, Values and Intimacy*, Basingstoke: Macmillan, 239–60.

Hollows, J., 2000, *Feminism, Femininity and Popular Culture*, Manchester and New York: Manchester University Press.

Hunt, P., 2001, *Children's Literature*, Oxford and Malden, MA: Blackwell Publishers.

Huyssen, A., 1986, *After the Great Divide: Modernism, Mass Culture, Postmodernism*, Bloomington, IN: Indiana University Press.

Jackson, C., 2000, 'Little, Violent, White: *The Bad Seed* and the Matter of Children', *Journal of Popular Film and Television*, 28 (2), 64–73.

Jackson, P., Stevenson, N. and Brooks, K., 2001, *Making Sense of Men's Magazines*, Cambridge: Polity.

Jensen, J., 1992, 'Fandom as Pathology: The Consequences of Characterisation', in Lewis, L. A. (ed.), *The Adoring Audience*, London and New York: Routledge, 9–29.

Jhally, S. and Lewis, J., 1992, *Enlightened Racism:* The Cosby Show, *Audiences and the Myth of the American Dream*, Boulder, CO: Westview Press.

Johnson, R., 1997, 'Grievous Recognitions', in Steinberg, D. L., Epstein, D. and Johnson, R. (eds), *Border Patrols: Policing the Boundaries of Heterosexuality*, London: Cassell.

Jones, S., 1988, *Black Culture, White Youth: The Reggae Tradition from JA to UK*, London: Macmillan.

Kaplan, E. A., 1992, *Motherhood and Representation: The Mother in Popular Culture and Melodrama*, London and New York: Routledge.

Keating, P., 1991, *The Haunted Study: A Social History of the English Novel*, London: Fontana Press.

Kett, J. E., 1977, *Rites of Passage: Adolescence in America, 1790 to the Present*, New York: Basic Books.

Kinsey, A., 1948, *Sexual Behaviour in the Human Male*, W. B. Saunders.

Kinsey, A., 1953, *Sexual Behaviour in the Human Female*, W. B. Saunders.

Kramer, P., 1998, 'Would You Take Your Child To See This Film? The Cultural and Social Work of the Family-Adventure Movie', in Neale, S. and Smith, M. (eds), *Contemporary Hollywood Cinema*, London and New York: Routledge.

Krutnik, F., 1998, 'Love Lies: Romantic Fabrication in Contemporary Romantic Comedy', in Evans, P. W. and Deleyto, C. (eds), *Terms of Endearment: Hollywood Romantic Comedy of the 1980s and 1990s*, Edinburgh: Edinburgh University Press.

Krutnik, F., 2000, 'Comedy', In Cook, P. and Bernink, M. (eds), *The Cinema Book*, London: BFI Publishing.

Lauret, M., 1998, 'Hollywood Romance in the Aids Era: *Ghost* and *When Harry Met Sally*', in Pearce, L. and Wisker, G. (eds), *Fatal Attractions: Rescripting Romance in Contemporary Literature and Film*, London: Pluto Press.

Lee, N., 2001, *Childhood and Society: Growing Up in an Age of Uncertainty*, Buckingham and Philadelphia: Open University Press.

Lewis, C., 1986, *Becoming a Father*, Oxford: Oxford University Press.

Lewis, J., 1992a, 'Gender and the Development of Welfare Regimes', *Journal of European Social Policy* 2 (3), 159–73.

Lewis, J., 1992b, *The Road to Romance and Ruin: Teen Films and Youth Culture*, New York and London: Routledge.

Lewis, L. A., 1992, *The Adoring Audience: Fan Culture and Popular Media*, London and New York: Routledge.

Liebes, T. and Katz, E., 1991, *The Export of Meaning*, Oxford: Oxford University Press.

Lupton, D. and Barclay, L., 1997, *Constructing Fatherhood: Discourses and Experiences*, London, New York and Delhi: Sage Publishing.

Lusane, C., 1999, 'Addressing the Disconnect between Black and White: The Race, Class and Gender Politics of *Married . . . With Children*', *Journal of Popular Film and Television* 27 (1), 12–20.

McCracken, A., 2002, 'Study of a Mad Housewife: Psychiatric Discourse, the Suburban Home and the Case of Gracie Allen', in Thumin, J. (ed.), *Small Screens, Big Ideas: Television in the 1950s*, London and New York: I.B. Tauris.

MacDonald, I., 1994, *Revolution in the Head: The Beatles' Records and the Sixties*, London: Random House.

McRobbie, A., 1978, 'Working-Class Girls and the Culture of Femininity', in Women's Studies Group (ed.), *Women Take Issue*, London: Hutchinson, 96–108.

McRobbie, A., 1981, 'Settling Accounts with Subcultures: A Feminist Critique', *Screen Education* 34, 46–57.

McRobbie, A., 1991, *Feminism and Youth Culture*, London: Routledge.

McRobbie, A., 1996, 'More! New Sexualities in Girls' and Women's Magazines', in Curran, J., Morley, D. and Walkerdine, V. (eds), *Cultural Studies and Communication*, London: Edward Arnold, 172–95.

Maltby, R. (ed.), 1989: *Dreams for Sale: Popular Culture in the Twentieth Century*, London: Harrap.

Maltby, R, 2003, *Hollywood Cinema*, 2nd edn, Oxford, Melbourne and Berlin: Blackwell Publishing.

Marc, D., 1992, *Comic Visions: Television Comedy and American Culture*, London and New York: Routledge.

Marling, K. A., 1994, *As Seen on TV: The Visual Culture of Everyday Life in the 1950s*, Cambridge, MA: Harvard University Press.

Marshment, M., 1988, 'Substantial Women', in Gamman, L. and Marshment, M. (eds), *The Female Gaze: Women as Viewers of Popular Culture*, London: The Women's Press, 27–43.

Masters, W. and Johnson, V., 1966, *Human Sexual Response*, London: Churchill.

Medhurst, A., 1995, 'It Sort of Happened Here: The Strange, Brief Life of the British Pop Film', in Romney, J. and Wootton, A. (eds), *Celluloid Jukebox: Popular Music and the Movies Since the 50s*, London: BFI Publishing.

Miller, M. C., 1990, 'Prime Time Deride and Conquer', in Alvarado, M. and Thompson, J. O. (eds), *The Media Reader*. London: BFI Publishing.

Millet, K., 1977 (originally published 1970), *Sexual Politics*, London: Virago.

Mink, G., 1991, 'The Lady and the Tramp: Gender and Race in the Formation of American Welfare', in Gordon, L. (ed.), *Women, Welfare and the State*, Madison, WI: University of Wisconsin Press.

Mitchell, J., 1971, *Woman's Estate*, Harmondsworth: Penguin Books.

Modleski, T., 1982, *Loving With a Vengeance: Mass-Produced Fantasies for Women*, London and New York: Methuen.

Modleski, T., 1991, *Feminism Without Women: Culture and Criticism in a 'Post-Feminist' Age*, London: Routledge.

Moores, S., 1988, 'The Box on the Dresser: Memories of Early Radio', *Media, Culture and Society* 10 (1), 20–36.

Morley, D., 1992, *Television, Audiences and Cultural Studies*, London and New York: Routledge.

Mount, F., 1983, *The Subversive Family: An Alternative History of Love and Marriage*, London: Unwin Paperbacks.

Mundy, J., 1999, *Popular Music on Screen: From the Hollywood Musical to Music Video*, Manchester: Manchester University Press.

Murdock, G., 1997, 'Reservoirs of Dogma: An Archaeology of Popular Anxieties', in Barker, M. and Petley, J. (eds), *Ill-Effects: The Media/Violence Debate*, London and New York: Routledge, 67–86.

Musgrove, F., 1964, *Youth and the Social Order*, London: Routledge and Kegan Paul.

Nava, M., 1996, 'Modernity's Disavowal: Women, the City and the Department Store', in Nava, M. and O'Shea, A. (eds), *Modern Times: Reflections on a Century of English Modernity*, London and New York: Routledge, 38–76.

Neale, S., 1992, 'The Big Romance or Something Wild?: Romantic Comedy Today', *Screen* 33 (3), 284–99.

Neale, S., 1999, 'Teenpics', in Cook, P. and Bernink, M. (eds.), *The Cinema Book*, London: BFI Publishing, 218–20.

Neaverson, B., 1997, *The Beatles Movies*, London: Cassell.

Newson, E., 1994, *Video Violence and the Protection of Children: Report of the Home Affairs Committee*, London: HMSO.

Newson, J. and Newson, E., 1963, *Patterns of Infant Care in an Urban Community*, London: Allen and Unwin.

Norman, P., 1981, *Shout! The True Story of the Beatles*, London: Corgi.

Oakley, A., 1974, *The Sociology of Housework*, Oxford: Basil Blackwell.

Osgerby, B., 1998, 'The Good, the Bad and the Ugly: Post-war Media Representations of Youth', in Briggs, A. and Cobley, P. (eds.), *The Media: An Introduction*, Harlow: Longman.

Parks, L., 2000, 'Cracking Open the Set: Television Repair and Tinkering with Gender 1949–1955', in Thumin, J. (ed.), *Small Screens, Big Ideas: Television in the 1950s*, London and New York: I. B. Tauris, 223–43.

Pearson, G., 1983, *Hooligan: A History of Respectable Fears*, London: Macmillan.

Pfeil, F., 1995, *White Guys: Studies in Postmodern Domination and Difference*, London: Verso.

Philips, D. and Tomlinson, A., 1992, 'Homeward Bound: Leisure, Popular Culture and Consumer Capitalism', in Strinati, D. and Wagg, S. (eds), *Come On Down? Popular Media Culture in Post-war Britain*, London: Routledge.

Philips, M., 1999, *The Sex-Change Society: Feminized Britain and the Neutered Male*, London: Social Market Foundation.

Postman, N., 1985, *The Disappearance of Childhood: How TV Is Changing Children's Lives*, London: Comet.

Pym, B., 1981 (originally published 1953), *Jane and Prudence*, London: Grafton Books.

Radford, J., 1986, *The Progress of Romance: The Politics of Popular Fiction*, London: Routledge and Kegan Paul.

Radner, H., 1998, 'New Hollywood's New Women: Murder in Mind – Sarah and Margie', in Neale, S. and Smith, M. (eds), *Contemporary Hollywood Cinema*, London and New York: Routledge.

Radway, J., 1987, *Reading the Romance: Women, Patriarchy and Popular Literature*, London and New York: Verso.

Riley, D., 1983, *War in the Nursery: Theories of the Child and the Mother*, London: Virago.

Roberts, E., 1995, *Women and Families: An Oral History, 1940–1970*, Oxford: Blackwell.

Rose, N., 1989, *Governing the Soul*, London: Routledge.

Rowe, K., 1995, *The Unruly Woman: Gender and the Genres of Laughter*, Austin, TX: University of Texas Press.

Ryan, D. S., 2000, 'All the World and her Husband: The Daily Mail Ideal Home Exhibition 1908–39', in Andrews, M. and Talbot, M. M. (eds), *All the World and her Husband: Women in Twentieth-Century Consumer Culture*, London and New York: Cassell, 10–22.

Schwarz, B., 1996, 'Night Battles: Hooligan and Citizen', In Nava, M. and O'Shea, A. (eds), *Modern Times: Reflections on a Century of English Modernity*, London and New York: Routledge.

Segal, L., 1988, 'Look Back in Anger: Men in the Fifties', in Chapman, R. and Rutherford, J. (eds), *Male Order: Unwrapping Masculinity*, London: Lawrence and Wishart.

Segal, L., 1990, *Slow Motion: Changing Masculinities, Changing Men*, London: Virago.

Seiter, E., 1996, 'Notes on Children as a Television Audience', in Hay, J., Grossberg, L. and Wartella, E. (eds), *The Audience and its Landscape*, Westview Press.

Seiter, E., 2004, 'Qualitative Audience Research', in Allen, R. C. and Hill, A., *The Television Studies Reader*, London:Routledge.

Shumway, D., 1999, 'Rock 'n' Roll Sound Tracks and the Production of Nostalgia', *Cinema Journal* 38 (2), 36–51.

Silva, E. B. and Smart, C. (eds), 1998, *The 'New' Family?*, London, Thousand Oaks, CA and New Delhi: Sage Publications.

Silverstone, R., 1997, 'Introduction', in Silverstone, R. (ed.), *Visions of Suburbia*, London and New York: Routledge.

Skirrow, G., 1990, 'Hellivision: An Analysis of Video Games', in Alvarado, M. and Thompson, J. O. (eds), *The Media Reader*, BFI Publishing, 321–38.

Smart, C. and Neale, B., 1999, *Family Fragments?*, Cambridge: Polity.

Smith, J., 1998, *The Sounds of Commerce: Marketing Popular Film Music*, New York: Columbia University Press.

Smith, M., 1998, 'Theses on the Philosophy of Hollywood History', in Neale, S. and Smith, M. (eds), *Contemporary Hollywood Cinema*, London and New York: Routledge.

Speed, L., 2000, 'Together in Electric Dreams: Films Revisiting 1980s Youth', *Journal of Popular Film and Television* 28 (1), 22–9.

Stopes, M., 1918, *Married Love*, London: Putnam.

Street, P., 2003, *Long Live the Queen! Britain in 1953,* Stroud: Sutton Publishing.

Taylor, E., 1986, *The Blush*, London: Virago.

Thompson, K., 1998, *Moral Panics*, London and New York: Routledge.

Thornton, S., 1995, *Club Cultures: Music, Media and Subcultural Capital*, Cambridge: Polity Press.

Thumin, J., (ed.), 2002, *Small Screens, Big Ideas: Television in the 1950s*, London and New York: I. B. Tauris.

Tibbett, J. C., 2001, 'Mary Pickford and the American "Growing Girl"', *Journal of Popular Film and Television* 29 (2), 50–62.

Tincknell, E., 1988, 'Family Fortunes: Women, Class and Power in the Popular Family Saga', unpublished MA dissertation.

Tincknell, E., 1991, 'Enterprise Fictions, Women of Substance', in Franklin, S., Lury, C. and Stacey, J. (eds), *Off-Centre: Feminism and Cultural Studies*, London and New York: Harper Collins Academic, 260–73.

Tincknell, E. and Chambers, D., 2002, 'Performing the Crisis: Fathering, Gender and Representation in Two Nineties Films', *Journal of Popular Film and Television* 29 (4), 146–56.

Tincknell, E. and Raghuram, P., 2002, '*Big Brother*: Reconfiguring the "Active" Audience of Cultural Studies?', *European Journal of Cultural Studies* 5 (2), 199–216.

Tincknell, E., Chambers, D., Van Loon, J. and Hudson, N., 2003, 'Begging for It: "New Femininities", Social Agency, and Moral Discourse in Contemporary Teenage and Men's Magazines', *Feminist Media Studies* 3 (1), 47–64.

Tompkins, J., 1989, 'West of Everything?', in Longhurst, D. (ed.), *Gender, Genre and Narrative Pleasure*, London: Unwin Hyman.

Turner, G., 1992a, *British Cultural Studies: An Introduction*, London and New York: Routledge.

Turner, G., 1992b, 'Suburbia Verite', *Australian Left Review*, October, 37–9.

Vallone, L., 1995, *Disciplines of Virtue: Girls' Culture in the Eighteenth and Nineteenth Centuries*, New Haven: Yale University Press.

Viviani, C., 1980, 'Who Is Without Sin? The Maternal Melodrama in American Film 1930–39', *Wide Angle* 4 (2), 4–17.

Wagg, S., 1992, '"One I Made Earlier": Media, Popular Culture and the Politics of Childhood', in Strinati, D. and Wagg, S. (eds), *Come On Down? Popular Media Culture in Post-war Britain*, London: Routledge.

Walkerdine, V., 1997, *Daddy's Girl: Young Girls and Popular Culture*, Basingstoke: Macmillan.

Walley, J., 1960, *The Kitchen*, London: Constable.

Weeks, J., 1989, *Sex, Politics and Society: The Regulation of Sexuality Since 1800*, 2nd edn, Harlow: Longman.

Weeks, J., Donovan, C., Heaphy, B. and Dunne, 1998, 'Everyday Experiments: Narratives of Non-heterosexual Relationships', in Silva, E. and Smart, C. (eds) *The 'New' Family?*, London: Sage.

Whelehan, I., 2000, *Overloaded: Popular Culture and the Future of Feminism*, London: The Women's Press.

Williams, R., 1961, *Culture and Society*, Harmondsworth: Pelican.

Williams, R., 1977, *Marxism and Literature*, Oxford: Oxford University Press.

Williams, Z., 2001, 'The Lady and the Vamp', *Guardian Weekend*, 17 November, 35–36.

Willis, P., 1977, *Learning To Labour: How Working-Class Kids Get Working-Class Jobs*, London: Saxon House.

Willis, S., 2000, '"Style", Posture and Idiom: Tarantino's Figures of Masculinity', in Gledhill, C. and Williams, L. (eds), *Reinventing Film Studies*, London and New York: Arnold.

Willmott, P. and Young, M., 1960, *Family and Class in a London Suburb*, London: Routledge and Kegan Paul.

Wilson, A. N., 2003, *The Victorians*, London: Arrow Books.

Wilson, E., 1977, *Women and the Welfare State*, London: Tavistock.

Wilson, E., 1980, *Only Halfway to Paradise: Women in Postwar Britain 1945–68*, London: Tavistock.

Winn, M., 1985, *The Plug-In Drug*, Harmondsworth: Viking Penguin.

Winship, J., 1984, 'Nation Before Family: *Woman*, The National Home Weekly 1945–1953', in Formations Editorial Board (ed.), *Formations of Nation and People*, London, Boston, Melbourne and Henley: Routledge and Kegan Paul.

Winship, J., 1987, *Inside Women's Magazines*, London: Pandora.

Winship, J., 1991, 'The Impossibility of Best: Enterprise Meets Domesticity in the Practical Women's Magazines of the 1980s', in Strinati, D. and Wagg, S. (eds), *Come On Down? Popular Media Culture in Post-war Britain*, London: Routledge.

Wood, R., 1986, *Hollywood from Vietnam to Reagan*, New York: Columbia University Press.

Zaretsky, E., 1976, *Capitalism, the Family and Personal Life*, London: Pluto Press.

Index